● Scapa Flow

● Cuxhaven

◇ Gallipoli Naval Campaign 1915

Escape of Goeben *and* Breslau *1914* ◇

ATLANTIC

OCEAN

◇ *Sinking of SMS*
Königsberg *1915*

INDIAN

OCEAN

Battle of
Coronel ◇
1914

Battle of the
◇ *Falkland Islands*
1914

THE HISTORY OF WORLD WAR I

NAVAL WARFARE
1914–1918

FROM CORONEL TO THE ATLANTIC AND ZEEBRUGGE

TIM BENBOW

FOREWORD BY DENNIS SHOWALTER

amber
BOOKS

Special thanks to my parents, George and Diana Benbow, for their meticulous proof-reading

This edition first published in 2008
Reprinted in 2012

Published by
Amber Books Ltd
Bradley's Close
74–77 White Lion Street
London N1 9PF
United Kingdom
www.amberbooks.co.uk

Copyright © Amber Books Ltd 2008

ISBN: 978-1-906626-16-7

Series Commissioning Editor: Charles Catton
Editorial: Ilios Publishing, Oxford, UK
Picture Research: Terry Forshaw and Susannah Jayes
Design: Hawes Design
Cartography: Patrick Mulrey
Indexer: Alison Worthington

For editorial or picture enquiries please contact editorial@amberbooks.co.uk

Printed in Dubai

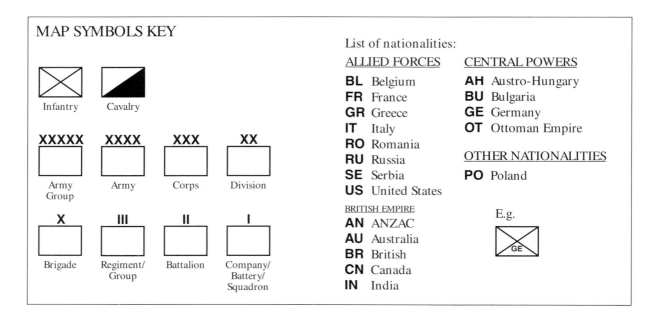

MAP SYMBOLS KEY

Infantry   Cavalry

XXXXX   XXXX   XXX   XX
Army   Army   Corps   Division
Group

X   III   II   I
Brigade   Regiment/   Battalion   Company/
             Group   Battery/
                                     Squadron

List of nationalities:

ALLIED FORCES

BL Belgium
FR France
GR Greece
IT Italy
RO Romania
RU Russia
SE Serbia
US United States

BRITISH EMPIRE
AN ANZAC
AU Australia
BR British
CN Canada
IN India

CENTRAL POWERS

AH Austro-Hungary
BU Bulgaria
GE Germany
OT Ottoman Empire

OTHER NATIONALITIES
PO Poland

E.g.
GE

Contents

Foreword

World War I was limited in time and space, lasting only four years. Its outcome was determined in a single region—northern France and Flanders. Yet its unprecedented scale and cost created a spectrum of consequences, earning it another name: the Great War. That war was a Great Surprise. It was expected to be decisive and short. Instead it drew the entire world into an attritional death grapple whose outcome was uncertain until the end, and whose graves are scattered from Nova Scotia to Singapore. The Great War marked the end of European hegemony, the rise of the US and the Soviet Union as superpowers, and the emergence of the non-Western world on its terms. This conflict truly was the defining event of the twentieth century.

For all its impact, World War I remains shrouded in myth, mystery, and mourning. It exists as a series of disjointed images: old photographs and fragments of poems; devastated landscapes; anonymous soldiers scrambling over the top; above all, the endless cemeteries of the Western Front. *The History of World War I* returns that tragic conflict to the sphere of history. Based on a half-century of sophisticated research, incorporating state-of-the-art graphics, the six volumes of the series present the war on land, at sea, and in the air in a global context, and in human terms.

Dennis Showalter

A German sailor from SMS *Emden*.

The Coming of War

At the end of the Napoleonic Wars, Britain enjoyed an unrivalled predominance on the seas. The British rule of the waves sustained the 'Pax Britannica' throughout the nineteenth century, deterring great power rivals as well as permitting expansion of the empire. By the end of the century, however, as storm clouds began to gather over Europe, this maritime strength had changed utterly in composition.

Britain's maritime strength also appeared to be losing much of its value as the industrial revolution threatened to reduce the advantages of Sea Powers relative to Land Powers. A new Continental enemy arose, which was less dependent on the sea and hence less vulnerable to naval power. This might have marginalized the struggle at sea in any future conflict. Yet when the great powers of Europe fought each other once again, the war at sea was to prove just as important as in almost all of the previous or later conflicts.

The Royal Navy battleships that would fight World War I were all but unrecognizable from those that had fought under Nelson. Steam propulsion, iron hulls and great advances in guns and armour revolutionized navies. Sea power was central to the causes and outcome of the war.

The nineteenth century saw the sailing warship, which for centuries had been the key instrument of naval warfare, displaced by a very different kind of vessel, as the effects of the industrial revolution were felt at sea. Changes in technology gave rise to major developments in naval tactics and strategy, and also affected wider issues such as the place of naval power within national policy. The most significant of these were the adoption of steam power, the advent of iron hulls, rapid advances in guns and armour and the development of underwater weapons.

STEAM POWER

The most momentous change was the gradual move from sail to steam as the means of ship propulsion. Adopting steam power freed warships from dependence on the wind, reducing journey times as well as making them more predictable, and making feasible some routes that had previously been impossible. In battle, warships became easier to manoeuvre, which greatly simplified tactics as well as changing the range of skills required to handle a ship or a squadron effectively. A steam-powered warship also had a good chance of either securing a favourable tactical position against a sailing ship or, alternatively, of avoiding battle altogether. This freedom, however, came at the cost of the need for fuel – initially coal, though the move to oil began just before the outbreak of World War I – which tied ships to their bases far

The great powers in Europe on the eve of World War I were very different to those that had fought the Napoleonic Wars, mainly due to the unification of Italy and Germany.

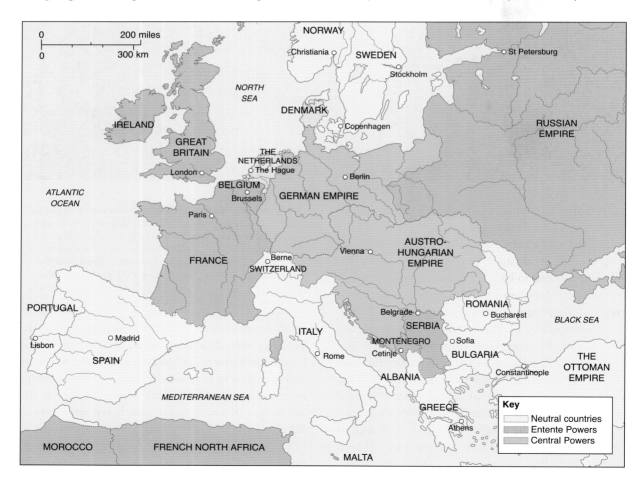

more closely than hitherto. Strategically, this favoured local over more distant powers and also made the acquisition of overseas bases more important. At the widest level, it changed the physical and human resources needed to be a great naval power, although Britain still enjoyed an early lead in the production of coal and steel, and industrial capacity.

Steam power was initially taken up with greatest enthusiasm by merchant shipping. It was first introduced to navies on a large scale by Britain, with France also showing considerable interest, and some experiments took place in the United States. It seemed to offer particular advantages for short-ranged warships such as the small gunboats so often used in minor wars during the nineteenth century, not least due to their ability to use shallow waters and rivers.

J.M.W. Turner's painting *The Fighting Temeraire tugged to her last berth to be broken up* (1838). This picture, recently voted Britain's most popular, symbolizes the demise of the old sailing battleships that had dominated naval warfare for centuries, replaced by the steam-powered offspring of the Industrial Revolution. The ship depicted was launched in 1798, and was named after a ship captured from the French; she also fought at the Battle of Trafalgar.

Steam warships and gunboats performed well in the Crimean War (1853–56); most of the British and French battleships deployed to the Black Sea were sailing ships, but the majority of the smaller warships were steam powered. This war established the advantages of steam ships, which not only proved extremely efficient in bombardment of targets ashore, but also at times inflicted the indignity on their sail-powered colleagues of towing them into position. By

HMS *Wivern* was one of two ironclad steam ships initially built for the Confederate Government. They could have helped to change the balance at sea in the American Civil War, but were taken over by the Royal Navy.

the end of the war, sailing warships were well on the way to becoming a thing of the past, with sails used only to supplement steam, and then only temporarily.

The use of steam power on land in the form of railway engines raised some doubts about the impact of military power landed from the sea, given that large armies could be swiftly deployed by Continental powers. Napoleon had complained that if the British had 30,000 troops at sea, he had to tie down 300,000 in garrisoning all of the places where they might land. In contrast, when Bismarck was asked what he would do in the event that the British Army landed in Germany, he is said to have responded that he would send out the local police force and arrest it. However, if the ability of navies to influence events ashore was reduced by steam power, so too was the ability of armies to guarantee a swift victory over the mobilized army of another great power. Without such a knockout blow, there could still be an important wartime role for sea power.

IRON HULLS

Following soon after the adoption of steam power by navies came the increased use of iron in warships. At first, this took the form of plates of iron bolted to the outside of wooden ships, to provide protection against shell guns. While the old wooden hulls had been able to take considerable punishment from solid shot, guns firing explosive shells threatened to blow them apart. This was demonstrated at the Battle of Sinope (1853), with the destruction of a Turkish fleet by Russian warships using the new Paixhans shell gun. Protection was needed against this threat, so the 'ironclad' was born. Moves to adopt iron for the construction of the ship, rather than simply as additional armour, proceeded slowly because of its tendency to splinter. However, advances in metallurgy changed this. Iron (and then steel) construction proved attractive because it permitted larger as well as more robust vessels that were not as vulnerable to fire as wooden ships, and were able to carry the ever heavier guns and armour that were developed during the century.

National rivalries helped to drive the process of innovation. The first ironclad battleship was the French *La Gloire*, launched in 1859. The advance represented by this ship drove an urgent counter-reaction in Britain, as would the German naval expansion at the start of the twentieth century. The British response was to build HMS *Warrior*, launched in 1860 and commissioned the following year, which was not an ironclad but rather the world's first iron-hulled warship. She carried an 11.4cm (4.5in) belt of iron armour, backed by 45.7cm (18in) of teak between it and the iron hull, and was divided into internal compartments to further reduce her vulnerability. She was steam powered, although she was also fitted with sails to save fuel, and heavily armed. *Warrior* never fired her guns in anger and was considered obsolete after just 10 years – in stark contrast to HMS *Victory*, which was over 40 years old at the Battle of Trafalgar (1805) yet still at the cutting-edge of quality. This tendency of warships to become obsolete more quickly, and the related importance of retaining technological parity with rivals, was an important new development in naval warfare.

GUNS AND ARMOUR

Shortly after the launch of *Warrior*, guns and projectiles that could penetrate her armour were already being tested. This illustrates the ongoing duel waged over the course of the nineteenth century between guns and armour.

The effect of explosive shells, as opposed to solid shot, against wooden hulls has already been noted. Solid shot remained better for penetrating armour for some years, though this would change as armour-piercing shells were developed. Other advances that enhanced the offensive side of the balance included improvements in metallurgy (which resulted in stronger guns, able to withstand more powerful charges), rifled barrels firing cylindrical projectiles

HMS *Warrior*

HMS *Warrior*, the world's first iron-hulled warship, was theoretically a frigate due to her single gun deck, but was at her launch the most powerful battleship in the world, armed with 26 x 68-pounder guns (as opposed to the usual 32-pounders) and 10 massive 110-pounder, breech-loading guns. She was nicknamed 'The Black Snake', after the reported comment of the French emperor Napoleon III that, against his warships, *Warrior* would be like a 'black snake among rabbits'. She can be visited today at the Portsmouth Historic Dockyard.

HMS *Hercules* (at centre) together with HMS *Warrior* and HMS *Bellerophon*. These vessels demonstrate the changing character of warships as a result of the impact of the Industrial Revolution.

(which increased both the range and accuracy of fire) and slower-burning powder (which increased range and penetrative power). When perfected, breech loading, as opposed to loading by the muzzle of the gun, both eased and increased the speed of reloading. From the 1860s onwards, guns began to be mounted in rotating turrets rather than firing through ports in the side of the vessel, as warships tended to carry fewer and larger guns. Turrets were not compatible with sails and all of the rigging they involved; as steam power increasingly become the sole means of propulsion, so turreted guns became more widely used. These improvements went alongside an increase in the size of main armament, up to the 16in guns of HMS *Benbow* (1885). As the range of guns increased, a need arose for a better means of aiming than simply sighting along the barrel. Thus, more sophisticated sights and director gear were introduced, allowing all of the ship's main guns to be fired together in a single salvo, followed by more elaborate fire-control systems that took into account factors such as the relative movements of the firing ship and its target.

One further effect of the growth in the size, range and striking power of artillery was a swing in the balance of advantage from ships to guns ashore, which were less constrained by weight and size. Warships still enjoyed some advantages over static shore batteries, but the saying often (and falsely) attributed to Nelson that 'a ship's a fool to fight a fort' became increasingly pertinent.

Armour improved alongside advances in naval artillery, first simply increasing in thickness – culminating in the 61cm (24in) belt of the aptly named HMS *Inflexible* – and then in quality, as steel was introduced. The latter was initially used as an outer plate attached to iron armour, and then in the form of all-steel armour, which provided better protection for less weight. The increasing weight of

The Battle of the Hampton Roads (1862)

The famous Battle of the Hampton Roads (March 1862) saw the first clash between two ironclads (wooden-hulled ships with plates of iron armour). The *Merrimack* (actually its former name – the ship had been renamed the *Virginia* after being captured and rebuilt by the Confederates) successfully sank several wooden Union ships, but was then confronted by the more formidable *Monitor*. The two ships blasted each other indecisively for four hours. However, the most modern guns were more than capable of inflicting severe damage on armoured ships. The engagement was an aberration rather than the shape of things to come, because of the short range at which it was fought and the overall indecisiveness of the encounter.

armour led to a divergence and greater specialization in ship design, with cruisers concentrating on speed and range at the expense of armour, while battleships featured the heaviest protection and firepower. Also, to save weight, the whole ship could not be equally protected, so armour was concentrated around the most vital parts, giving rise to what would become known as the 'citadel' in US ships. Later, the longer range of guns meant that ships would be hit from above by plunging fire, as well as from the sides, so horizontal deck armour was introduced over some parts of the ship. At times, it was even thought that armoured warships might prove impervious to naval guns (partly due to the inconclusive result of the *Virginia (Merrimack)–Monitor* action during the American Civil War). However, armour could never guarantee the invulnerability of warships, although it could make them less vulnerable and more capable of absorbing fire, particularly against smaller-calibre guns or at longer ranges.

All of these changes together meant that warships had changed dramatically in appearance compared to those from the days of Nelson. There was also a greater distinction within the fleet between ships intended for different roles. The other effect of all of this was a steady and dramatic increase in the cost of warships – with an increasing penalty for lagging behind the leading edge of technology – and hence a decrease in the number of battleships in the main fleets. This tendency encouraged some states to think more creatively about how they might seek to exercise sea power, or prevent their enemies from doing so.

UNDERWATER WEAPONS

Rather than simply opposing a fleet of battleships with a similar force, some thinkers sought a different approach to countering them through the use of underwater weapons. They held the appeal of making possible a stealthy attack, as well as targeting vulnerable areas of the ship below its main armour. There were unsuccessful attempts to use submarines as early as the American War of Independence (1775–83). Further experiments with submarines and naval mines (often referred to, confusingly, as 'torpedoes') followed during the period of the Napoleonic Wars (1793–1815), as well as during some regional conflicts in the nineteenth century; Russia, for example, made widespread use of mines during the Crimean War, albeit to little effect. They first saw widespread use and some positive results during the American Civil War. Several attacks were made by mines and spar torpedoes (an explosive charge at the end of a pole), including the first sinking of a ship by a submarine, the Confederate *Hunley*. What would today be called a torpedo – that is, a weapon that is self-propelled rather than simply floating – was invented by Robert Whitehead in 1866 and was first used in the Russo-Turkish War of 1877. As with other innovations, early examples were flawed but their evident potential encouraged swift evolution in reliability, range and accuracy. The Royal Navy eagerly took up the torpedo boat from 1875 and, at the same time, sought to counter the threat such vessels posed by fitting battleships with small batteries of quick-firing guns. In addition, in the early 1890s the Navy created a new class of ship, the 'torpedo boat destroyer'. This was fast and well armed, and also had

The submarine *Resurgam II*. Her name translates as 'Would that I might rise again'. This apparent lack of confidence was rather appropriate, since very often early submarines failed to do so, with fatal consequences for their brave crews.

its own torpedo tubes for an offensive role. Success in countering torpedo boats placed more value on submarines, the pre-war development of which will be explored in the later chapter on the U-boat war.

GREAT POWER RIVALRIES

Changes in technology during the nineteenth century had a fundamental effect on sea power, altering the shape of the navies that would vie for supremacy with each other during the course of World War I. They were accompanied by wider changes in international politics, which redrew the map of the world in an equally significant fashion. The 'Concert of Europe' represented an attempt by the European great powers to prevent the Continent from being plunged into another conflict like the Napoleonic Wars. It had some successes, but was gradually undermined by the new forces of political nationalism and the industrial revolution. Some European powers flourished (Britain and France) while some moved towards collapse (Austro-Hungary and the Ottoman Empire), yet new powers also emerged (Italy

and, with greater consequence, Germany). Moreover, by the end of the century the international system was no longer synonymous with Europe, as the United States and Japan entered the world stage to the west and east.

Underwater weapons were relatively primitive during the American Civil War, which saw the first sinking of a surface ship by a submarine, the *Hunley* (pictured below), in February 1864. Still, they showed signs of becoming an important element of naval warfare, which could not be ignored by the great sea powers.

Kaiser Wilhem II, the German emperor, was a keen supporter of sea power and of expanding the German Navy. His hope was to copy the Royal Navy and earn the respect of Britain, but his naval expansion programme helped to bring the two countries into conflict.

Naval power itself helped to play a role in creating the conditions for war. A new power arose with ambitions outside Europe and on the high seas, with the result that the traditional and familiar rivalry between Britain and France gave way to something much more dangerous.

BRITAIN AND THE TWO-POWER STANDARD
In the decades after the end of the Napoleonic Wars, Britain had the luxury of looking away from Europe and towards the wider world. This was not due to any lack of vital interests on the Continent; as the long clashes with France demonstrated, Britain clearly could not afford to ignore the rise of a hostile power that threatened to dominate Europe. Rather, in the absence of any such threat, Britain could concentrate on commerce, empire and industrialization. While never anything more than 'first among equals' in terms of military power, the economic strength of

Alfred T. Mahan (1840–1914)

Alfred Thayer Mahan was a US naval officer, historian, lecturer at the Naval War College and a great advocate of sea power. His notable books include *The Influence of Sea Power on History 1660–1783* (1890), *The Interest of America in Sea Power* (1897) and *Naval Strategy: Compared and Contrasted with the Principles and Practice of Military Operations on Land* (1911). The British were delighted by his writings, which seemed to vindicate their policy and praised the Royal Navy. He was more influential in driving change in the United States, Japan and Germany, where both Kaiser Wilhelm II and Alfred von Tirpitz were avid readers. The (rather over-simplified) conclusions that they took from his work were, first, that a great power needed an empire and a great navy to secure its wealth, status and security, and, second, that this navy should not look to cruisers and commerce raiding, which would amount to mere harassment of the enemy's shipping, but rather to a battlefleet to win command of the sea.

Britain during this period was unique, and it rested, above all, on the protection afforded by sea power. As explained by Alfred T. Mahan, the American naval historian, there seemed to be a virtuous circle enjoyed by the leading sea power, with superiority on the oceans providing trade and colonies. This increased the wealth of the country, which in turn sustained superior sea power. British strategy turned on a small but high-quality army and, mainly, on the superiority of the Royal Navy over any challenger – or, indeed, over any two challengers.

The concept of a 'two-power standard' – that is, that the Royal Navy should be superior to a combination of the second and third largest fleets – was initially coined in 1817, shortly after the end of the Napoleonic Wars. It was designed to ensure that Britain's sea power would remain unchallenged not only by any state but by any alliance. Critically, it did not specify any particular navies, but rather applied to whichever were the second and third most powerful. This was sensible: given the long lifespan of warships, it was not possible to be certain whom one might wish to deter 10 or 20 years after they were built. In practice, however, it tended to apply to France and Russia, Britain's main rivals throughout the century. The two-power standard officially became policy with the 1889 Naval Defence Act, following a popular and press campaign for naval expansion in response to a French naval build-up and a worsening in relations with her and with Russia. It was reaffirmed in 1893, with specific reference to France and Russia, which had accelerated their own building programmes. The technological developments previously explained made it increasingly expensive to maintain the two-power standard – yet Britain continued to commit the resources to meet it. At its heart, the policy was a reflection of Britain's dependence on the sea for her security and even survival. It also suggested just how seriously the country would view any new challenge on the oceans.

GERMANY'S *WELTPOLITIK*

For Britain, the international system was changing. The rise of the United States caused some disputes, but these were handled diplomatically. The creation of a new European power with the unification of Italy in the early 1860s was not a matter of concern, since it had good relations with Britain and – crucially – was economically dependent on trade with her. Potentially more serious was the unification of Germany a few years later, which created a new great power in the centre of the Continent. Yet this was not unwelcome to Britain, which had for generations allied with the German states to balance against France. Britain's main security concerns lay well beyond Europe in the shape of threats to the empire, from France in the Near East and Africa and, in particular, from Russia over the 'Great Game' in Central Asia (especially Persia and Afghanistan), which had implications for India. The Russian threat seemed to be growing, as the development of railways meant that Russia could transport large armies to disputed areas far more rapidly than Britain could reinforce her local troops. The acquisition of empires by the European powers accelerated in the 1880s with what has become known as the 'scramble for Africa', as informal influence was replaced by more formal control. No state wanted to be left out of a carve-up that would affect the balance of power back in Europe, so this new wave of imperialism not only included the usual suspects of Britain and France, but also the older imperial powers of Spain and Portugal, as well as less familiar participants including Belgium and Italy, and also the united Germany, which acquired colonies in Southwest

The unification of Germany, achieved without turning Britain into a potential enemy, was the great achievement of Prince Otto von Bismarck's diplomatic machinations. However, his successors were more ambitious, looking to build up an overseas empire and a great navy to go with it, which caused great alarm in London.

Africa, the Cameroons and Tanganyika. This was hugely significant as it marked the early stages of Germany's *Weltpolitik* (world politics). In 1888, Wilhelm II became kaiser and in March 1890, he dismissed the chancellor Otto von Bismarck. Bismarck, the principal architect of German unification, had concentrated on Europe and had been wary of colonial entanglements precisely because they risked souring relations with Britain. Far better,

he thought, to use the world outside Europe to gain concessions from Britain, exploiting her rivalries with France and Russia. The new Kaiser, however, wanted a more activist overseas policy, believing that joining the other leading European states as an imperial power was crucial. To miss out on the new wave of imperialism would weaken Germany at home, restricting her growth in power and status.

The German pursuit of *Weltpolitik* gave rise to some disputes with Britain, notably over Portuguese colonies, a railway to Baghdad and Germany's overt support for the Boers in their confrontation with London, in addition to increasing trade rivalries between the two. The fact that Germany was late to join the push for empire meant that other European states were alarmed by how great her gains were, while Germany was dissatisfied by their modesty. More concern was, perhaps, caused by the blustering and aggressive style of the German policy, as opposed to its substance. Far more serious, however, and central to the breach between the two, was a policy that was intimately connected with *Weltpolitik*, namely the expansion of the German Navy.

THE HIGH SEAS FLEET
Up to the mid-1890s, the German Navy had been designed mainly for use against France and Russia, particularly in the Baltic, with an emphasis on cruisers

The Battle of Onganjira (1904). This colonial engagement, fought by Germany against the Hereros in Southwest Africa, symbolized the country's ambitions to build up an overseas empire like that of the other European great powers. The resulting imperial rivalries helped to stoke mutual suspicion back home in Europe.

and local defence. The more ambitious foreign policy now being pursued seemed to require a larger fleet capable of operations at greater distance from home. Such a fleet, it was hoped, would also demand the attention of Britain and help to force concessions, making Germany an indispensable partner. Kaiser Wilhelm II was heavily influenced in his enthusiasm for naval power by the writings of Mahan; in 1894, he described himself as 'not reading but devouring Captain Mahan's book'. The aspiration therefore arose to build a fleet of 25 battleships. To oversee this programme and to persuade the Reichstag (the German Parliament) to fund it, in June 1897 the Kaiser appointed Alfred von Tirpitz as Secretary of State of the Imperial Navy Office, a position equivalent to Britain's First Lord of the Admiralty.

Tirpitz justified the navy on the basis of securing Germany's trade and enhancing her diplomatic influence, but he clearly saw its main purpose as challenging British command of the seas. He rejected the option favoured by some in France of attacking British commerce with asymmetric means such as cruisers and torpedo boats. He believed that Germany would be in a poor position for a war on Britain's trade because of her own lack of overseas bases and restricted access to the Atlantic. Tirpitz therefore looked to challenge the Royal Navy in the North Sea by building up a battlefleet. The idea behind this plan was the concept of a 'risk fleet': the new navy would provide a shield for Germany's rise to great-power status by deterring any attack by Britain – since although the Royal Navy would win any naval war, in doing so it would lose enough warships to weaken itself against its principal naval rivals, namely France and Russia. In this sense, Tirpitz's strategy rested on the British two-power standard. The problem with this idea was that the building programme and the formidable cost it entailed were justified to the

The four battleships of the *Nassau* class (*Nassau, Posen, Rheinland* and *Westfalen*) were the first German Dreadnoughts, and were completed in 1910. All four took part in the Battle of Jutland, forming the 2nd Division of the 1st Battle Squadron of the High Seas Fleet.

Reichstag not only by references to expanding and protecting trade and the empire, but also with immoderate and strongly anti-British rhetoric. This was taken up by much of the German press, with its British counterpart responding enthusiastically in like manner. While the initial rationale for the naval programme had been to make Germany an unavoidable partner for Britain, this aspect became submerged by the passions unleashed, as the means became the end. Tirpitz could argue that it was only natural for a growing European power to want to go to sea, but his subtle conceptual approach was more intellectual than realistic.

In 1898, Germany's First Naval Law set a target of 19 battleships and eight armoured cruisers. This was then expanded by the Second Naval Law of 1900, which envisaged 38 battleships (compared to the 32 then in Britain's Home Fleet) and 20 armoured cruisers. Britain's reaction was initially calm, partly because the Royal Navy was already growing in response to the perceived challenge from France and Russia. At first, the main concern in London was the possibility of Germany's fleet being allied to those of

Alfred von Tirpitz (1849–1930)

Alfred von Tirpitz joined the Prussian Navy in 1865, rising to become Chief of the German Naval Staff in 1892. Kaiser Wilhelm II appointed him to head the expansion of the German Navy, seeing a series of naval bills through the Reichstag on the back of well crafted publicity campaigns. Although much of his naval experience was in the torpedo arm, he favoured building battleships. His 'risk theory' proved disastrous: not only was it undermined by the British naval response, but it also helped drive Britain into an alliance with France. When war came, Tirpitz believed it was too soon for Germany's naval plans (as his successors would also believe in 1939). He later became an advocate of greater reliance on U-boats. He was made a Grand Admiral in 1911, but resigned as Secretary of State in March 1916 and dedicated his time to right-wing politics.

BELOW The dreadnought *Prinzregent Luitpold*, one of the five-ship *Kaiser* class, with larger guns and thicker armour than the *Nassau* class. Laid down in 1911 and commissioned in December 1913, she fought at Jutland, surviving unscathed, and was scuttled at Scapa Flow after the war.

ABOVE SMS *Markgraf* was one of the *König*-class Dreadnoughts, which were similar to the *Kaiser* class. She was completed after the beginning of the war, in October 1914. She fought at Jutland, where she was hit five times by heavy British shells, taking 25 casualties.

France and Russia. However, the publicity campaign that Tirpitz engineered to ensure parliamentary support for his programme, and the hostile language it fostered in the German press and Reichstag, could not go unnoticed in Britain. The German naval build-up therefore gradually began to cause a growing alarm, not least because the German fleet was concentrated close to home (rather than being dispersed and more distant, like the fleets of Britain's other rivals). Moreover, the German Navy was judged to have highly professional personnel and impressive warships, which were clearly intended for use against Britain rather than France. When the British Government and public opinion saw a powerful fleet being built, across the narrow northern seas, and publicly justified by remarkably hostile rhetoric, this was inevitably perceived as a serious threat directed against Britain – and one to which it had to respond. This was not simply a matter of great power vanity over having a big navy, but rested on awareness of a major threat to critical national interests, even survival: as was often stated, if a hostile power gained command of the seas around Britain, the threat was not even invasion, it was starvation. When Winston Churchill later referred to the German Navy as a 'luxury fleet' it might have seemed dismissive, but it did demonstrate the contrast between the German desire and the British need for sea power. Tirpitz might well have seen his fleet as a deterrent, but it represented too great a threat to Britain to go unanswered.

The first element of Britain's response lay in the area of diplomacy. The two-power standard was in theory directed against France and Russia, but this was showing signs of changing as Germany continued to increase construction while France actually reduced naval spending. The first big diplomatic move came in 1902, with the Anglo-Japanese alliance. While mainly directed against France and, especially, Russia in the Far East, it also freed up British warships to face the growing threat at home. An equally striking development occurred in 1903, when London announced the creation of a North Sea fleet to be based at a new naval base at Rosyth in Scotland, which was better placed to counter Germany than existing ports on the south coast. Still more startling for Germany was the 1904 entente between Britain and France (also increasingly alarmed by German power), which saw the two former rivals settle many of their existing colonial disputes and begin a relationship that quickly moved on to military and naval discussions and cooperation. Germany was alarmed by this

rapprochement and sought to force them apart with an aggressive and high-risk policy regarding Morocco – further alarming Britain by raising the possibility of Germany acquiring a base on the Atlantic coast. In fact, by seeking to test and even end the Entente, this policy only deepened it, with Britain and France embarking on 'military conversations' in 1906. The following year, Britain concluded a similar entente with Russia; although Russian ambitions still seemed a threat to the empire, her defeat in the Russo-Japanese War (1904–05) made her seem less worrying while also increasing Russia's own desire to come to an accommodation with Britain. Moreover, while Russia, like France, still represented a potential threat to overseas possessions, this was far less worrying than that of Germany, with its hostile policy and growing navy just across the North Sea.

Diplomacy alone was not enough, however. Between 1900 and 1905, Germany launched 14 battleships, compared to Britain's 16, so inevitably Britain began to increase its own naval construction. The response was not limited to increasing the size of the navy, which to many observers seemed rather complacent and old fashioned. Unlike the British

SMS *Ostfriesland*, part of the *Helgoland* class. This ship had a chequered history, surviving the main Battle of Jutland without being hit, but then being damaged by a mine on the way home. *Ostfriesland* was transferred to the United States after the war, and was sunk in 1921 by Brigadier-General Billy Mitchell to prove that aircraft could sink battleships.

Admiral of the Fleet John Fisher (1841–1920)

John Fisher, known as 'Jacky' to the sailors whose living conditions he did so much to improve, joined the Royal Navy in 1854. He showed great interest in new technology and reforms throughout his career as an instructor at the gunnery school, head of the torpedo branch, Director of Naval Ordnance, commander of the Mediterranean Fleet and Second Sea Lord (in charge of personnel). He championed technical education, long-range gunnery, torpedo-boat destroyers, the submarine, aircraft and switching the navy's fuel from coal to oil. As First Sea Lord, he drove revolutionary change through the Royal Navy, vastly improving its preparedness for war. He supported his protégés, but was ruthless with sceptics and created much opposition among colleagues, which forced him from office in 1910. He was recalled at the start of the war, at the age of 74, but resigned again in 1915 over a clash with Winston Churchill concerning the Dardanelles campaign. His character was undoubtedly abrasive, but the Royal Navy needed such a forceful personality to shake it out of its nineteenth-century complacency.

Army, it had not received a shock like the Boer War to blow away its post-Trafalgar lethargy. However, a similar effect was achieved by the combination of the challenge from Germany and the impact of a visionary new leader.

On the eve of Trafalgar Day in October 1904, Admiral John Fisher became First Sea Lord, the professional head of the Royal Navy. He embarked on a radical and much-needed programme of reform both to reduce the naval budget and to increase the navy's efficiency. First, he slashed the reserve fleet and older vessels overseas, cutting 154 obsolete ships which he felt 'could neither fight nor run away' to free up men (in part to serve as nucleus crews for the remaining reserve ships, increasing their readiness) and to save money. Second, he rebalanced the Royal Navy, taking advantage of the government's diplomatic moves that reduced overseas threats to bring much of the fleet home for a new focus against Germany. This included recalling battleships from the Far East and from the Mediterranean Fleet, which declined from 14 battleships in 1902 to just six in 1906, and even these were to return home on the outbreak of war. Fisher eagerly took up the challenge posed by Tirpitz, and some of his public comments took on a distinctly and robustly anti-German tone. He caused considerable alarm in Germany, not least in speculating about the possible need to 'Copenhagen' the German fleet – a reference to Nelson's pre-emptive attack on the Danish fleet in 1801 (a more modern equivalent might be to 'Pearl Harbor'). Fisher was keen to build smaller warships, including submarines and destroyers for coastal defence. He is perhaps best known, however, for shifting the naval arms race with Germany from a competition based solely on numbers to one resting on quality, as he oversaw the adoption of a radical new type of battleship.

THE DREADNOUGHT

Fisher was an enthusiast for long-range gunnery and also a great believer that speed was the critical strategic and tactical asset for a warship. These two became the key principles for the design of the *Dreadnought*. Previous battleships had several different sizes of guns, with one or two calibres of secondary armament in addition to the main batteries. This made the task of observing and correcting the fall of shells far more difficult as well as reducing the number of the largest guns on the ship. The *Dreadnought* was therefore an all-big-gun battleship, with nothing between her ten 12in guns and small quick-firing guns for use against torpedo boats. The intention was to maximize her fighting power at long range. She was also fast, with a speed of 21 knots, two or even three knots faster than potential adversaries, and was the first battleship driven by turbine engines. She was heavily armoured, with 28cm (11in) of armour compared to 22.8cm (9in) earlier ships. These attributes came with a greater displacement – 18,187 tonnes (17,900 tons), some 1,524 tonnes (1,500 tons) greater than the previous class.

Critics were unhappy about the lack of the secondary armament of medium-calibre guns that such vessels usually carried and the fact that the programme meant Britain would have fewer, albeit more capable, battleships. Some questioned the wisdom of this innovation, since in rendering obsolete all current foreign battleships, it did the same to Britain's existing fleet – which, being larger, suffered more. On the other hand, it was believed that such a development was bound to happen (with the United States, Japan, Russia, Italy, Austria and Germany already looking towards similar developments) so it was better to initiate the change rather than to follow others.

HMS *Dreadnought*. The warship came to symbolize the naval rivalry between Britain and Germany. She was the most famous element of Jackie Fisher's naval revolution, although the true heart of his vision of future naval warfare was the *Invincible*-class battlecruiser.

HMS *Dreadnought*

HMS *Dreadnought* radically changed the nature of first-rank battleships, with capital warships in future being categorized as either 'Dreadnoughts' or 'pre-Dreadnoughts'. On her launch, like *Warrior* before, she was faster, better armed and better armoured than any other warship, compelling foreign navies to adopt similar designs. She displaced 18,410 tonnes (18,120 tons), carried ten 12in guns, was protected by 28cm (11in) of armour and her four Parsons turbines gave her a top speed of 21 knots. Her name was appropriately illustrious: previous Royal Navy warships of the same name had fought against the Spanish Armada and at Trafalgar; the name was later used for Britain's first nuclear-powered submarine, echoing the revolutionary change represented by the 1906 vessel.

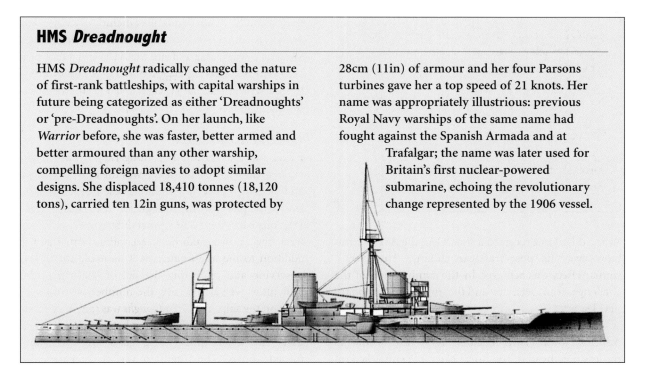

The British fleet photographed in 1907. The Royal Navy struggled to keep pace with the changing technology of the nineteenth century, but was galvanized by the challenge posed by the rise of the German Navy. Under the leadership of Admiral Jackie Fisher, it had transformed itself by the outbreak of World War I.

Dreadnought was laid down in October 1905 and completed as early as December 1906. She represented such a leap in power that not only were other navies compelled to follow suit, but her name also became the benchmark for classification, with fleets being divided into 'Dreadnoughts' and 'pre-Dreadnoughts'. Warship development did not end with the *Dreadnought*, as 1909 saw Britain launch the 'super-Dreadnought' *Orion* class with 13½in guns, and then, in 1915, *Queen Elizabeth* was completed with 15in guns. Significantly, this vessel was the first battleship to be powered by oil rather than coal, increasing the range of warships, as well as introducing a new resource that great powers would seek to control.

While the *Dreadnought* has received more attention, Fisher's true passion lay with his other new type of ship, the battlecruiser. He saw this ship as the future of naval power, but was persuaded to concentrate on battleships, in part because of the nature of the German challenge. The battlecruiser would have a similar heavy armament to the *Dreadnought*, but would sacrifice protection for even greater speed. Its role would be to scout for the battlefleet – being able to defeat the enemy's armoured cruisers while doing so – and to hunt down fast commerce raiders, as well as playing the useful auxiliary role in a major fleet engagement. This was the origin of the *Invincible* class, displacing 17,476 tonnes (17,200 tons) – just 711 tonnes (700 tons) less than *Dreadnought* – and carrying an all-big-gun armament of eight 12in cannons, which outgunned pre-Dreadnought battleships. To allow the high speed of 25 knots sought by Fisher, the battlecruisers only featured medium armour. Some critics felt that this represented too great a sacrifice, and controversy was to accompany the wartime performances of both the *Invincible* and *Lion* classes; the latter, launched in 1909, was even faster than the *Invincible* (at 27 knots, as against 25) and was armed with 13½in guns.

Far from ending the arms race between Britain and Germany, the launch of the *Dreadnought* intensified it. Tirpitz swiftly responded with further naval laws increasing construction in 1906 and 1908 with the aim of achieving a 2:3 ratio of capital ships with Britain. Given the worldwide commitments of the Royal Navy, this would give the High Seas Fleet a good chance of local superiority in the North Sea. Britain kept pace, urged on by popular opinion and the press in continuing the spiral of suspicion. In 1909, as Churchill later quipped, the Admiralty asked for six battleships, the economists would only allow four, and the Cabinet compromised on eight. The two-power standard was becoming too expensive to be supported, but it was also becoming less relevant as relations with France and Russia improved and a single predominant threat arose in the shape of

Germany. A tentative thawing of relations between the two in 1910 was insufficient to reverse the mutual suspicion already built up. In 1911, another German attempt to split Britain and France by bullying the latter over Morocco in the Agadir crisis only served to bring them closer.

The two-power standard was heavily modified, if not abandoned altogether, in March 1912 when Winston Churchill (who had been appointed First Lord of the Admiralty – the navy minister – in 1911) announced that the Royal Navy would now be planned on the basis of a 60 per cent advantage over Germany. The same year saw a naval agreement between France and Britain, with the former taking the lead in the Mediterranean and the latter in the Channel, thus permitting a further concentration of the British fleet against Germany. At this point, Germany's commitment to the naval race began to weaken, not least because her army intensified its demands for a greater focus on preparations for war on land. Yet in terms of Germany's foreign policy and grand strategy, the damage was done.

SET FOR WAR
The plan for the creation of the German High Seas Fleet had not only failed, but also had the disastrously counter-productive effect of turning Britain into an enemy. Tirpitz's policy had been based on exploiting Britain's two-power standard, taking for granted the continuing hostility between Britain on the one hand and France and Russia on the other. Yet his naval construction programme was clearly directed against Britain and demanded a response. The result was for Berlin a combination of the probably predictable (Britain expanding her own fleet), the unexpected (concentrating naval strength at home) and the unthinkable (rapprochement with France and Russia). The threat posed by a modern, high-quality and overtly hostile battlefleet so close to Britain's home waters was so great that colonial squabbles with France and Russia seemed trivial in comparison. These powers gradually came to be seen no longer as enemies but as potential allies. Whereas Germany had planned her naval expansion to exploit the international balance of power, the policy ended up overturning it, to the detriment of Germany's cause.

'Whereas Germany had planned her naval expansion to exploit the international balance of power, the policy ended up overturning it, to the detriment of Germany's cause.'

In addition to changing unfavourably the pattern of international alliances, Germany's naval build-up failed to provide a fleet capable of standing up to the Royal Navy. The two-power standard had always been a means to an end – naval security – rather than an end in its own right. Thus, as a single, growing threat loomed above all others, Britain not only rebalanced its naval power by bringing most of the fleet home, it also took up the challenge with its own build-up in quantity and also quality. This locked Germany into a naval arms race that it could not win. In challenging Britain at sea, it faced the same problem that had undermined the naval strength of Spain and, even more, France: lacking the benefits of being an island, they had to devote much of their resources to countering rivals on land. As Germany developed from a coastal fleet, through cruisers, to a battlefleet, its navy rapidly ascended the learning curve of key technologies and expertise required of a first-class naval power. The creation, from such meagre beginnings, of a battlefleet of such high quality in such a short time was a stunning achievement. Yet, the resources diverted from the army weakened Germany on land, while its navy never attained the strength that would allow victory on the seas. It could therefore be seen as having inflicted a double blow on German strategy, helping to bring Britain into the war without providing a decisive weapon against her, while also depriving the army of resources, thus rendering it incapable of delivering swift and decisive success against France and Russia.

CHAPTER 1

Distant Waters

At the start of the war in August 1914, there were three challenges to the Royal Navy's command of the seas: German cruisers stationed outside Europe, the German battlefleet based across the North Sea and the novel threat of the submarine. While in northern European waters, the opposing battlefleets remained cautiously outside their opponent's reach, in more distant waters the threat from the cruisers would dominate the opening stages of the war, predominantly in the Indian, Pacific and South Atlantic oceans.

The Royal Navy had long deployed powerful squadrons on many overseas stations. Despite Fisher's rebalancing of the fleet, the outbreak of the war still saw British warships spread across the world, although these were not first-rank ships. Their responsibilities were considerable and widespread, though they benefited from an impressive network of bases and support facilities.

Survivors from SMS *Gneisenau* floating in the water during the Battle of the Falkland Islands, 8 December 1914. The early months of the war saw two major engagements take place far from European waters; the first (Coronel) was a German victory, the second (the Falklands) a British one.

Germany, albeit on a smaller scale, had sought to gain diplomatic benefits from her growing naval power. In the early years of the century, her warships had seen action in the Far East and the Caribbean, and off South America and North Africa. At the beginning of the war, Germany had a number of cruisers patrolling foreign waters. The light cruiser *Königsberg* was off East Africa, the *Dresden* was in the western Atlantic and the *Karlsruhe* was en route to relieve her. Their standing orders in the event of war were to conduct classic cruiser operations against enemy commerce. The idea of creating a chain of fortified bases from which these ships could operate had been dropped, in view of the high probability that such bases would fall and any warships stationed there would be lost. As an alternative, Germany built up a network of agents in neutral ports to arrange the supply of fuel, food and other materials.

Vice Admiral Maximilian Graf von Spee (1861–1914)

Spee was born in Copenhagen to a noble German family ('graf' equates to 'count') and entered the Imperial German Navy in 1878. He was a gunnery specialist who gained much experience in overseas service. This was to stand him in good stead in 1912, when he was appointed commander of Germany's principal overseas naval force, the East Asiatic Squadron. On the outbreak of war, Spee took this powerful, modern force across the Pacific – a formidable achievement in terms of arranging refuelling and resupply in an increasing hostile region – before reaching the coast of Chile. Here, at the Battle of Coronel he inflicted on the Royal Navy its first defeat in over a hundred years. Thereafter, he steamed into the South Atlantic, where he took the risky decision to raid the British base at the Falkland Islands. The resulting battle cost Spee's life and also those of his two sons, who were serving in other warships of the East Asiatic Squadron.

Spee (left) was responsible for an early boost to the prestige of the Imperial German Navy, but it was only a matter of time before his force was run to ground.

SPEE IN THE PACIFIC

Germany's principal overseas force was the East Asiatic Squadron, under the command of Vice Admiral Maximilian Graf von Spee. It operated from the only major German overseas base at the fortified port of Tsingtao (Qingdao) in China. This force was centred on the modern armoured cruisers *Scharnhorst* and *Gneisenau*, each displacing 12,900 tonnes (12,700 tons) and carrying eight 8.2in and six 5.9in guns, with light cruisers in support. Both had well trained and experienced crews, and their gunnery was impressive even by the high standards of the German Navy.

Britain had powerful forces east of Suez, but, reflecting the importance and spread of its trading and imperial commitments, these were widely dispersed. Thus, the China Station had a force including the pre-Dreadnought *Triumph* (armed with comparatively feeble 10in guns) with two armoured cruisers and two light cruisers; the East Indies were protected by the battleship *Swiftsure* (sister ship of *Triumph*), with two light cruisers; and Australia and New Zealand contributed a battlecruiser and four light cruisers. Many of these ships were effectively obsolete, but in wartime they would be reinforced by Allied vessels from the French and Russian navies, and perhaps even the powerful and modern Japanese fleet. Furthermore, the British Grand Fleet provided distant support by hindering additional German cruisers in their efforts to menace the shipping lanes. The Admiralty was well

As part of Spee's East Asiatic Squadron, the light cruiser *Nürnberg* finished off the badly damaged HMS *Monmouth* at the Battle of Coronel. At the subsequent Battle of the Falkland Islands she sought to escape, but was chased down and sunk by HMS *Kent*, inflicting some damage in return.

aware of the strength of the German East Asiatic Squadron, viewing it with a wary respect, and realized that British forces would need to concentrate to be sure of defeating it.

Spee's orders gave him considerable freedom to act according to his own appreciation of the situation. At the start of the war, his squadron was scattered, but its core ships, *Scharnhorst* and *Gneisenau*, together with the light cruiser *Nürnberg*, were training in the Caroline Islands. Spee led his force to Pagan Island in the Marianas, where he was met by the light cruiser *Emden*, escorting the supply ships and colliers (coaling ships) that had departed Tsingtao in anticipation of its being blockaded. He decided to keep his force concentrated rather than dispersing it. Some historians later suggested that he would have achieved more by splitting his force and having it prey on British shipping, to maximize disruption and to force Britain to disperse its navy to hunt each vessel down. However, Spee believed that keeping them together would prevent individual ships from being cornered and destroyed. Moreover, keeping the force concentrated offered him the prospect of engaging at an advantage a smaller enemy squadron. Some of his

Rear Admiral Sir Christopher Cradock (1862–1914)

Cradock joined the Royal Navy at the tender age of 13. His formative experiences ranged from fighting ashore in Egypt and the Sudan, to helping suppress the Boxer Rebellion in China, to serving on the Royal Yacht. He also found the time to publish three books. Cradock was an experienced and brave officer, popular with his crews and his fellow officers and well regarded by his superiors. In 1913, he was appointed to command the North America and West Indies Station, becoming responsible on the outbreak of war for protecting shipping over a huge area. His action at the Battle of Coronel, leading the British force from his flagship HMS *Good Hope* against a far superior German force, showed immense courage and determination, but he has subsequently been criticized as reckless. He could have avoided the battle that cost his life, but chose not to.

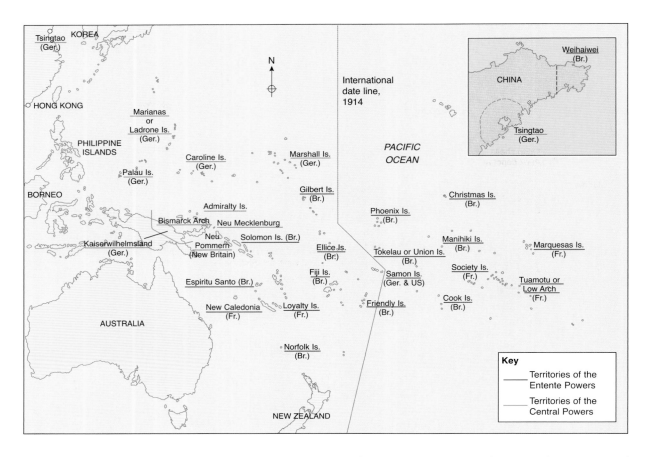

Key
— Territories of the Entente Powers
— Territories of the Central Powers

The Pacific, 1914. The naval balance in this region was generally favourable to the Entente powers, particularly after they were joined by Japan. Nevertheless, the sheer size of the area and the amount of shipping that needed protection meant that Allied naval forces would be stretched.

captains, particularly Karl von Müller of the light cruiser *Emden*, put the case for conducting classic cruiser warfare against British trade. Spee accepted that a single cruiser could cause significant disruption and would be able to refuel itself from captured vessels. He therefore detached *Emden*, as the fastest light cruiser, to attack British merchant shipping in the Indian Ocean.

Spee was aware that British and Dominion forces were patrolling near Hong Kong and Australia, and had been warned that, at best, Japan would be neutral. This meant that the base at Tsingtao would be untenable and made the option of raiding British

trade in East Asia unappealing. His decision proved prudent, as on 23 August Japan declared war on Germany. The rising power in Asia was keen to use the opportunity presented by the war in Europe to enhance its position in the Pacific, while its navy was equally eager to improve its prestige in comparison with the army. The Japanese Navy made a valuable contribution to the Allied cause, escorting convoys as far as Europe, as well as occupying German-owned islands in the Pacific, including the Carolines, Marianas and Marshalls, all names that would become familiar in the next world war. In September 1914, Japan launched an amphibious assault against Tsingtao. Her forces advanced over land, besieged the base and captured it in November. In the meantime, other German colonies were mopped up, with New Zealand seizing Samoa, and Australia taking New Guinea, New Britain and the Solomons.

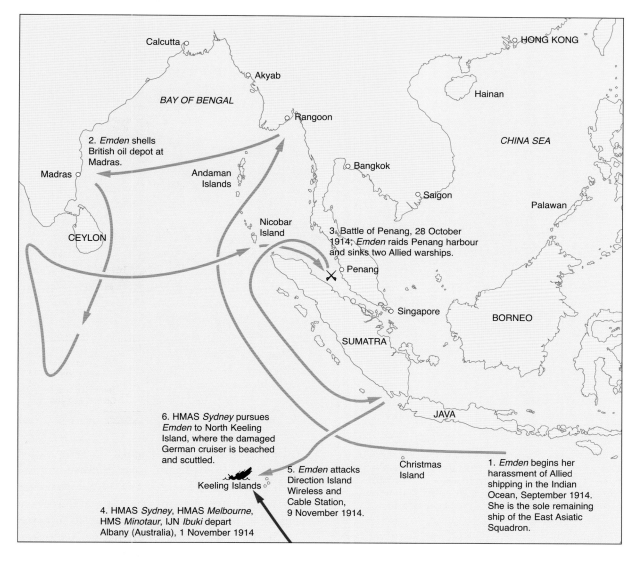

2. *Emden* shells British oil depot at Madras.

3. Battle of Penang, 28 October 1914; *Emden* raids Penang harbour and sinks two Allied warships.

6. HMAS *Sydney* pursues *Emden* to North Keeling Island, where the damaged German cruiser is beached and scuttled.

5. *Emden* attacks Direction Island Wireless and Cable Station, 9 November 1914.

4. HMAS *Sydney*, HMAS *Melbourne*, HMS *Minotaur*, IJN *Ibuki* depart Albany (Australia), 1 November 1914

1. *Emden* begins her harassment of Allied shipping in the Indian Ocean, September 1914. She is the sole remaining ship of the East Asiatic Squadron.

The Pacific was therefore rapidly becoming hostile to German forces. However, it was to Spee's advantage that many of the British and Allied warships in the area were occupied in supporting operations to capture German colonies (a far from urgent task, which could have waited until his force had been dealt with) and in escorting troop convoys heading for Europe. Despite the network of colliers and friendly agents in neutral ports built up by Germany before the war, the availability of fuel was the main consideration for Spee.

Emden's area of operations. Spee was persuaded to allow the light cruiser *Emden* to separate from the rest of his squadron in order to raid enemy shipping in the Indian Ocean. She took 23 vessels and caused great disruption for two months before being sunk by HMAS *Sydney*.

He therefore headed south and east, towards the coast of Chile, where he expected to be able to acquire coal. On the way, he was joined at Easter Island by the light cruisers *Leipzig* (which had steamed south from the coast of California) and *Dresden* (which had rounded Cape Horn, having been in the South

Atlantic at the outbreak of war). Each had taken two British merchant ships before joining the main force. Spee then managed largely to disappear into the vast expanses of the southern Pacific. Britain had no firm idea of his location, but the best guess of naval commanders was that he was heading for South America, which was supported by occasional sightings of his force. On 14 September, he was spotted off Samoa; on 22 September, a French steamer radioed a sighting of the German ships at Tahiti; and in mid-October they were spotted at Easter Island. These sightings confirmed indications gleaned from intercepted wireless messages that he was heading for South America, though this was far from certain.

Rear Admiral Sir Christopher Cradock was in command of the North America and West Indies Squadron, responsible for a huge area with a great deal of merchant traffic. His squadron of cruisers was in the Caribbean at the outset of the war. It had been hunting German cruisers in the North Atlantic, but as the threat there declined and reinforcements arrived, it moved south. His forces were small relative to the vast area for which they were responsible, and though capable of taking on a raiding light cruiser, they were old and greatly inferior to Spee's squadron. Cradock's flagship was the armoured cruiser HMS *Good Hope*, which displaced 14,325 tonnes (14,100 tons). Her two 9.2in guns were backed by 16 outdated 6in guns, although it was generally known that these low-mounted weapons could not be used in heavy seas, further weakening their offensive power. She was accompanied by the 9750-tonne (9600-ton) armoured cruiser *Monmouth*, carrying 14 of the same 6in guns. These cruisers were very much second-line warships, and had not been retained for service with the Grand Fleet precisely because of their age and limited armament. Furthermore, the policy of concentrating forces at home – which had involved disbanding the South Atlantic Squadron – and reinforcing overseas stations only on mobilization, meant that their crews were inexperienced reserves. The ships were supported by the more modern light cruiser *Glasgow* (4880 tonnes/4800 tons, armed with two 6in and ten 4in guns) and the armed merchant cruiser *Otranto*, which was expected to fight similar vessels among the enemy forces rather than warships. While the light cruisers on either side were comparable, *Scharnhorst* and *Gneisenau* had an enormous advantage over Cradock's armoured cruisers in the range and power of their guns; the main armament of each comprised eight 8.2in guns spread across two twin and four single turrets, backed by a secondary armament of six 5.9in guns. In addition, Spee's crews were well trained and filled with men of experience.

German Cruiser Operations

Accounts of naval warfare often focus on great clashes between fleets, but no less significant were the activities of cruisers. They patrolled the seas, often at some distance from home and for long periods, either defending or attacking merchant shipping. Targeting trade could damage an enemy's economy and hinder his transportation of key war materials and troops, as well as forcing him to devote disproportionate resources in dispersing his fleet to hunt down the attackers. The American historian Alfred T. Mahan dismissed the impact of cruisers in harassing shipping, as opposed to a full blockade. Nevertheless, in the early months of World War I they tied down considerable Allied resources and brought some striking German successes.

German cruiser operations caused considerable disruption and achieved favourable publicity, but their impact was negligible next to that of the U-boats.

As it became clearer that Spee was probably heading towards South America, there was discussion within the Admiralty of despatching three or four armoured cruisers to reinforce Cradock, but this option was rejected. Some even raised the possibility of sending battlecruisers, but Admiral John Jellicoe, commander of the Grand Fleet, vetoed any such weakening of his force. The only reinforcement provided, despite an awareness of Spee's strength, was the pre-Dreadnought battleship HMS *Canopus*. This 13,160-tonne (12,950-ton) vessel was obsolete; indeed, she was scheduled to be scrapped in 1915. She mounted four 12in guns that were comfortably outranged by the main armament of Spee's armoured cruisers, and had less armour protection than they had. Never a fast ship, she was slowed further by mechanical problems, and her crew comprised inexperienced reserves. At one point it was decided to send the modern armoured cruiser HMS *Defence*, carrying four 9.2in and ten 7.5in guns, to join Cradock, but this decision was reversed. Crucially, Cradock was never informed of this decision, and set off thinking that *Defence* would shortly join him.

HMS *Monmouth* was an obsolete armoured cruiser, too old and weak to serve with the Grand Fleet, that served overseas with a scratch crew of inexperienced reservists. When she faced Spee's modern force at the Battle of Coronel she was hopelessly outclassed and was sunk with all hands.

THE BATTLE OF CORONEL (1 NOVEMBER 1914)

Believing that he was acting in accordance with his orders from London (which were at best ambiguous), Cradock took his squadron from the South Atlantic into the Pacific to seek out Spee. He was under the impression that *Canopus* could only make 12 knots, so he left her behind to escort his colliers; she was in fact capable of 16 knots, though awareness of this might not have changed his decision. While the old battleship would have been useful in an engagement with Spee, Cradock believed that she would slow down the rest of the force and hence make any such engagement less likely. Moreover, the German commander would have enough of a speed advantage easily to avoid battle with a force including *Canopus* if he desired. Cradock faced an impossible dilemma: with *Canopus* he would probably be unable to force a battle, while without her (and, in all probability, even

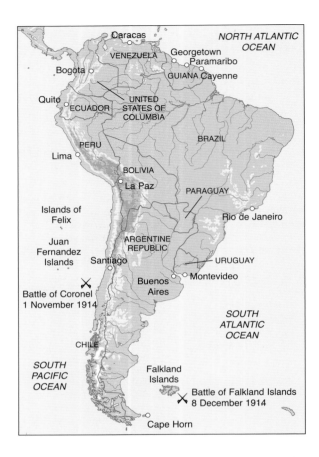

with her), he would lose any battle that occurred. His best hope was to pounce on ships separated from Spee's force, defeating it one ship at a time. Hence, having intercepted radio signals suggesting that at least one German warship was nearby, on 31 October he was heading north along the west coast of Chile. While Cradock was seeking the German force, the latter was heading south from Valparaiso and was hunting him, having been informed that *Glasgow* had been sighted off Coronel.

At 4.20pm on 1 November, *Glasgow* spotted smoke and steamed towards what was assumed to be one of the German light cruisers. Five minutes later, *Scharnhorst* and *Gneisenau* were recognized. At this point, discovering that his opponent was not just a single light cruiser, Cradock had to make a fateful decision between attacking what he knew to be a far superior force or avoiding battle. He chose the former course. Just after 6pm, he tried to force an action, seeking to gain any slight advantage he could by ensuring that the setting sun would be behind him, to dazzle the German gunners. As Cradock sought to close to within the comparatively short range of his main armament, Spee turned away and used his superior speed to maintain his distance until the sun

ABOVE **The large amount of British merchant shipping off the west and east coasts of South America presented a lucrative and tempting target to German raiders. Initially, they were faced only by second-rate British warships, providing them with an early opportunity to boost German morale.**

BELOW **HMS *Canopus* was a nineteenth-century pre-Dreadnought, rescued from the scrap yard at the start of the war and pressed into overseas service. She was so slow that Rear Admiral Sir Christopher Cradock left her behind when he went into the Pacific in search of Spee's squadron.**

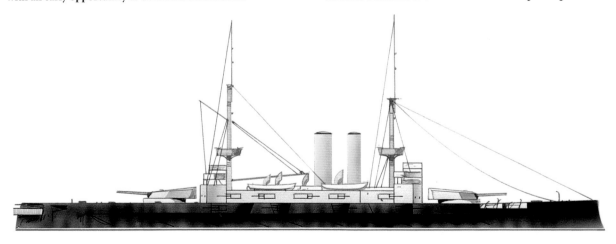

had gone down far enough to silhouette the British ships and leave his own in darkness. Just after 7pm, the German armoured cruisers opened fire, at a range that allowed 12 of their 8.2in guns to fire; only the two 9.2in guns of *Good Hope* were able to respond, and one of these was knocked out by the third salvo from *Scharnhorst*. As the two flagships fired at each other, *Gneisenau* concentrated her fire on *Monmouth*, *Leipzig* on *Glasgow* and *Dresden* on *Otranto*. (*Nürnberg* was not involved in the early stages of the battle, having been slowed by problems with her engine and propellers.) The British warships returned fire, but their targets were hardly visible and the fall of their shells could not be seen at all. Cradock sought to take

his already badly damaged ships in closer, to bring the German force within the range of the old 6in guns of his cruisers, but this simply intensified the fire directed against them.

At about 7.50pm, the fires on the battered *Good Hope* reached her main magazine and she exploded, sinking with all hands by 8pm. *Monmouth*, also grievously damaged, broke away from the battle only to be discovered and finished off by the late-arriving

At the Battle of Coronel, Cradock sought to exploit his initial advantage in visibility, but Spee was able to use the superior speed of his force to decline battle until it suited him. His better-armed and better-protected warships then swiftly destroyed their opponents.

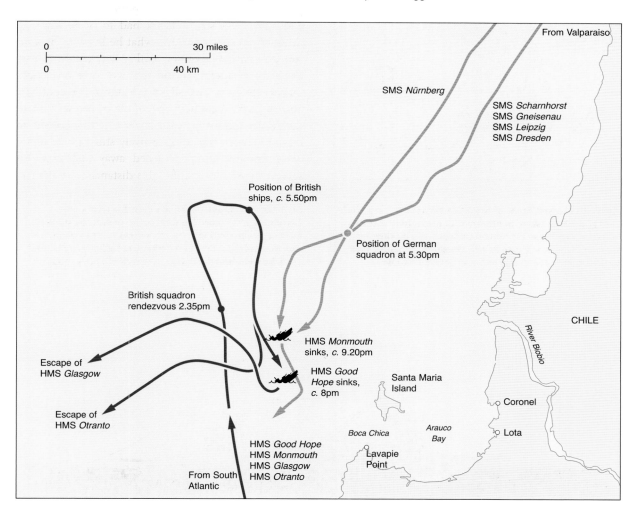

Nürnberg, capsizing and sinking at about 9pm, again leaving no survivors. *Glasgow* escaped with only light damage and casualties from five hits, and *Otranto* also managed to slip away into the darkness. On the German side, neither *Scharnhorst* nor *Gneisenau* suffered anything more than very minor damage while the light cruisers were unscathed.

The result of the Battle of Coronel was a major blow to the prestige of the Royal Navy and a corresponding boost to that of Germany. The Imperial German Navy had inflicted on Britain its first naval defeat in more than a century. News of the battle was greeted in Britain with a combination of shock and anger. Opinion then and since has been divided over where to lay the blame. Some have criticized Cradock for taking his force into an action that could have been avoided, against a force that he knew to be far superior

HMS *Defence* was a more modern and more powerful armoured cruiser than either *Good Hope* or *Monmouth*, with four 9.2in guns. Cradock requested that she be sent to reinforce him, but the decision to do so was not taken until too late. HMS *Defence* was later sunk at the Battle of Jutland.

to his. Whether this was due to his calculation of the balance of risks or simply down to a reluctance to retreat in the face of the enemy, it was an error. He had an alternative course of action open to him: he could have fallen back towards *Canopus*, which at the time Spee's force was sighted was some 500km (300 miles) behind, escorting the squadron's colliers. Had he done this, however, he would have risked allowing Spee to slip past him into the South Atlantic, where his powerful cruisers could have wreaked havoc on British trade as well as threatening the crucial base on the Falklands. Cradock would have been aware that if he declined battle at this point, he could well fail to find Spee at a later time.

Another factor in favour of embracing the traditional offensive spirit of the Royal Navy was the consideration that the lack of bases or friendly ports for the German ships meant that even if not sunk, they would be hard pressed to repair any major damage, which would compel them to accept internment in a neutral port, thus taking them out of the rest of the war. Yet the gross inequality in the fighting power of

the two squadrons meant that such damage was unlikely to be inflicted. Finally, Cradock was aware that another British admiral had just been court-martialled for failing to engage what many considered to be a clearly superior enemy force; indeed, he had explicitly said that he had no intention of repeating the fate of Rear Admiral Ernest Troubridge (an account of Troubridge and the escape of the *Goeben* is provided in the later chapter on the Dardanelles).

Others have directed their criticism at the Admiralty War Staff, which must indeed share the blame. During this early stage of the war, it undoubtedly suffered organizational weaknesses – not least due to the fact that it was still a young institution, having only been established in 1912 – and errors were made. It should be noted in mitigation that there were pressing concerns elsewhere, with the main German fleet and also an operation to defend Antwerp dominating attention in London. The situation was not helped by the disruption caused by personal attacks on the First Sea Lord, Admiral Prince Louis of Battenberg, which culminated in his resignation on 29 October. Further uncertainties arose from problems with signals. There was no direct contact between Cradock and the Admiralty; signals had to go through intermediaries, so there was always a possibility of a critical message being delayed or even failing to arrive at all. On top of this practical difficulty, both parties sent signals that were misunderstood. Cradock seems genuinely to have believed that the Admiralty wished him to engage Spee and that it viewed his force as adequate for the task. Conversely, however, it seems clear that the Admiralty did not intend their signals to be read this way. Similarly, whilst Cradock thought he had made his intentions clear to the Admiralty, their understanding of his signals was quite different, and they believed him to be fulfilling their intentions and remaining at the Falklands. Then, when they realized

> '*The most serious error by the Admiralty and the principal cause of the defeat at Coronel lay in the failure to provide Cradock with additional forces.*'

he had steamed into the Pacific, they failed to stop him because they believed he was accompanied by *Canopus*. Yet, when he explicitly stated that he was leaving *Canopus* behind, they did not query this decision, let alone countermand it.

The most serious error by the Admiralty and the principal cause of the defeat at Coronel lay in the failure to provide Cradock with additional forces. London overestimated the fighting power of *Canopus*, which would probably not have changed the outcome of the battle even if present. The known strength of Spee's force should have resulted in greater reinforcement. Eventually, the Admiralty seems to have recognized this and unambiguously ordered Cradock to avoid taking on Spee before *Defence* arrived. It was too late: the signal was sent on 3 November, after the battle had been fought and decided. While the Royal Navy was overstretched with many widespread commitments, by failing to send more warships to the South Atlantic the authorities were over-insuring against other, uncertain risks while neglecting to strengthen a commander facing an enemy force that was known to be greatly superior. Cradock may justly be criticized for making the wrong choice between two unpleasant options, but the Admiralty had left him in that invidious position.

THE NEXT MOVES
In the aftermath of the battle, *Canopus* joined up with *Glasgow* and headed back to the Falkland Islands to defend the base there, arriving at Port Stanley on 8 November. Meanwhile, swift and important decisions had been taken in London. The German victory was clear in tactical terms, but far greater in terms of prestige and morale, so there was a burning desire to strike back. There was also a practical reason to do so, since Spee's victorious squadron represented a serious threat to British trade. Hence, Churchill (First Lord of

the Admiralty) and Jackie Fisher (who had returned as First Sea Lord) took rapid action.

They ordered a series of redeployments – demonstrating the worldwide stage on which the Royal Navy operated – to cover all of the options open to Spee and ensure that the net would gradually be closed on him. In case he should head back across the Pacific, a Japanese squadron of one battleship and two battlecruisers was deployed to Suva, while the

Vice Admiral Sir Frederick Doveton Sturdee (1859–1925)

Sturdee joined the Royal Navy in 1871 and passed out of initial training at the top of his class. He became a torpedo specialist and commanded a series of squadrons, before becoming Chief of the Admiralty War Staff, a position he held on the outbreak of war. He was perhaps better suited to command afloat than to staff work; he was criticized for his role in the sinking of the three cruisers (HMS *Cressy*, *Aboukir* and *Hogue*) in September 1914, as well as for the decisions leading to the Battle of Coronel, though he had advocated reinforcing Cradock with two battlecruisers. This suggestion was over-ruled, but when just such a force was despatched to avenge Cradock, Sturdee was appointed to command it. At the Battle of the Falklands, Sturdee was presented with a favourable situation, but handled it professionally, avoiding potential mistakes and securing a decisive victory without any serious damage to the precious battlecruisers. He was later appointed to command a squadron of Dreadnoughts in the Grand Fleet, and retired in the rank of Admiral of the Fleet.

battlecruiser HMAS *Australia*, accompanied by the light cruiser HMS *Newcastle* and two Japanese warships, was sent to the southern coast of California. Spee might head north and seek to cross between the Pacific and the Atlantic via the newly opened Panama Canal, so another battlecruiser, HMS *Princess Royal*, was sent to Halifax (to strengthen the forces off New York) and then, with the old battleship HMS *Glory*, to the West Indies to link up with three cruisers already there. Forces off the west and south of Africa were also reinforced by armoured cruisers and the old battleship *Vengeance* from the Channel Fleet.

Finally, Spee might pass Cape Horn and head into the South Atlantic. *Glasgow* was therefore ordered to join up with the cruiser squadron operating off Montevideo; *Canopus* was to have accompanied her, but further engine troubles led to her remaining to guard the Falklands. This force was under strict instructions not to engage Spee until reinforced by warships more powerful than the German admiral could ever have anticipated having to fight. Churchill suggested sending a battlecruiser, but Fisher recommended sending two; Jellicoe protested, but had to accept the decision. The two modern battlecruisers *Invincible* and *Inflexible* were therefore rapidly made ready, being pushed through the dockyards two days faster than was initially thought possible. This was not the last time that a capital ship called *Invincible* would be rushed through the dockyards to head for the Falklands in order to avenge a serious blow against Britain. The battlecruisers were modern capital ships of 17,780 tonnes (17,500 tons), with the main armament of a battleship (eight 12in guns) and with little armour to allow high speed. The fact that the Admiralty was prepared to risk weakening the Home Fleet by detaching three battlecruisers – leaving it with a four to five inferiority against the High Seas Fleet – shows just how seriously Spee's force was taken.

On 11 November, *Invincible* and *Inflexible* headed south under the command of Vice Admiral Sir Frederick Doveton Sturdee. His force was not only adequate for its task, but his orders were in clear contrast to the ambiguous ones given to Cradock: 'search for the German armoured cruisers *Scharnhorst*

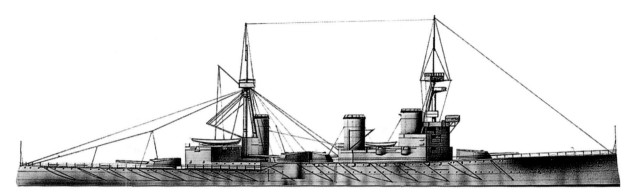

HMS *Inflexible* was the second of Fisher's battlecruisers. After the victory at the Falkland Islands, she was involved in the escape of the *Goeben* in the Mediterranean and then served in the Dardanelles in support of the Gallipoli operation. She also took part in the Battle of Jutland.

and *Gneisenau* and bring them to action. All other considerations are to be subordinated to this end.'

On 26 November, Sturdee's force met up with the cruisers off Montevideo, replenished coal and stores, and then on 28 November headed south again. He arrived at the Falkland Islands on 7 December, after a surprisingly leisurely passage, and began to take on coal to be ready the next day to round the Horn and begin searching for Spee in Chilean waters.

Spee, as it happened, was on his way to him. He had realized that heading back across the Pacific would only lead him towards powerful British or Japanese forces, so he steamed into the South Atlantic, which offered the prospect of lucrative commercial targets as

HMS *Invincible* steaming into action at the Falklands. Her rapid deployment to the South Atlantic and her victory in the battle represented exactly what Jackie Fisher had intended the battlecruisers to do. However, they did not fare so well in the full fleet engagement at Jutland.

well as the possibility of a dash for home. He seemed to be in no great hurry and did not display the resolution he had previously; he could have made the passage much sooner, attacking the Falklands and departing well before Sturdee arrived. In fact, he put into port in Chile and then remained at anchor for 10 days; on 15 November – four days after the *Invincible* and *Inflexible* had left Britain – he headed south, and was then further delayed by bad weather. Spee entered the South Atlantic on the night of 1/2 December. He captured a collier and paused to distribute its precious cargo, since shrinking coal stocks were his main concern. Once again, he lacked accurate information; he had been informed that a large cruiser force was at Port Stanley in the Falkland Islands, but was subsequently assured that it had departed for South Africa. German agents in South America did learn of the presence of the British battlecruisers, as Sturdee did little to keep their passage secret, but this critical intelligence never reached Spee.

> 'At around 10am the German lookouts recognized the distinctive tripod masts of not one but two battlecruisers. The presence of these two fast capital ships must have been an enormous shock.'

On 6 December he called his captains together and explained his intention to attack the British base on the Falkland Islands. This was an important facility, with a radio station and coal reserves as well as harbour facilities; destroying these would seriously harm the Royal Navy's operations in the South Atlantic as well as inflicting another hammer blow to British prestige and morale. Some of his captains were concerned about the risk involved, but Spee expected to find only a modest cruiser force there, which he would either destroy with his superior firepower, repeating the success of Coronel, or evade with his superior speed. His decision to attack Port Stanley has been criticized, much like Cradock's decision to give battle just over a month before. In Spee's defence, it was remarkably bad luck that when he closed on the Falklands on the morning of 8 December, he was to encounter a powerful British force, even though it was as surprised by his appearance as he was to discover it.

THE BATTLE OF THE FALKLAND ISLANDS (8 DECEMBER 1914)

Spee ordered *Gneisenau* and *Nürnberg* to go ahead to scout the harbour, with the rest of the force a few kilometres behind. He might have been wiser to send just a light cruiser as a scout, with the bulk of his squadron lying further off. At about 9am, as they approached to attack the wireless station, they spotted warships in the harbour, though smoke made it difficult to be sure of their identity. *Gneisenau*'s captain dismissed the claim that one lookout had recognized a battlecruiser. About 20 minutes later, they came under the fire of heavy guns, having been spotted at 7.50am by lookouts posted ashore for just such an eventuality. At last, *Canopus*, absent from Coronel, was able to play a brief but important role. She had been beached to provide some protection for the harbour before Sturdee arrived and she now shielded his deployment, driving off the German squadron while the British force left the harbour.

The British force was a powerful one, comprising not only the two battlecruisers *Invincible* and *Inflexible*, but also the armoured cruisers *Carnarvon*, *Cornwall* and *Kent*, the light cruisers *Bristol* and *Glasgow*, and the armed merchant cruiser *Macedonia*. Initially, however, the squadron was in a highly vulnerable position. Quite unaware of the approaching enemy, most of the ships had not even begun to take on coal, others still had coal piled on their decks, and some had started on lengthy repairs and maintenance. All but *Kent* were at two hours' notice to depart and would take some time to get up steam. Nevertheless, Sturdee calmly ordered his force to begin preparations to put to sea while *Canopus* provided covering fire, shooting blind over the land. *Gneisenau* and *Nürnberg* initially manoeuvred to attack *Kent* at the mouth of the harbour, but turned back on taking accurate fire from *Canopus*.

It has been suggested that a rapid attack to exploit the great early disadvantage of the British force might have brought Spee success, either bombarding the British ships at anchor – perhaps even ordering his light cruisers to take the risk of launching torpedo attacks against stationary enemies – or engaging the British ships at a disadvantage as they left port one by one. Such a bold move would have had a good chance of at least inflicting serious damage that would have slowed any pursuit. Instead, Spee ordered his two ships to rejoin the squadron and withdrew at top speed to the southeast. His reasons are not clear but it seems that while he realized that a powerful force was present, he was confident that, even if it included Dreadnoughts, he had the advantage in speed and could make his escape. At around 10am, however, the German lookouts recognized the distinctive tripod masts of not one but two battlecruisers. The presence of these two ships must have been an enormous shock – even worse than that experienced by Cradock on sighting *Scharnhorst* and *Gneisenau*, since Cradock had at least been aware that they were in the area.

It took about two hours for Sturdee's force to put to sea, but when it did so, it had not only escaped from its earlier vulnerability but was now in a strong position. The weather was fine, visibility was good and there was plenty of daylight left. The German ships were less than 30km (20 miles) away and would soon be within range of the battlecruisers' 12in main armament. At about 10.20am, Sturdee signalled 'general chase'. He realized that he had ample time and so reduced speed somewhat to allow his armoured cruisers to catch up and to reduce the smoke being generated. At about 11.30am he even ordered that his crews should eat a meal.

The three German colliers supporting Spee were spotted by an alert resident of the islands, who telephoned the British base. Sturdee ordered their interception by the armed merchant cruiser

HMS *Canopus* opens fire, over the land, from within the harbour at Port Stanley. Although absent from the Battle of Coronel, Canopus played a useful role in the early stages of the Battle of the Falkland Islands by driving away Spee's force while the British squadron deployed.

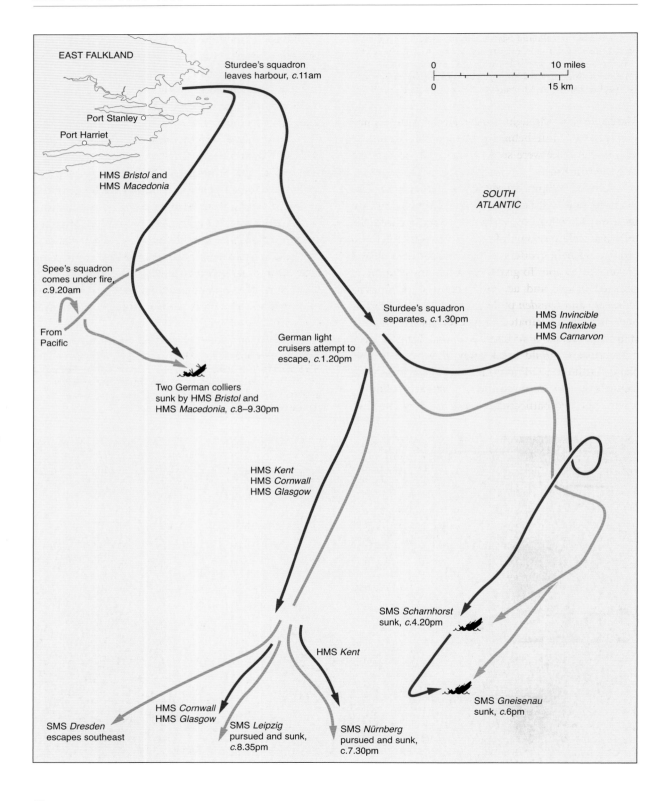

EAST FALKLAND

Sturdee's squadron
leaves harbour, c.11am

0   10 miles

0   15 km

Port Stanley ○

Port Harriet ○

HMS *Bristol* and
HMS *Macedonia*

SOUTH
ATLANTIC

Spee's squadron
comes under fire,
c.9.20am

From
Pacific

Sturdee's squadron
separates, c.1.30pm

HMS *Invincible*
HMS *Inflexible*
HMS *Carnarvon*

German light
cruisers attempt to
escape, c.1.20pm

Two German colliers
sunk by HMS *Bristol* and
HMS *Macedonia*, c.8–9.30pm

HMS *Kent*
HMS *Cornwall*
HMS *Glasgow*

SMS *Scharnhorst*
sunk, c.4.20pm

HMS *Kent*

SMS *Gneisenau*
sunk, c.6pm

HMS *Cornwall*
HMS *Glasgow*

SMS *Dresden*
escapes southeast

SMS *Leipzig*
pursued and sunk,
c.8.35pm

SMS *Nürnberg*
pursued and sunk,
c.7.30pm

The Battle of the Falkland Islands saw the faster British battlecruisers emerge from Port Stanley to chase down and sink the German armoured cruisers *Scharnhorst* and *Gneisenau*. Spee ordered his light cruisers to attempt to escape, but *Leipzig* and *Nürnberg* were caught and sunk.

Macedonia and the light cruiser HMS *Bristol*, which was lagging a little behind the rest of the squadron. Two of the three were sunk, while the third escaped into internment.

At about 12.20pm, Sturdee increased speed to close the range, and just before 1pm opened fire at a range of some 14,500m (16,000 yards). Spee realized the only plausible outcome of the battle, and at 1.20pm ordered his light cruisers to break out of the line and make their escape. To give them a fighting chance, he changed course and accepted action while *Leipzig*, *Nürnberg* and *Dresden* pulled away. However, Sturdee had already anticipated this eventuality and his standing orders to his cruisers were that if the German light cruisers should break away, they were to give chase. Without needing additional instructions, the captains of *Kent*, *Cornwall* and *Glasgow* duly followed, leaving the two battlecruisers and the slower cruiser

Carnarvon to continue the pursuit of *Scharnhorst* and *Gneisenau*. Even divided in this way, the British force still enjoyed a considerable superiority.

By about 1.30pm, the main units were on parallel courses at a range of some 12,500m (14,000 yards). The British battlecruisers fired broadsides and the German armoured cruisers returned fire. Few British shells found their target, but those that did caused serious damage. Sturdee sensibly sought to keep the range ideal for his purposes – within the range of the main armament of his battlecruisers but outside that of the German cruisers. Spee, on the other hand, sought to close the range to assist his main armament and also to allow his secondary 5.9in guns to be brought into play. Sturdee aimed to avoid this, and at times changed course to maintain the range as well as to escape the clouds of smoke from his guns that obscured their targets.

The sinking of the *Leipzig*. This vessel, a *Bremen*-class light cruiser, sought to escape at the Battle of the Falkland Islands, pursued by two British cruisers. She initially managed to maintain her lead over HMS *Cornwall*, but was hit and slowed by HMS *Glasgow* and then sunk.

HMS *Invincible* and *Inflexible* at the Battle of the Falkland Islands. The *Scharnhorst* and *Gneisenau* had overpowered the obsolete British armoured cruisers at Coronel, but at the Falkland Islands they faced two battlecruisers that outclassed them in speed and firepower.

Throughout various changes of course over the next two hours, the warships continued to fire at each other, with the British inflicting more damage with their heavier guns, yet being impressed by the ability of the German crews to keep up their own rate of fire. Gradually, though, the damage began to tell on the guns and machinery of the German ships. At about 3.30pm, Spee changed course in an attempt to bring his undamaged broadsides to bear. Sturdee crossed his wake to take the leeward position (so his smoke would be blown away) and to widen the range once again, and continued to pound the *Scharnhorst*. At about 4pm, the German flagship stopped firing and shortly afterwards began to list. At 4.17pm, the grievously damaged ship sank with all hands, having ordered *Gneisenau* to escape if she could. Her sister ship was in no position to do so, however, and as she slowed she now became the target for both the British battlecruisers as well as for the *Carnarvon*, which had caught up. As *Gneisenau*'s return fire diminished under the attacks of the three British warships, they closed the range to finish her off. By about 5.30pm, having run out of ammunition, *Gneisenau* stopped

SMS *Dresden* was the only ship of Spee's squadron to survive the Battle of the Falkland Islands, using her high speed to escape the pursuing British cruisers. Despite her captain's subsequent caution, she was hunted down, cornered and sunk in March 1915 by two of the ships she had evaded.

firing and the British warships followed suit. Unable to fight on and with his engines out of action, her captain had scuttling charges fired and then ordered the surviving crew members to abandon ship. *Gneisenau* slowly capsized and at about 6pm sank, leaving just under 200 survivors (the sole ones out of the 1500 crew of the two armoured cruisers) to be picked up by the British ships. *Invincible* had been hit more than 20 times, but had suffered just one casualty and no noteworthy damage beyond one of her anti-torpedo boat guns being knocked out. *Inflexible* had lost one man killed and two wounded, but took no significant damage. This outcome was as stark a demonstration as Coronel of the effect of a distinct qualitative disparity.

The three light cruisers, for which Spee had sacrificed himself and his two most powerful units, were also at a disadvantage. They were being pursued by two armoured and one light cruiser, and given the length of their operations without full maintenance, could not rely on speed to save themselves.

At first *Cornwall* chased *Leipzig*, *Kent* pursued *Nürnberg*, while *Glasgow* went after *Dresden*, which was in the best state mechanically and started to pull away. Rather than continue after *Dresden* and possibly seeing both escape, *Glasgow* switched target to *Leipzig*. Several times *Glasgow* opened fire beyond the effective range of her main guns, and when *Leipzig* – realizing escape was unlikely – turned to bring her broadside to bear, *Glasgow* pulled away once again. Each time this occurred, the better-armed and armoured *Cornwall* was able to close the gap, and eventually was able to add her own fire. As more damage was inflicted on *Leipzig* she slowed down, and *Cornwall* was able to close in and intensify her fire, with *Glasgow* in support. By about 7.30pm, *Leipzig* was out of ammunition and her captain gave the order to scuttle, his ship sinking with him at 9.23pm. Just 18 of her crew survived. *Glasgow* had been hit twice, losing one man killed and four wounded while *Cornwall*, against which *Leipzig* had concentrated her fire, was hit 18 times, but was saved from casualties or significant damage by her armour.

Meanwhile, *Kent* was pursuing *Nürnberg*. The German warship should have been faster, but she was in far from top condition and *Kent*'s engine room managed to bring her up to a speed two knots above her theoretical maximum (partly by burning much of the ship's wooden furniture). At about 5pm, after the distance between the two had closed, *Nürnberg* opened fire and found that her 4.1in guns outranged the 6in armament of *Kent*. However, the latter's armour prevented damage that might have slowed her down, and at 5.35pm two of *Nürnberg*'s hard-pressed boilers burst, ending the hope that she might escape into the thickening mist and rain. *Kent* closed in and her heavier armament proved decisive. Just before 7pm, *Nürnberg* struck her colours and half an hour later capsized and sank, with just seven of her crew surviving. *Kent* had been hit repeatedly, taking four dead and 12 wounded. One hit started a fire that threatened to ignite a magazine, but damage control and the flooding of the compartment prevented this.

HMS *Cornwall* was an armoured cruiser, sister ship of the ill fated *Monmouth*. At the Battle of the Falkland Islands, she took on an opponent more appropriate to the capabilities of her class, and, with the assistance of HMS *Glasgow*, sank the *Leipzig*. She later served in the Dardanelles operations.

Dresden was the only ship of the East Asiatic Squadron to escape, helped by her high speed and by the poor weather, which had finally changed to favour the Germans. She avoided British patrols, returned to the Pacific and hid out in isolated bays, hindered in pursuing cruiser warfare by her lack of coal. She sank one British merchant ship in February 1915, but her luck finally ran out in March, when she was confronted once again by two of the ships she had evaded at the Falklands. A deciphered signal ordering a collier to join her brought *Kent* to the planned rendezvous on 8 March. *Dresden* outran her, but six days later was cornered in Cumberland Bay (in Juan Fernandez Island, off the west coast of Chile), by *Kent* and also *Glasgow*, the survivor of Coronel. After a brief battle she was scuttled by her crew.

Sturdee had won a great victory – indeed, the most decisive victory won at sea throughout the war. Admittedly, he enjoyed considerable luck in arriving at the Falklands just at the right time for Spee's force to fall into his lap, and had further good fortune in the favourable weather on the day of the battle. However, he showed commendable calm in recovering from the unpleasant surprise of having his force caught in a vulnerable position in harbour. He then avoided various mistakes that could have had serious consequences and, crucially, adopted precisely the right tactics to destroy the two armoured cruisers that were his main objective, without risking serious damage that might deny the Grand Fleet the return of its precious battlecruisers in fighting condition. His foresight in providing clear orders to his accompanying cruisers was vindicated when they broke off to chase down the German light cruisers.

The effect of the battle was, like that of Coronel, far greater than the significance of the ships actually sunk. First, British prestige and morale rebounded

Like *Cornwall*, HMS *Kent* was another sister ship of the *Monmouth* that joined in the chase of the German light cruisers at the Battle of the Falkland Islands. She successfully pursued the *Nürnberg*, her crew squeezing crucial additional speed from her old engines by burning wooden furniture.

after the shock of the previous month. Second, with the destruction of Spee's force, the pressure on British merchant shipping – much of which had been kept in port while the threat existed – was now relieved. Moreover, many cruisers could now be freed for other tasks, either with the Grand Fleet or to support other operations.

Fisher was positively exultant, not only that his bold decision to accept the risk of weakening the Grand Fleet had paid off, but also at the vindication of the design of his cherished battlecruisers. Here, they had been used precisely as he had intended, using their speed to close with an opponent and to shape the tactics of the battle to their advantage, holding the enemy at an ideal range and then using their heavy armament to decisive effect.

The wreck of the *Königsberg*. One of the German light cruisers stationed overseas at the outbreak of war, *Königsberg* operated against British shipping off East Africa before being chased up the Rufiji River. She was blockaded there and was sunk in July 1915 by two British monitors.

The battle did provide some cause for concern for the Royal Navy. The accuracy of its gunnery had been poor. There were mitigating circumstances, notably the long range of the engagement, the effect of smoke and the difficulties of aiming while steaming at high speed with frequent course changes. Nevertheless, in a more evenly balanced encounter, the consequences might have been more serious. The circumstances of the battle were such that the great weaknesses in the design of British warships, particularly the battlecruisers, did not become apparent: the range and power of the German guns was not enough to threaten them, while the German armour was easily defeated by the main armament of *Invincible* and *Inflexible*.

The battles of Coronel and the Falklands shared a number of important features. First, they had only occurred because of imperfect information: with more accurate intelligence, one side would have sought to avoid battle. Second, the result of both engagements was determined by an overwhelming difference in fighting power of the respective forces

involved. Finally, both actions were, in a way, a throwback to the past: few battles in the future would be waged solely by surface warships, without any role for mines, submarines or aircraft.

SURFACE RAIDERS AGAINST COMMERCE

With the destruction of Spee's force, the sting had been taken out of the campaign waged by German surface warships against merchant shipping. In addition to commissioned warships, Germany followed the practice of previous centuries by arming merchant ships to prey on enemy commerce. Some of these vessels were away from home at the beginning of the war and were converted at sea, receiving guns and ammunition from warships in isolated anchorages. Some of these ships achieved a measure of success: like the cruising warships, they not only sank merchant ships but also caused wider disruption to commerce and diverted the efforts of British warships. On the whole, however, they represented less of a threat than Britain had feared, being severely restricted by their

As captain of the *Emden*, Karl von Müller convinced Spee to allow him to detach and operate against Allied merchant shipping. He showed considerable courage and flair, earning the admiration of his opponents before his ship was caught and sunk. He was interned and survived the war.

inability to acquire coal. Some were hunted down and sunk by warships or by Britain's own armed merchant ships, others had to accept internment as their fuel ran out. Overall, their direct and indirect effects were less marked than those of Germany's regular cruisers.

The most famous German raider was the light cruiser *Emden*, under Karl von Müller. As previously noted, Spee detached her from the East Asiatic Squadron to raid commerce, with a collier for refuelling, while he kept the rest of his force concentrated and headed across the Pacific. For two months *Emden* attacked merchant shipping in the Bay of Bengal and the Indian Ocean, often disguising herself as a British cruiser with fake additional funnels. She took 23 vessels totalling 69,100 tonnes (68,000 tons) and caused enormous wider disruption as ships were kept in port due to her presence. She also

bombarded oil tanks at Madras and sank a Russian light cruiser and a French destroyer at the Battle of Penang on 28 October 1914 in Malaya. Critics of cruiser warfare argue that it is only a matter of time before a raider's luck will run out. This fate befell *Emden* on 9 November 1914, when she sought to attack a cable station in the Cocos Islands. Officials ashore saw through her disguise and their frantic signal reached an Australian convoy that happened to be just over 80km (50 miles) away. It sent the light cruiser HMAS *Sydney* to respond. This warship outgunned and outranged *Emden*, with 6in guns against her 4.1in armament, and though she suffered some damage, *Sydney* had by far the better of the engagement. *Emden* was so badly damaged that Müller beached her and surrendered.

East Africa, 1914. The Royal Navy had an overwhelming superiority over Germany in the waters off East Africa at the beginning of the war. Once the light cruiser *Königsberg* was bottled up and sunk, this superiority was unchallenged, though German forces on land continued to fight.

The other German light cruisers stationed overseas at the beginning of the war were the *Karlsruhe* and the *Königsberg*. *Karlsruhe* was in the Caribbean at the outbreak of war and had a narrow escape early on, when HMS *Suffolk* (commanded by the ill fated Cradock) happened upon her while she was helping to convert a merchant ship into a commerce raider. She relied upon her speed to slip away from *Suffolk* and shortly afterwards from HMS *Bristol*. She then headed south to prey on commerce off South America, capturing 17 merchant ships of over 77,200 tonnes (76,000 tons). In November, she headed towards Barbados to attack British facilities there, but on 4 November, south of Trinidad, she was torn in half by an internal explosion that killed two-thirds of her crew. The cause of this accident is unknown, but may have been due to defective ammunition or her cordite stores overheating in the warm tropical climate. Even after her destruction, she caused continuing disruption to commerce, since Britain did not discover that she had sunk until March 1915.

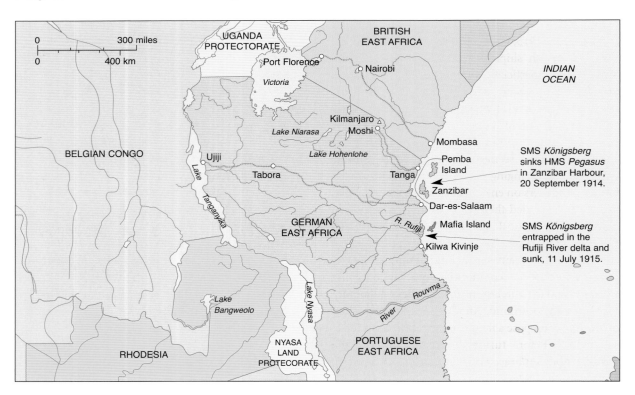

The *Königsberg* was the name ship of her class. Her main armament comprised ten 4.1in guns mounted in single turrets, backed by ten 2in guns and two 18in torpedo tubes. She had a top speed of 24 knots. Operating off East Africa, she sank a British liner in August 1914, and sank the obsolete and outranged British light cruiser HMS *Pegasus* at anchor on 20 September. Britain then successfully targeted her supplies, sinking a supporting collier and buying up stocks of coal ashore. *Königsberg* evaded the forces hunting her by taking refuge in the Rufiji River delta where she was discovered on 30 October. British cruisers were unable to follow her, so they sank a collier to block her in, and maintained a blockade to prevent her crew from clearing the blockage or receiving supplies. She was thus effectively contained, though she tied down several British ships before two shallow-draught monitors – warships purpose-built for bombarding targets ashore – were brought up to destroy her, with the aid of aircraft to spot for their gunfire, on 11 July 1915. Her guns were taken ashore and used to considerable effect by the German forces in East Africa.

By January 1915, German surface raiders had sunk some 75 British ships of 277,400 tonnes (273,000 tons). While superficially impressive, this figure was a tiny fraction – some two per cent – of the total strength of the British merchant fleet, while Britain had captured nearly three times as many German merchant ships. Alfred Mahan's low opinion of commerce raiding seemed vindicated once again. It appeared that changing technology had reduced the impact of cruisers on enemy commerce. The adoption of steam power tied them more closely to bases and made fuel a critical vulnerability, while it also dispersed their quarry by removing restrictions on the courses that merchant ships could adopt. Moreover, improvements in communications with cable telegraph and the wireless meant that they could more easily be run to ground. Another technology existed that would soon pose a far greater threat to commerce: submarines. Before turning to these, however, the German Navy embraced a more traditional strategy, centred on the battlefleet.

Germany's Armed Merchant Cruisers

Kaiser Wilhelm der Grosse operated around the Canary Islands, sinking two merchant ships before being intercepted and sunk by the cruiser HMS *Highflyer* on 26 August 1914. *Cap Trafalgar* was sunk on 14 September in a battle in which she was outgunned by the British armed merchant cruiser *Carmania,* but still managed to inflict considerable damage on her attacker. *Prinz Eitel Friedrich* sank 11 ships before being interned in the United States in March 1915. *Kronprinz Wilhelm* accounted for 15 ships, but when she was interned in the United States in April 1915, after British cruisers had taken her supply ship, the last of the early armed merchant cruisers was out of the war. Perhaps the strangest auxiliary cruiser was the sailing ship *Seeadler,* which operated from 1916 to 1917. Although such a ship might have seemed old fashioned, she was free of the dependence on coal that proved to be the key vulnerability of other raiders. She captured and sank 16 ships before being wrecked in September 1917.

Germany followed previous common practice and converted merchant vessels – including *Prinz Eitel Friedrich,* pictured here – to act as commerce raiders.

CHAPTER 2

The North Sea Raids

While naval operations around the world had an impact on the war, they were something of a sideshow in comparison with the main event in the North Sea. It was here that the battlefleets confronted each other, and where the war at sea would be decided – and if Britain lost here, then Germany would win the war.

The British Grand Fleet, under Admiral Sir John Jellicoe, comprised 21 Dreadnought and eight pre-Dreadnought battleships, together with four battlecruisers under the command of Vice Admiral Sir David Beatty. Its base was Scapa Flow in the Orkney Islands, north of Scotland. The Channel Fleet, with 18 pre-Dreadnoughts, was based at Portland. There were various forces of light cruisers, destroyers and submarines based at other ports including Rosyth, Invergordon on the Cromarty Firth, the Humber, Harwich and Dover. The German High Seas Fleet comprised 13 Dreadnoughts and 16 pre-Dreadnoughts, under Admiral Friedrich von Ingenohl, with four battlecruisers (plus one armoured

The German High Seas Fleet manoeuvring off Heligoland in 1914. The German Navy confidently expected to be able to fight a decisive battle on its own terms against the British Grand Fleet. Instead, the early months of the war saw the two fleets play a cat-and-mouse game, seeking out advantage.

cruiser often counted with them) under Admiral Franz von Hipper. They were mainly based at Wilhelmshaven on the Jade River in the North Sea, behind the heavily fortified island of Heligoland, and Kiel in the Baltic, with a canal connecting the two. There were other bases at Bremerhaven, Cuxhaven and Ems on the North Sea.

While Britain enjoyed a clear advantage in warship numbers, its effect was reduced by the global responsibilities of the Royal Navy. The balance in terms of quality was more favourable to Germany. In general, British warships were faster and had greater endurance at sea than German ships, and also tended to have heavier guns. German warships tended to have better armour and superior underwater protection, and their offensive power was boosted by more accurate gunnery and better quality shells, torpedoes and mines.

The two fleets were more equal in the new asset of air power. In 1914, the Royal Naval Air Service had seven airships, 31 seaplanes (which took off from and alighted on the water) and 40 aeroplanes, while the German Navy had one airship and 36 seaplanes. Other navies had air arms, including the United States, France, Russia, Italy and Austria.

The major North Sea naval bases of Britain and Germany. The North Sea was the principal arena for the surface naval war. It witnessed a number of small-scale engagements in the first months of the conflict, as well as raids conducted by each side against targets on their enemy's coast.

INITIAL WAR PLANS

Both the Royal Navy and the High Seas Fleet expected the naval war to begin with a major engagement between the two battlefleets. However, there was a critical difference in how they expected such a clash to occur.

The commanders of the High Seas Fleet were conscious of its numerical inferiority, but were confident that the strong offensive tradition of their opponent would see the Royal Navy seek battle close to the German bases. Such a bold move would allow German mines and torpedoes to weaken the British fleet sufficiently to change the balance of advantage.

The British Admiralty, on the other hand, was well aware that changes in naval warfare had made it impossible to attempt the sort of 'close blockade', with the fleet poised just off the enemy coast, that it had successfully imposed on its adversary in previous centuries. Modern warships, with their voracious appetite for coal, could not be kept on station for long periods, while new means of attack made it too dangerous to linger near enemy bases. The Royal Navy had therefore secretly abandoned plans for close blockade in 1912.

While technology closed off one option, geography provided an alternative; the location of the British Isles naturally restricted German access to the Atlantic and made possible a distant blockade. Stationing the main battlefleet in Scotland, with a smaller fleet backed by minefields in the English Channel, would imprison the German fleet in the North Sea. The occasional raider might slip through to threaten overseas trade, but not

The Birth of Air Power at Sea

Dirigible airships appeared in the late nineteenth century, and then in 1903 the Wright brothers made the first powered flight. The obvious advantages of aircraft for reconnaissance led to naval trials, which the German Navy began with Zeppelins in 1906, while the Royal Navy in 1909 acquired the imaginatively named Airship *No. 1* for the same purpose. In 1910, an aeroplane took off from an anchored United States cruiser. In 1911, one landed on a United States battleship and took off again; in the same year a seaplane took off and landed. In 1912, an aeroplane took off from a Royal Navy battleship that was underway, and experiments began in dropping bombs and in detecting submarines from the air. Then in 1913, the cruiser HMS *Hermes* was modified to operate seaplanes, and Britain began the construction of the world's first purpose-designed aircraft carrier, *Ark Royal*. Aircraft went to war at a very early stage of their development, and their roles expanded rapidly as their capabilities matured.

Admiral Sir John Jellicoe took over as commander-in-chief of the British Grand Fleet at the beginning of the war. His force bottled up the German High Seas Fleet and prevented it from both interfering with British trade and breaking the British blockade of Germany.

Admiral Friedrich von Ingenohl was commander-in-chief of the German High Seas Fleet at the beginning of the war. He devised a series of raids against the British coast, aiming to entice a small part of the Grand Fleet into battle.

a whole squadron. This approach would not defeat the High Seas Fleet, but would contain and neutralize it, while leaving open the possibility that it might be brought into an ambush.

Denied battle on ideal terms, the German battlefleet was held back at the start of the war. While Germany was confident of swift victory on land, there was little point in risking the fleet, which could be preserved as a useful bargaining chip for peace negotiations. As the war dragged on without a victory, Germany's naval strategy shifted from relying on attrition against attacking British forces, to more actively trying to catch a small part of the British fleet at a disadvantage, thus seeking parity in that way.

The early months of the war therefore saw both sides keen to test their strength in battle, but reluctant to risk losing their expensive battleships and cautious of being drawn into combat on unfavourable terms. The practical effect of this was that the two sides warily circled each other, while undertaking a series of raids that aimed to lay traps for the opponent.

THE BATTLE OF HELIGOLAND BIGHT (28 AUGUST 1914)

The first significant engagement of the war came about as a result of early patrols into the Heligoland Bight, just off the German bases, by British submarines. These revealed the routine of German destroyer patrols. Commodore Reginald Tyrwhitt, commander of the Harwich Force, and Commodore Roger Keyes, in command of British submarines, proposed a plan to attack these forces, aiming to seize the initiative by hitting the German Navy close to home. Winston Churchill, First Lord of the Admiralty, was delighted by their bold suggestion and it was put into effect, albeit in a revised form.

The plan was for a small force of British submarines to draw the enemy destroyers out into the North Sea, where they would be pounced upon by two light cruisers and a flotilla of destroyers from the Harwich Force. Another group of submarines would be in position to attack any heavier German units attempting to assist their destroyers, while a force including the two battlecruisers *Invincible* and *New Zealand* would provide more distant support. When Jellicoe heard of the plan on the eve of its execution, he expressed concern that the British force risked being overwhelmed by a sortie of the main German battlefleet. He urged that the Grand Fleet should be committed – as, indeed, the original plan had envisaged. The Admiralty turned down this request, but did permit him to send Beatty with three additional battlecruisers (*Lion*, *Queen Mary* and *Princess Royal*) and Commodore William Goodenough with six *Town*-class light cruisers, to strengthen the supporting force. Neither of these two commanders had complete information about the planned operation, and the signal informing Tyrwhitt and Keyes of these additional forces never reached them. This failure caused considerable confusion and came very close to having serious consequences.

The plan was implemented on 28 August, in conditions of thickening mist and poor visibility near the coast. The first contact between opposing forces occurred at dawn, when the German destroyer *G194* spotted and pursued a British submarine, only to be engaged at 7am by the leading British destroyers. Admiral Hipper believed that no British forces larger than destroyers were present, and hence initially ordered only two light cruisers, *Stettin* and *Frauenlob*, to assist, with others ordered to prepare to put to sea. He later requested that heavier units be committed but they were prevented by the tide of the Jade River. By about 8am, the two light cruisers were engaging their British counterparts, and although they were damaged they succeeded in covering the retreat of their destroyers, while also damaging and slowing Tyrwhitt's flagship *Arethusa*. The engagement rapidly became confused as reinforcements joined, left and rejoined the battle, fading in and out of the mist.

As Tyrwhitt's ships withdrew, they cut off and sank the destroyer *V187* just after 9am. Goodenough detached two of his cruisers to support the withdrawal of the Harwich Force, but their unexpected appearance added to the confusion: Tyrwhitt's ships initially believed them to be hostile, but recognized them before opening fire. The British submarines were less quick to realize that they were friendly: *E6* fired a torpedo at the cruiser *Southampton* but missed, while her target's attempt to ram the submarine in response also failed.

Further German light cruisers joined the battle piecemeal rather than as a single force. At about 11am, *Strassburg* attacked and further damaged *Arethusa*, but

Heligoland had been a British possession until ceded to Germany in 1890. The island was converted into a heavily defended naval base and was used extensively by the German fleet during the war.

Winston Churchill, First Lord of the Admiralty

Churchill became First Lord of the Admiralty in 1911. He was often carried away by his enthusiasm and exaggerated his own mastery of naval warfare, exercising excessive control over commanders around the world. He was seen by many contemporaries, both politicians and navy officers, as highly intelligent and a persuasive debater, but also as a nuisance or, worse, a danger. This view seemed vindicated by doubtful schemes such as the deployment of the Royal Naval Division to Antwerp in 1914 (for which he suggested himself as commander, to the considerable amusement of the rest of the Cabinet) and the Gallipoli expedition. However, there were also signs of the characteristics that came to the fore later in his career, notably his boldness, imagination and determination to seize the initiative. He needed the right partner as First Sea Lord, which for a while he had in Jacky Fisher. Though their relationship was rather stormy, there was a core of mutual respect, and Fisher could restrain Churchill's wilder impulses.

The Battle of Heligoland Bight (28 August 1914). This engagement represented a bold attempt by the Royal Navy to seize the initiative at the outset of the war. In the midst of a confusing engagement, the Germans lost the ships *Köln*, *Mainz* and *Ariadne* plus a destroyer (*V187*). The Royal Navy, by comparison, lost only one light cruiser. The British victory owed much to Beatty's bold and offensive-minded disposition, a throw-back to the age of Nelson, and provided a tonic for popular morale. However, a series of errors in planning came close to throwing away this success.

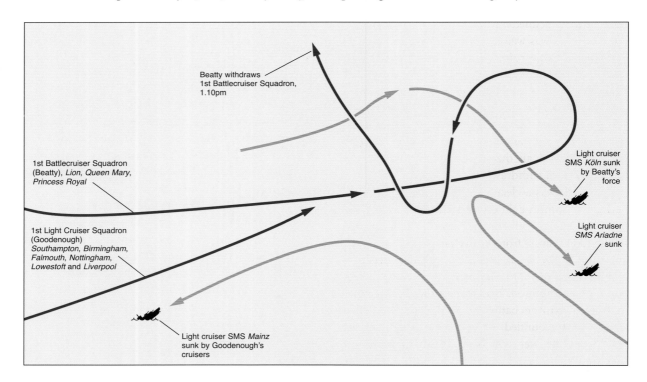

Beatty withdraws
1st Battlecruiser Squadron,
1.10pm

1st Battlecruiser Squadron
(Beatty), *Lion, Queen Mary,
Princess Royal*

1st Light Cruiser Squadron
(Goodenough)
*Southampton, Birmingham,
Falmouth, Nottingham,
Lowestoft* and *Liverpool*

Light cruiser
SMS *Köln* sunk
by Beatty's
force

Light cruiser
SMS *Ariadne*
sunk

Light cruiser SMS *Mainz*
sunk by Goodenough's
cruisers

was driven off by the determined attacks of her accompanying destroyers. At 11.45am, *Mainz* entered the action, but was chased into the path of Goodenough's cruisers, hit repeatedly by shells and torpedoes and sank at 1.10pm. Meanwhile, the Harwich Force came under increasing pressure, driving off two attacking light cruisers at 12pm, but was then attacked by three more at 12.30pm, which threatened to overwhelm it.

Just at the right moment, however, Beatty's battle-cruisers appeared on the scene. His squadron had been poised some 50km (30 miles) away from the developing engagement until about 11.30am, when he received an urgent call for assistance. This presented him with a considerable dilemma. On the one hand, he could seize the initiative, rescue the lighter forces and inflict substantial damage on the enemy. On the other hand, committing his squadron to battle so close to the enemy's main bases would not only risk running into mines or torpedo attack – just as Germany's initial war plan had hoped – but would also risk falling victim to attack by superior forces should the High Seas Fleet put to sea. Beatty's temperament inclined him towards the bold, offensive choice, but he was well aware that the loss of one or more of his battlecruisers would represent a serious blow to the strength and the reputation of the Grand Fleet. Nevertheless, at 11.35am, he ordered his force into the Bight at top speed. His battlecruisers overpowered the German light cruisers, sinking two more and driving the others off. At 1.10pm, realizing he had achieved all that he could, he ordered the British forces to withdraw.

The result was a clear victory for the Royal Navy. Germany lost three light cruisers, the *Köln*, *Mainz* and *Ariadne* (which had emerged from the mist just 3500m (3800 yards) from Beatty's flagship, *Lion*), with three more seriously damaged, and one destroyer also sunk; a total of 1240 German sailors were killed, wounded or captured. Britain had one light cruiser and three destroyers badly damaged, and lost 35 men killed and 40 wounded. At a time when most of the news from the war was bad, British opinion was delighted by this success in the first encounter between the Royal Navy and its young challenger. The popular reaction was rather more than was justified, but it was a welcome tonic for morale to see a victory that seemed to echo Drake and Nelson, entering the enemy's back yard and giving him a bloody nose.

Vice Admiral Sir David Beatty (1871–1936)

Beatty joined the Royal Navy in 1884, and his qualities of bravery and leadership ensured rapid promotion. He won a medal for gallantry and promotion to commander for his service in Nile gunboats during the Sudan Campaign (1896–98). Further heroics in China hastened his promotion to captain and then, at 39, he was promoted to rear admiral, becoming the youngest flag officer since Nelson. A period as naval secretary to the First Sea Lord, Winston Churchill, helped him to the command of the 1st Battle Cruiser Squadron in 1913. Beatty was dashing, a keen sportsman and devotee of fortune tellers, a socialite who enjoyed his fame and cultivated his popular image, always wearing his cap at a jaunty angle and flaunting a personalized uniform jacket with two buttons fewer than the regulation version. He was a decisive and offensive-minded commander, more willing to take a risk than Jellicoe, but far from reckless. He expected his subordinate captains to be as swift as he was to appreciate a situation, and to act on their own initiative. In November 1916, he became commander-in-chief of the Grand Fleet on Jellicoe's appointment as First Sea Lord (a position that Beatty would take on after the war).

There was a considerable degree of good fortune involved. Disjointed planning, poor coordination and a failure to keep all commanders fully informed caused great difficulties, and could easily have had far worse consequences. Disaster was averted, but the chance of greater success was thrown away: Keyes believed that if the British forces had been properly united, they could have sunk twice as many German cruisers. Beatty's rapid calculation of the risks and decision to press on into the Heligoland Bight, in full awareness of the danger he faced, proved critical. Had Hipper's battlecruisers sortied earlier, or had German U-boats been able to intervene, the outcome could have been quite different.

While the result of the battle was not the triumph the British press believed, it had a great psychological impact on the German Navy, not least because their enemies had done exactly what it had hoped, taking offensive action near the German bases. Unaware of how lucky its attackers had been, the German Navy was perhaps more impressed by the British performance than it should have been. The Kaiser further restricted the deployment of his precious High Seas Fleet, confirming its cautiously defensive strategy. There were later attempts by the Royal Navy to repeat the operation, but they were found not to be feasible due to the increasingly dense defensive minefields laid – another reaction to this battle.

THE LOSS OF THE CRESSYS

The high morale enjoyed by the Royal Navy did not last. Submarines had already had an impact on the war: on 5 September 1914, *U21* torpedoed and sank the cruiser HMS *Pathfinder* to become the first U-boat to sink a British warship. A bigger shock was to come.

On 22 September, three old armoured cruisers, *Aboukir* (whose captain, John Drummond, was the senior officer and hence in command of the small force), *Cressy* and *Hogue*, were patrolling against enemy minelayers off the Dutch coast. They lacked supporting destroyers because of earlier bad weather, though some were en route to join them. They were steaming on a straight course, at a speed of less than 10 knots to conserve coal, and could not have been

easier targets for submarine attack. Suddenly, at about 6.25am, *Aboukir* was badly damaged by an underwater explosion and began to sink. Her captain, assuming she had hit a mine, ordered her sister ships to close and pick up survivors. The warship had actually been hit by a torpedo fired by the U-boat *U9*. Its captain, Lieutenant Commander Otto Weddigen, was surprised to see the other two cruisers presenting

Admiral Franz von Hipper (1863–1932)

Hipper joined the Imperial German Navy in 1881 and followed a career path more characterized by ship command than by staff appointments ashore. In 1912, he was promoted to rear admiral and in October of the following year became commander of the Scouting Group of the High Seas Fleet. Like Beatty, Hipper seemed to have the ideal qualities for a commander of battlecruisers: he was bold and brave, and often hugely frustrated by the restrictions placed on his actions by his superiors. Criticized by some for his actions at the First Battle of Heligoland Bight and reviled by the British press as a 'baby killer' for his attacks on towns in eastern England, he did well to extricate his battlecruisers from the clutches of the British ships at the Battle of the Dogger Bank, albeit at the cost of the armoured cruiser *Blücher*. His most celebrated achievement was his command of the Scouting Group at the Battle of Jutland in May 1916. In August 1918, he replaced Scheer as commander-in-chief of the High Seas Fleet, and had the melancholy task of overseeing mutinies and then surrender.

themselves as such easy targets, but this did not prevent him from taking advantage of this opportunity, and he torpedoed and sank them both. The Royal Navy had lost three cruisers, together with 1459 officers and men.

As is standard procedure when a Royal Navy ship is lost, a Court of Inquiry was held. It criticized Drummond for failing to take the normal precaution of following a zigzag rather than a straight course, to

complicate the aim of any U-boat, and also for ordering in the other two cruisers when he did not know whether his ship had been hit by a mine or a torpedo. Tragically, concern had previously been expressed about the danger to these old, slow cruisers. It was widely believed that they were vulnerable to attack – hence their nickname of 'the live bait squadron' – although the threat envisaged was from surface warships. These concerns had led Churchill to recommend that their patrols be ended, but the change of policy had not been implemented: there were not enough light cruisers to take over the role and the predominantly bad weather prevented destroyers from fulfilling it. While it is true that the

The crew of *U9* with Lieutenant-Commander Otto Weddigen at centre. The main impact of the German U-boats was against merchant shipping, but there were some striking successes against allied warships. *U9* sank three old *Cressy*-class armoured cruisers in a single day.

HMS *Audacious*. **When this new battleship was sunk by a mine on 27 October 1914, the Admiralty took the unusual step of keeping her loss a secret, to conceal the worrying decline in the strength of the Grand Fleet.**

three cruisers were not following the precautions that they should have been, the formidable threat posed by submarines could no longer be doubted.

The German submariners were not the only ones to make their mark. On 13 September, the British submarine *E9* sank the German light cruiser *Hela*, and on 6 October a destroyer. Overall, though, submarines caused more concern to the Royal Navy, not least because it had more warships at sea and hence offered more targets than its opponent. The main cause of alarm on the British side was the uncomfortable awareness of the poor defences of the main base at Scapa Flow against submarines. For much of September 1914, and then again between mid-October and late November, this vulnerability caused the Grand Fleet to beat an undignified retreat from Scapa Flow to the west of Scotland and then to the north of Ireland. Such concerns seemed to be vindicated on 23 November, when *U18* managed to penetrate the defences of Scapa Flow, although she was sunk on the way out. By mid-1915, British bases were far better defended against submarines.

There was also a considerable threat to shipping from naval mines. In contrast to the hesitation over its use of U-boats, from the very start of the war Germany laid mines in international waters, which resulted in loud protests from neutrals. The Royal Navy's capabilities for laying mines and also for countering them were very limited, but they gradually improved. Mines constrained the activities of the fleet, not least due to the concern that reducing speed to allow minesweeping would make ships more vulnerable to submarine attack. Then, on 27 October, came the most significant loss of a warship to date in the war, when the new super-Dreadnought HMS *Audacious* was sunk by a mine laid by a surface raider.

Shortly afterwards, a familiar face returned to the Admiralty. On 29 October, Admiral Prince Louis of Battenberg was replaced as First Sea Lord by Jacky Fisher, returning at the age of 74 to a position that he had left in 1910. He quickly created a more businesslike atmosphere and initiated a new building programme, focusing particularly on submarines, destroyers and smaller anti-submarine vessels, which would become critical later in the war.

Fisher's counterparts had begun to look to a more ambitious strategy. Rather than simply waiting for the Royal Navy to dash itself against the defences around the High Seas Fleet's bases, the German commanders now embraced a more active policy of seeking to tempt isolated elements of the Grand Fleet into action against superior forces. This new approach was initiated on 3 November 1914, when four German battlecruisers, with two battle squadrons providing distant support, bombarded the town of Yarmouth in Norfolk, in part to test the Royal Navy reaction. Little damage was inflicted, and on the way home the armoured cruiser *Yorck* sank after blundering into a German minefield.

Ingenohl now devised a plan for a larger-scale repeat of the raid on Yarmouth. Hipper's battlecruisers would attack Scarborough and Hartlepool, with the battle squadrons of the High Seas Fleet in the North

Sea for support, despite the Kaiser's order to avoid risking high losses. The British battlecruisers would be drawn out to respond to the raid, allowing Hipper to lead them across a newly laid minefield and then onto the waiting guns of the battlefleet. The operation was delayed in November due to technical problems. Then in December, the defeat at the Falkland Islands made a compensating success more urgent, while also providing an opportunity, given the absence of two British battlecruisers. However, when the plan was put into effect, the British had been forewarned by progress in what was to become an increasingly central element of modern warfare: wireless.

BREAKING THE GERMAN CODES: ROOM 40

The use of wireless presented considerable benefits, but also opened up new vulnerabilities. One was the excessive central control it made possible, not least when the First Lord of the Admiralty was a character like Churchill. Others were the various ways in which the enemy could exploit one's own use of wireless.

In November 1914, a motley group of civilians and a few naval officers moved into modest new accommodation in the Admiralty. This small office gave its name to their nascent organization: Room 40 OB (Old Building). During August 1914, the Royal Navy had established a body to work on intercepted enemy signals and to break their codes. It answered to Rear Admiral Sir Henry Oliver, the Director of the Intelligence Division of the Admiralty, who appointed as its nominal head the Director of Naval Education, Sir Alfred Ewing. He in turn recruited a number of staff from the naval colleges at Greenwich, Dartmouth and Osborne and also from Oxford and Cambridge universities. They became the initial staff of Room 40.

Its pioneering work was greatly assisted by three windfalls that helped to reveal the secrets of the principal German codes. First, on 11 August, a German steamer was captured in Australia. This yielded a copy of the code-containing *Handels-verkehrsbuch* (HVB), a book used by the German naval staff to communicate with German merchant ships and also by some German small craft, U-boats and Zeppelins. It reached the Admiralty by the end of

October. Second, on 25 August, the German cruiser *Magdeburg* ran aground off Estonia. The crew failed to destroy their confidential papers, and the Russians acquired copies of the *Signalbuch der Kaiserlichen Marine* (SKM), which contained codes and current keys, as well as the map grids used by the German Navy. By the middle of October, Britain had been given a copy. Third, on 17 October, four German destroyers sent to lay mines in the Thames estuary were attacked and sunk. According to some sources, this interception was itself the result of information from Room 40. It certainly led to a further intelligence

Sir Alfred Ewing (1855–1935) had been a professor of engineering at the universities of Tokyo, Dundee and Cambridge before becoming director of naval education in 1903, implementing Fisher's reforms. Early in the war he became the head of Room 40, a position he held until 1916.

gain: on 30 November, the lead-lined box for code books thrown overboard from *S119*, one of the sunk destroyers, was found in the nets of a British trawler. This box contained a copy of the *Verkehrsbuch* (VB) and its code used to communicate with naval attachés and warships stationed overseas, and also by senior officers at sea.

These captures helped to make nearly all German wireless signals vulnerable to deciphering. Two other factors increased Germany's vulnerability to this process. First, all their telegraph cables were cut early in the war, forcing them to rely on wireless communication. Second, they were careless with security: they failed to acknowledge the likelihood that their codes had been compromised, they failed to replace codes often enough and they made remarkably promiscuous use of wireless. The result was that Room 40 was provided with a wealth of material from a chain of listening stations established early on in the war. The expertise built up meant that when the captured codes were eventually replaced later in the war, their successors were also swiftly broken. The German

Captain Reginald 'Blinker' Hall (right), Director of Naval Intelligence. The nickname 'Blinker' stemmed from a noticeable mannerism. He oversaw the work of Room 40 and often used its product to great effect. The US ambassador to Great Britain described him as 'a clear case of genius'.

Government had a vague awareness that the British were probably reading some of its signals, but had no idea of just how well they were doing. There were some German successes against British codes, but, in general, British security was considerably better with codes frequently changed and the use of wireless limited.

Signals intelligence is easily misunderstood. Only in the rarest cases does it provide an all-seeing clarity comparable to turning on a light in a darkened room. Rather, it offers limited, partial clues as to what is going on; there will be gaps and uncertainties, things one does not know and questions that one does not even know to ask. These limitations are the best case: there will also be missed messages, delays, incorrect inferences and, critically, instances where information is available but is not passed in a timely fashion to those who can best act upon it. Signals intelligence can deliver great successes, but just as often it proves tantalizingly incomplete and inadequate. Some useful information will result not from individual dramatic decryptions, but rather from the general picture, built

up by painstaking work over a long period, of enemy organization and procedures. Some of the work of Room 40 did not even involve cracking codes and ciphers: much information was gained from direction finding, using Y Stations, or listening posts, to triangulate the position of German ships using wireless. Moreover, even if signals could not be read, studying changes in their pattern (known as traffic analysis) could also produce valuable intelligence.

The natural limitations of signals intelligence were worsened by some of the teething problems that were inevitable in such a new craft. First, there were inefficiencies in the organization. Room 40 was too closely under the control of Oliver, and for a while it lacked naval expertise to provide the specialist understanding necessary to make sense of the intercepted signals. The former problem was never solved, but the latter was by attaching naval officers, such as Commander Herbert Hope, and also by the closer involvement of the new director. In November 1914, Oliver became chief of staff and was replaced as Director of Intelligence by Captain Reginald 'Blinker' Hall, who proved to be truly outstanding in this role.

Second, there were problems in using the information gleaned from intercepts. There is always a trade off in signals intelligence between, on the one

A light cruiser commissioned in 1912, *Magdeburg* was operating in the Baltic in August 1915 when she ran aground. Her crew failed to destroy her code books, which were seized by the Russians and later passed on to Britain, greatly assisting the work of Room 40.

The Zimmermann Telegram

On 16 January 1917, the German foreign minister Arthur Zimmermann sent a telegram to the German ambassador in Mexico. The latter was instructed to offer Mexico a military alliance directed against the United States, for which Germany would give financial support and territory in Texas, New Mexico and Arizona. Mexico politely declined this offer, but the damage was done: the telegram was intercepted and deciphered by Room 40. Concealing the source of the message from the Americans as well as the Germans, London passed on its contents to the United States Government, which published it as its own work. There was some initial scepticism that it was genuine, until Zimmermann himself publicly confirmed it. There was already growing hostility in the United States towards Germany, largely due to unrestricted submarine warfare, but the Zimmermann telegram, and hence Room 40, helped to tip the balance and bring about the entry into the war of the United States.

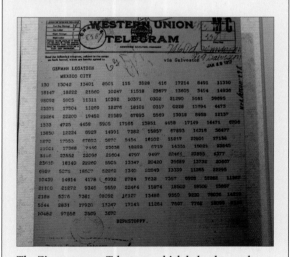

The Zimmermann Telegram, which helped provoke the United States entry into the war, was intercepted, decrypted and brilliantly used by 'Blinker' Hall.

hand, maintaining the secrecy of one's activities and, on the other, making practical use of the product. Too little secrecy and one jeopardizes the stream of intelligence; too much, and the value of having the material is greatly reduced. The appropriate balance to strike, as well as the most effective means of bringing together intelligence and operations, took some time to develop; initially, the Admiralty erred on the side of caution, restricting access too severely to the product of Room 40.

Nevertheless, over the course of the war Room 40 provided a vast amount of invaluable intelligence, not least making possible the operation to intercept the German forces conducting the Scarborough raid and also placing the Royal Navy in a favourable position for the Battle of the Dogger Bank. It also played a crucial role in the Battle of Jutland, the campaign against the U-boats and even helped to nudge the United States towards entry into the war. After the war, Room 40 was to merge with its army counterpart to form the Government Code and Cipher School, which, from its new location at Bletchley Park, would play an even more significant role in World War II.

THE SCARBOROUGH RAID (16 DECEMBER 1914)

The raid was to be conducted by Hipper's 1st Scouting Group, consisting of four battlecruisers plus the armoured cruiser *Blücher*, with a screen of light cruisers and destroyers. They would arrive off the Yorkshire coast at dawn on 16 December to bombard Scarborough and Hartlepool and to lay mines. They would be supported by the High Seas Fleet, which would patrol about 200km (125 miles) east of Scarborough, on the eastern edge of the Dogger Bank.

However, on the night of 14/15 December Room 40 intercepted and deciphered signals revealing that the battlecruisers were to attack the British coast on the 16th. The information provided was accurate but incomplete. First, the precise targets were not known,

The 1914 east coast raids. The early months of the war saw the German High Seas Fleet conduct a series of raids on British coastal towns, aiming to draw part of the Grand Fleet into a trap. Due to the work of Room 40, it was the German fleet that came close to suffering series setbacks.

so it was decided to seek to ambush the attackers as they returned home rather than scatter the fleet in an attempt to defend all possible targets. Second, and potentially more significant, the intelligence did not reveal that the German battlefleet would be at sea to support the raid. Thus, in addition to Hipper's

battlecruisers, any British force would also be facing Ingenohl's fleet of 22 battleships (14 Dreadnoughts and eight pre-Dreadnoughts), with supporting armoured cruisers, light cruisers and destroyers. This critical gap in the Admiralty's awareness of the enemy order of battle was a reminder of the limitations of

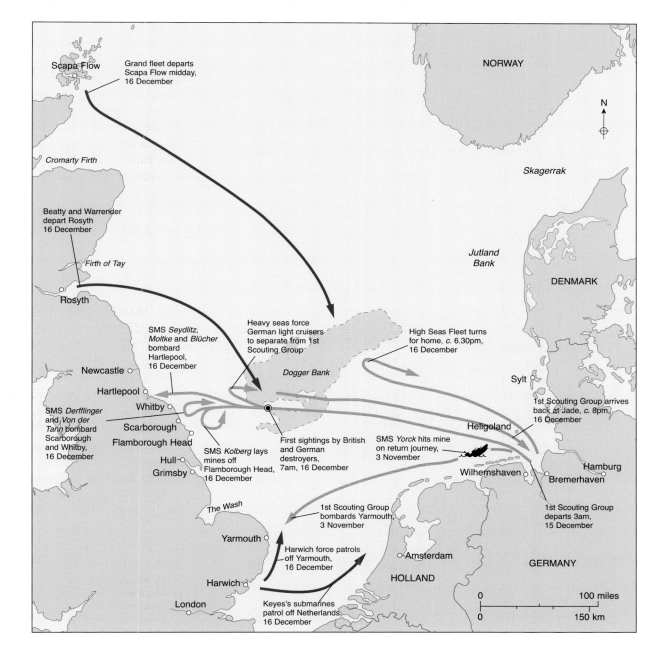

signals intelligence. In the event, both sides were hindered by imperfect information and a major action did not occur.

Jellicoe wanted the Grand Fleet deployed to meet the raid, but the Admiralty, unaware that the German battlefleet would be at sea, refused and committed only one of its battle squadrons, albeit the most powerful. Even given the incomplete information on which it rested, this decision represented a failure to concentrate strength against the enemy. The forces sent to meet Hipper (as was believed) were Beatty's

four battlecruisers, six Dreadnoughts of the 2nd Battle Squadron under Vice Admiral Sir George Warrender (the overall commander), with his flag in HMS *King George V*, four armoured cruisers under Rear Admiral William Pakenham and five light cruisers under Commodore William Goodenough. The plan was for these forces to meet in the North Sea, to the southeast of the Dogger Bank, before dawn on 16 December. Keyes's submarines would patrol off Holland, in case Hipper should head south, and Tyrwhitt's light cruisers and destroyers were off Yarmouth.

During the night, Hipper's force and the British passed close by each other (the nearest elements of the two forces being just 16km or 10 miles apart at about 1am) without discovering the other's presence. Meanwhile, the High Seas Fleet headed for its own

The German bombardment of the British east-coast towns, such as Scarborough (shown here), did little material damage but caused much public anger, directed both against Germany, for bombarding civilians, and against the Royal Navy, for failing to protect the public.

HMS *Southampton*, a *Chatham*-class light cruiser of the Royal Navy, at sea in 1917. The role of light cruisers was to scout ahead for the main elements of the battlefleet.

rendezvous, which happened to be remarkably close to Warrender's. At about 5.15am, before dawn, the lead British destroyers happened on the German destroyers acting as the forward screen of the High Seas Fleet. This was one of the potentially decisive moments of the engagement and, indeed, of the entire war at sea. Had Ingenohl only realized it, he was within touching distance of exactly what he had sought since the start of the war: 16km (10 miles) away was part of the British Grand Fleet, which his far larger force (22 capital ships against 10) comfortably outgunned.

His reaction was cautious, however, as he assumed that the British destroyers were the vanguard of the entire Grand Fleet. He feared a night attack by destroyers and was also painfully aware that he was acting against the orders of the Kaiser in risking a battle against superior forces. Hence, at 5.30am he ordered his fleet to turn away from the British, and shortly afterwards headed for home at high speed. If his decision to withdraw to safety was understandable, it is rather more difficult to comprehend his failure to inform Hipper, still heading for the British coast, either of his own withdrawal or of the presence of a powerful British force along the line of retreat.

The High Seas Fleet therefore let slip a potentially advantageous situation, while leaving the battlecruisers of its Scouting Group in a very perilous position. They were saved by similar confusion on the

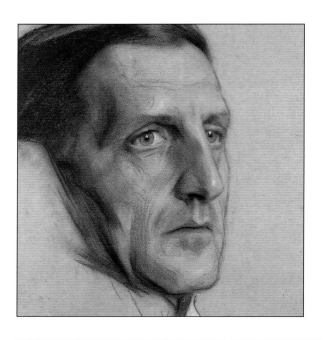

British side. For their part, the Royal Navy warships initially gave chase to the German light forces – unaware that they were pursing the main enemy battlefleet – before breaking off when they received word of the attacks on the Yorkshire coast.

Between 8am and 9.15am, Hipper's battlecruisers shelled Scarborough, Whitby and Hartlepool. The three 6in guns defending Hartlepool (which made it the only legitimate target of the three according to international law) returned fire to some effect, hitting *Moltke* and *Blücher*. The German bombardment had

Commodore William Goodenough was given command of the 1st Light Cruiser Squadron in 1913, with his flag on HMS *Southampton*. He fought at the battles of Heligoland Bight and Dogger Bank, and during the Scarborough Raid, for which he has been criticized for some errors. His performance at Jutland was highly praised, described by one historian as 'the model for scouting admirals'.

The Cuxhaven Raid, 25 December 1914

The first naval aircraft strike against a target ashore took place on Christmas Day 1914. The target comprised the Zeppelin sheds at Cuxhaven; this was the third time it had been targeted, following two abortive attempts in October and November. Three British cross-Channel steamers, *Empress*, *Engadine* and *Riviera*, had been converted to carry seaplanes. They headed across the North Sea, escorted by destroyers and submarines. Nine seaplanes were hoisted out from the carriers, but two were unable to take off due to the sea state and the rest were unable to attack their target due either to failure to recognize it or to fog, with four shot down (all the crews being rescued). In response, German Zeppelins and seaplanes conducted the first ever air attacks against warships, albeit unsuccessfully. Although the results of the operation were disappointing, it was a boost for British morale. It also indicated that the early use of aircraft from ships was beginning to foster some creative ideas.

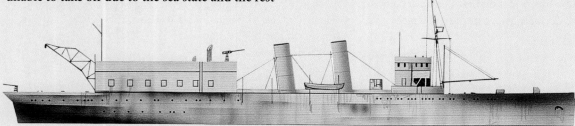

HMS *Engadine*, a converted seaplane carrier, took part in two of the great events of the war: the Cuxhaven Raid and – serving with the Battlecruiser Fleet – the Battle of Jutland.

little success, missing all of the defending guns as well as the submarine and the destroyers based there. It did inflict light damage to some facilities in the docks and shipyards and also hit various churches, public buildings, hotels and houses. Similarly light damage was done to the two seaside resorts to the south and over 120 civilians were killed. Hipper then headed for his rendezvous with the High Seas Fleet, unaware that it was well on its way home.

At about 11.25am, HMS *Southampton* (Goodenough's flagship) sighted Hipper's light cruisers and destroyers. The German commander had detached them from his battlecruisers at 6am to head back to the High Seas Fleet because they were having difficulty keeping up in rough seas. This turned out to be an enormous stroke of luck, since it meant that they were far enough ahead of his main force to provide sufficient warning time for him to change course and avoid the British trap.

Goodenough turned to engage, reporting to Beatty the presence of one light cruiser with destroyers. He then spotted two more German light cruisers with accompanying destroyers, but failed to inform Beatty, leaving the admiral unaware that he had encountered Hipper's screening forces. Hence, when three additional British light cruisers moved to assist Goodenough, Beatty ordered two of them to resume their position as his own screen, to continue searching for the main enemy force. His signal was poorly drafted by his flag lieutenant and was misunderstood: contrary to Beatty's intention, all of the British light cruisers broke off the action at 11.50am. This represented another error by Goodenough, who should have used his initiative to act on his more accurate understanding of the situation, continuing the engagement.

At about 12.15pm, Warrender's Dreadnoughts, which were some 25km (15 miles) away from Beatty, were next to spot Hipper's light forces but the latter were fast enough to evade him. At this time, Beatty was heading west on an ideal course to intercept the eastbound Hipper. At 12.30pm, on hearing of the further contact with the German light forces, however, he reversed course eastwards while Hipper (who at the closest had been fewer than 20km or 12 miles from Beatty), now alerted to the presence of British capital ships, turned north and then northeast. The British squadrons continued to seek their quarry, but as the weather deteriorated further, Hipper's force was able to complete its journey home. At just after 3.45pm, Warrender called off the search.

The reaction of the British press was a mixture of angry condemnation of the German Navy for killing civilians, and criticism of the Royal Navy for allowing the attacking warships to escape. The episode only heightened a popular feeling of disillusionment that the war at sea was not going well, as inflated expectations of a new Trafalgar were dashed. There was also considerable disappointment within the Royal Navy at having missed the chance to inflict a serious blow on the enemy. Jellicoe, in particular, regretted that he had not been authorized to bring down the whole Grand Fleet. There was similar anger on the German side, with commanders feeling that Ingenohl had deprived them of a good opportunity by turning away as soon as British forces were sighted.

Derfflinger **was the lead ship in the second, improved generation of German battlecruisers, having a heavier armament than** *Moltke,* **with a 12in as opposed to 11in main armament. She was a new ship, being commissioned just a month after the start of the war.**

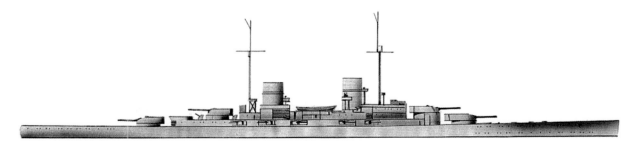

This battle that never was provides a useful indication of some of the constraints imposed on both sides by uncertainty, poor weather and the aversion to risk that characterized the activities of the major fleets. Chance and human error saw the advantage move from one side to the other, with neither seizing it. Although the capital ships of the two battlefleets had still not faced each other, this was about to change.

THE BATTLE OF DOGGER BANK (24 JANUARY 1915)

After the narrow escape following the Scarborough raid, the commanders of the German Navy were keen to achieve some success, regain the initiative and stem the decline in morale around the fleet. They were also aware that the Royal Navy seemed to have some kind of intelligence advantage, but were unsure as to the

source; suspicion fell on the possibility of spy vessels disguised as Dutch trawlers on the Dogger Bank. Further, it was known that Britain occasionally sent unsupported light forces there on patrol, which offered an additional tempting target.

A plan was therefore devised for a raid, which would lead to the war's first clash of capital ships. It involved three battlecruisers of the Scouting Group,

the flagship *Seydlitz*, *Moltke* and *Derfflinger* (the fourth, the *Von der Tann*, was in dock for repairs) with their usual companion, the large armoured cruiser *Blücher*. They were to make a swift attack on the fishing vessels and warships on the Dogger Bank while the rest of the High Seas Fleet remained back in the Heligoland Bight. The operation was delayed by bad weather until, at 10am on 23 January 1915, Hipper was ordered to proceed with the operation.

At about the same time that he was leaving port that evening, so was Beatty; once again, Room 40 had provided warning of the German fleet's activities, intercepting and deciphering the signal to Hipper. Beatty was in command of a powerful force, including three of the newer 13½in-gun battlecruisers *Lion* (his flagship), *Tiger* and *Princess Royal*, with two of the older 12in-gun battlecruisers, *New Zealand* and *Indomitable*, under Rear Admiral Sir Archibald Moore. They were accompanied by Goodenough's light cruisers and were to be joined by three light cruisers and two flotillas of destroyers from Tyrwhitt's Harwich Force. The objective of the German operation was not known, but it was assumed to be another attack on the east coast. Hence, the British forces were to rendezvous to the northeast of the Dogger Bank, with the aim of getting between Hipper and his base to cut off his line of retreat.

Later on the evening of 23 January, the Grand Fleet left Scapa Flow to be ready for a sortie by the High Seas Fleet, should it emerge. Jellicoe complained that he had not been alerted earlier; this appears to be another error by the Admiralty, resulting in a failure to concentrate potentially overwhelming force, just like that of 16 December.

At about 7.10am on the morning of 24 January, Beatty's force was joined at the rendezvous by the lead elements of Tyrwhitt's squadron, in conditions of good visibility and calm seas. Just 10 minutes later, gunfire was seen to the south. This was from the initial

The *Blücher* was an old armoured cruiser and should not really have accompanied the German battlecruisers, lacking their speed, protection and firepower. She was slowed and sunk at the Battle of the Dogger Bank, though in doing so she bought time for the battlecruisers to make their escape.

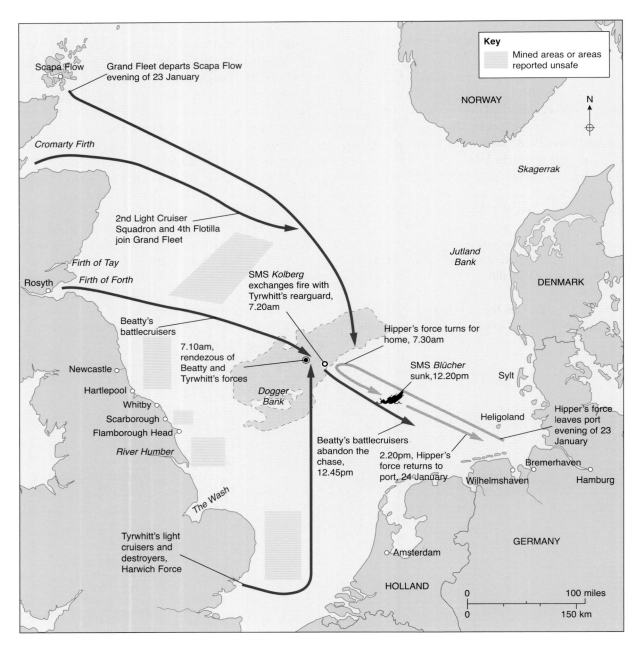

Key

Mined areas or areas reported unsafe

Grand Fleet departs Scapa Flow evening of 23 January

Scapa Flow

NORWAY

N

Cromarty Firth

2nd Light Cruiser Squadron and 4th Flotilla join Grand Fleet

Skagerrak

Firth of Tay

Jutland Bank

Rosyth

Firth of Forth

SMS *Kolberg* exchanges fire with Tyrwhitt's rearguard, 7.20am

DENMARK

Beatty's battlecruisers

Hipper's force turns for home, 7.30am

7.10am, rendezous of Beatty and Tyrwhitt's forces

SMS *Blücher* sunk, 12.20pm

Sylt

Newcastle

Dogger Bank

Hartlepool

Whitby

Scarborough

Flamborough Head

River Humber

Beatty's battlecruisers abandon the chase, 12.45pm

2.20pm, Hipper's force returns to port, 24 January

Heligoland

Hipper's force leaves port evening of 23 January

Bremerhaven

Wilhelmshaven

Hamburg

The Wash

Tyrwhitt's light cruisers and destroyers, Harwich Force

GERMANY

Amsterdam

HOLLAND

0   100 miles

0   150 km

exchanges between some of the ships of the Harwich Force, the departure of which had been delayed by fog, and Hipper's light cruiser vanguard. Once again, the German screening forces seemed to have done their job and, albeit with another considerable stroke of luck, provided the Scouting Group with enough

warning to avoid the main British force. Hipper turned away and headed homewards, confident that he had the speed to outrun what he believed to be British battleships.

In fact, like Spee at the Battle of the Falkland Islands the previous month, his pursuers were the

The Battle of the Dogger Bank. This engagement saw the British coming close to shattering the German battlecruiser fleet. Beatty's force was chasing the retreating Germans but was confounded by poor signalling, inaccurate gunnery, damage to the flagship and errors by commanders.

faster battlecruisers. Beatty gave chase, ordering his squadron to increase speed to 25 knots, then to 26, 27, 28 and finally, at 8.52am, to 29 knots – though the ships never quite reached this speed – by which point the older *New Zealand* and *Indomitable* began to fall behind despite attaining higher speeds than they had managed in their trials. Beatty was aware that this separation would occur, but accepted it in his eagerness to get at the enemy. By now, Hipper realized that he was facing battlecruisers and increased speed, but was held back by *Blücher*, which could only make 23 knots.

Shortly before 9am, the British battlecruisers began to fire from about 18,000m (19,500 yards) at *Blücher*, the rearmost of Hipper's force. Within five minutes

they had the range and began firing salvoes, with the German ships returning fire at about 9.15am. The latter sought to damage and slow the leading battlecruiser, which was the easiest and most visible target, and hence concentrated their fire on *Lion*. Beatty, on the other hand, wished to spread the fire of his force to damage and slow all of the enemy vessels. At 9.35am, when he had reduced the enemy's lead enough for most of his battlecruisers to open fire, he signalled, 'Engage the corresponding ships in the enemy's line'. This order could have been more clearly expressed, with five ships fighting four, and was misunderstood by Captain Henry Pelly of *Tiger*. His ship should have fired on *Moltke*, but he focused on *Seydlitz* instead – inaccurately, to make things worse – with the result that *Moltke* was not engaged and could fire undisturbed at *Lion*.

A shell from Beatty's flagship hit *Seydlitz*, causing a cordite fire that knocked out her two after turrets and came close to destroying the ship; luckily for Hipper, it

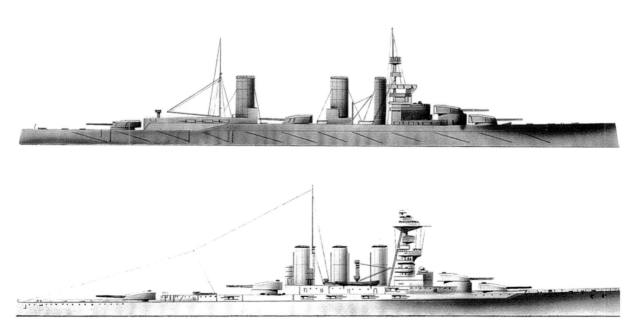

TOP **HMS *Lion* was the lead ship of a British class of improved battlecruiser, with heavier guns – 13½in as opposed to 12in – than her predecessors, as well as better armour and a higher speed. She served as Beatty's flagship at Dogger Bank, where she was damaged, and at Jutland.**

ABOVE **HMS *Tiger* was another of the 'splendid cats', a slightly modified version of the *Lion*-class battlecruisers; the arrangement of her turrets was altered to improve her firing arcs. She was involved in the thick of the action at the battles of Dogger Bank and Jutland.**

Admiral Hugo von Pohl (1855–1916) began the war as the chief of the naval staff, and replaced Ingenohl as commander-in-chief of the High Seas Fleet in February 1915. He served less than a year in the post before ill health compelled him to retire.

did not slow her down. *Lion*, though, was suffering badly, taking a series of hits that knocked out her electricity generation and caused serious flooding that gradually affected her engines and slowed her down. At 10.40am, two hits on *Blücher* destroyed two turrets and damaged her engines, further reducing her speed. Shortly afterwards, Hipper realized that she was lost and ordered his ships home, abandoning *Blücher*. His squadron looked to be in a desperate situation, with it being only a matter of time before more of his ships were slowed down to be picked off. At this moment, though, he was saved by errors and confusion in the British force.

To be fair, Beatty was experiencing serious practical difficulties. Not only was his flagship slowing down due to flooding, but further battle damage meant that her wireless was out of action. He could only communicate with the rest of his force by flags, difficult anyway in high winds, and could only send two groups of these at a time as the other halyards had been shot away. Just when these problems were limiting his ability to command the squadron, at about 10.54am what seemed to be a U-boat periscope was spotted off *Lion*'s starboard bow. It later transpired that there were no U-boats in the area, but the commander could only act on what he believed to be true. Beatty reasoned that where there was one U-boat, there could be several and feared that he might have been drawn into a submarine trap. He therefore ordered his force to turn. This was crucial because it not only allowed the German fleet to extend its lead, but since the signal was not accompanied by a warning of submarines, it also further confused his captains as to his intentions. Further, the new course meant following the wake of the German destroyers and it was feared that they might drop floating mines behind them, so Beatty signalled, 'Course N.E.'

As *Lion* fell out of the chase, Beatty sought to confirm to his captains his intention that they should leave *Blücher* to be finished off by the lagging *Indomitable* and continue after Hipper's battlecruisers. He therefore hoisted the signal 'Attack the rear of the enemy' (there being no established signal for 'Engage the main body of the enemy'). Unfortunately, in the confusion caused by the changes of course and the limited communications, this signal was read together with the previous one as a single order; his captains inferred that they should attack the enemy's rear to the northeast – the already doomed *Blücher*. Beatty could only watch in frustration as his battlecruisers slowed and turned to finish off this single ship, allowing the rest of the German force to escape. He tried desperately to save the situation by making Nelson's classic signal, 'Engage the enemy more closely', only to find that this, too, was lacking from the signal book.

Beatty transferred his flag to the destroyer HMS *Attack* and then at 12.20pm to the *Princess Royal*, by which time *Blücher* had finally capsized and sunk, fighting to the end. He briefly resumed the chase but called it off at 12.45pm, realizing that Hipper had enough of a lead to make it back to the main battlefleet before being caught.

The Royal Navy had won a clear victory, sinking *Blücher* and badly damaging *Seydlitz*, leaving over 950 German sailors dead and 300 wounded or captive. The cost was damage that kept *Lion* out of action for four months and minor damage to *Tiger*, with 15 men killed and some 40 wounded. The British press was overjoyed that the attacks on the coastal towns had been avenged, and much of the pressure on the Admiralty was eased. Within the Royal Navy, though, there was bitter disappointment and a widespread awareness that it was a success achieved but a triumph missed; the battle represented a wonderful opportunity that could have led to the annihilation of the German battlecruisers – one that was squandered.

Beatty did commit some errors, notably in failing to make his intentions clearer to his captains, so that they would know how to respond to the unexpected in the confused conditions of battle. Most historians agree, however, that the greater mistakes were made by his subordinates. Pelly of the *Tiger* has been criticized for failing to engage his opposite number as ordered, while all of the captains failed to press on against the rear of the enemy force. Most of the blame has been directed at Rear Admiral Moore, who took command when Beatty was incommunicado. He should have exercised more initiative and responsibility, acting according to what he should have known to be his superior's intent, rather than following what must

have seemed a very strange order. Beatty was reluctant to criticize him, but Fisher, as always, was not so diplomatic, writing a series of splenetic letters, sprinkled with his usual capital letters and multiple exclamation marks, describing Pelly as a 'poltroon' and Moore's action as 'despicable'. Still, the public and the press were delighted and an unwillingness to puncture this bubble of optimism explains why Pelly emerged unscathed and Moore suffered no worse than being transferred to a command in the Canary Islands.

Other worrying lessons should have been drawn from the battle. The accuracy of British gunnery had once again been poor, even allowing for the very high speed, the smoke from German battlecruisers and the thick smokescreen laid by their covering destroyers. This problem was tackled by speeding up the installation of new fire control apparatus. Some changes were also made to the signal book, including restoring a signal for the Nelsonian 'engage the enemy more closely'. However, the opportunity was missed for a more thorough overhaul of the signalling system, or for greater scrutiny of long-range gunnery or of the inadequate armour protection of the battlecruisers.

As is often the case, the defeated side proved more willing to identify and act upon lessons from the battle. The German Navy, despite believing wrongly that it had inflicted serious damage on Beatty's ships, concluded that it had been unwise to send *Blücher*

Moltke was one of the German battlecruisers, the heavy scouting forces which, like their British counterparts, saw more action than their compatriots in the battle squadrons of the main fleets. The German battlecruisers had better armour protection than their British opponents.

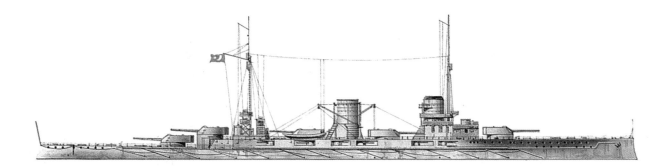

Destroyers at Dogger Bank. Although larger warships receive more attention, destroyers were the true work-horses of much of the naval war. They supported the fleets, hunted U-boats and fought some lively small-scale actions themselves.

with the battlecruisers and that the operation had not been coordinated with the U-boats (though it was a misplaced British fear of submarine attack that allowed Hipper's force to escape). One fortunate side effect of the battle for the High Seas Fleet came from the hit on *Seydlitz* that had started a fire; if this had spread, it would have reached the magazine, destroying the ship, but the flooding of two compartments prevented this. The correct conclusion was drawn from what Vice Admiral Reinhard Scheer called 'a very valuable lesson': all capital ships were provided with better arrangements to protect against flash from a hit in a turret reaching the magazine. Further, while German gunnery had been more accurate than that of its adversary, insufficient effort had been devoted to practising long-range firing. Hence, while the German battlefleet did not put to sea for a year, it used this time well to improve its armour, fire control and gunnery. The Royal Navy was perhaps lulled into complacency by success, and did not undertake such a rigorous programme of self-evaluation. The critical reaction of the German Navy served it well when the main fleets met at Jutland.

HMS *Lion* in action. The early skirmishes of the surface naval war in the North Sea left both sides feeling dissatisfied. The respective battlecruiser fleets had tested each other's mettle, but the main fleets had yet to come into contact.

The other longer-term effect of the Battle of the Dogger Bank was that criticism of Ingenohl increased still further, in the light of what seemed to be the latest in a series of errors. He was replaced on 2 February by the Chief of the Naval Staff, Admiral Hugo von Pohl. While the latter was bolder than his predecessor, he still had no intention of hazarding his battlefleet in an engagement with superior forces, and continued the attempt to whittle away the strength of the Grand Fleet. While this preserved the existence of the German battlefleet, it also eroded morale, the effect of which would not become apparent until later in the war.

The fact that the High Seas Fleet had, once again, only narrowly escaped disaster helped to tip the balance in a long-running dispute over a possible alternative strategy. Since attrition of the Royal Navy did not look like giving Germany command of the sea, a number of influential voices – notably Tirpitz – had long been urging the greater use of submarines to impose a full economic blockade on Britain. Dogger Bank tipped the balance, and the new commander-in-chief of the fleet added his voice to those calling for the unleashing of the U-boats.

CHAPTER 3

The U-Boat War Begins

As war got underway, it became quite clear to the Admiralty that the threat posed by German submarines had been grossly underestimated. The world's most powerful navy was even briefly forced to retreat to distant harbours by the U-boats. Their main impact, however, stemmed from their use against merchant shipping. During several periods of unrestricted warfare, events such as the sinking of the passenger liner *Lusitania* ensured the notoriety of this potent underwater weapon.

Experiments with submarines began as early as the seventeenth century. Various governments showed interest in the early work of such pioneers as Robert Fulton and J.P. Holland, not least because it seemed to offer the possibility of attacking hostile warships that were engaged in a blockade. This was how the Confederate submarines were used during the American Civil War, which saw the first sinking of an enemy ship by a submarine. Interest in the potential of this new weapon grew rapidly

A German U-boat in the Mediterranean. The impact of submarines in World War I was greater than anyone had anticipated beforehand. The U-boat campaign was perhaps Germany's best chance of forcing Britain out of the war.

85

towards the end of the nineteenth century. The internal combustion engine offered a superior source of propulsion compared to hand cranks operated by the crew, while torpedoes provided an effective weapon that could be used from a reasonable distance, as opposed to the spar torpedo, which had sunk as

The Submarine Enters the Stage

Although there had been earlier experiments, the first time a submarine sank a ship was on 18 February 1864. The CSS *H.L. Hunley* sank the sloop USS *Housatonic*, which was blockading the harbour of Charleston, South Carolina. The *Hunley* used a spar torpedo (an explosive charge at the end of a long iron pipe), but itself sank with the loss of all hands due to damage sustained in the attack. The danger to the submarine's own crew was a common feature during its early years: before this final operation, no fewer than 35 men had died on the *Hunley* in accidents, including its builder, H.L. Hunley himself. As with other earlier submarines, the boat could travel short distances underwater, but attacked its targets on the surface, albeit operating partially submerged and presenting a small target that was difficult to see.

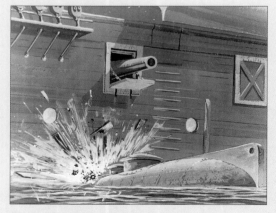

The Confederate submarine *Hunley*, the first submarine to sink an enemy warship.

many users as targets. There were still reasons for scepticism, however, due to limited seaworthiness, poor reliability and limited range; yet as these characteristics improved, the submarine had to be taken more seriously.

France showed particular interest in early submarines, which were seen as promising a means of neutralizing Britain's advantage in battleships, preventing naval blockades and allowing a more lethal campaign against merchant shipping. By 1901, France had 31 on order. Interest was also shown in the United States (which by 1902 had ordered seven) and also Greece, Italy, Japan, the Netherlands, Portugal, Russia, Spain, Sweden and Turkey.

Britain was a little slower to see the submarine as a useful weapon, with many in the government and the Royal Navy reluctant to encourage something that seemed to threaten the dominance of the surface warship, in which Britain held such an advantage. It was also seen by some as an immoral, even cowardly weapon: Admiral Sir Arthur Wilson called it 'underhand, unfair and damned un-English'. Indeed, at the 1899 Hague Conference on the laws of war (where the delegates included such naval luminaries as Mahan and Fisher), Britain suggested banning the submarine and the torpedo, but other states were reluctant, not least because Britain was less keen to see similar restrictions placed on battleships. However, the fact that so many states were acquiring submarines, not least France, meant that building some was prudent, even if only for experiments in how to counter them. Hence, in 1901, Britain ordered five. Some of the submarine's proponents in the Royal Navy recognized its wider potential and within a few years of commissioning the first boats, Britain envisaged using them for defending ports and narrow straits. Others, such as Jacky Fisher, conceived a more ambitious, offensive role than mere coastal defence, realizing that Britain could use them near the enemy's bases or in other areas where he was locally dominant. Many remained sceptical, however, with Admiral Beresford nicknaming them 'Fisher's toys'.

Germany was, ironically (in view of later events), one of the last great powers to adopt the submarine,

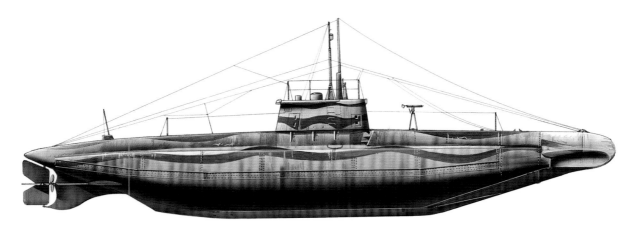

which it did by ordering a single one in 1905 and beginning trials in 1907. Thereafter, there was a swift technological advance, with the development of larger, longer-range boats and trials of a diesel engine in 1913, which was safer, more reliable and promised a genuinely ocean-going submarine. This delay was due in large part to the priority placed on the battlefleet by Tirpitz in his naval expansion plans, despite his experience as head of the torpedo arm.

U4, an early German submarine. Germany was a relatively late entrant to the submarine trade, due to the emphasis placed on battleships. At the beginning of the war, she had one of the smallest submarine forces of a major naval power, but these included some of the world's most advanced boats.

A British A-class submarine at sea. The A-class was one of the first to enter service in the Royal Navy, from around 1903. They were small boats, designed only for short-range, coastal operations and served during the war in harbour defence.

The gun on a British E-class submarine. This class represented a considerable advance on the A class, and entered service from 1911 onwards. The boats were capable of overseas operations and were used offensively during the war, including in the Baltic and in the Dardanelles.

At the beginning of the war in 1914, France had the largest submarine fleet with 77 boats, with Britain in second place with 55, the United States third with 38 and then Russia with 33. Germany had only 28 U-boats (the term being an abbreviation of *Unterseeboote*). These figures are somewhat misleading, however, since most of the French and British boats were very small and limited in capability, whereas 10 of the German boats were very modern and powered by diesel engines, and Germany had many more under construction.

The great advantage that submarines possessed was their stealth, due mainly to the ability to operate beneath the water for short periods of time, though also because their low profile made them hard to spot when they were operating on the surface at night. This characteristic was useful both for evading patrolling forces and for ambushing surface ships, and allowed a navy to operate even when its opponent was dominant in traditional terms. Their main weaknesses – some of which would reduce as the early technical capabilities of the submarine improved – were that they had limited range and speed, especially when operating underwater, that they were relatively fragile and that they carried only a limited stock of torpedoes – typically six at the beginning of the war.

Generally, the submarine was seen as useful for reconnaissance, and for the defence of coasts and harbours. Alternatively, for the more ambitious, it might be used to pick off enemy warships (especially dam-aged ones) in support of the battlefleet, which was still universally seen as the centrepiece of naval power. Ideas about using the submarine offensively and at a greater distance grew along with improvements in its capabilities, but the envisaged target was still enemy warships. None of the main powers anticipated the use of submarines against merchant shipping. Most policy makers and analysts doubted that they could be an effective weapon due to the restrictions imposed by international law, failing to appreciate how the pressures of war might lead to the casting aside of legal conventions. One exception was Jacky Fisher, who warned about the dangers of attacks conducted without warning against merchant ships; however, his prediction was dismissed as unthinkable.

'None of the main powers anticipated the use of submarines against merchant shipping. Most doubted that they could be an effective weapon due to international law restrictions'

EARLY USE AGAINST WARSHIPS

The initial use of submarines by both sides was, as expected, against warships. Both Britain and Germany established patrols near their own bases and then began to send their boats over greater distances, seeking out the enemy rather than waiting for him to attack. On 6 August 1914, Germany dispatched 10 U-boats to patrol the North Sea. On 8 August, this force made contact with the enemy and *U15* conducted the first, albeit unsuccessful, torpedo attack on a British warship, the pre-Dreadnought HMS *Monarch*. The following day, *U15* was spotted on the surface, apparently suffering mechanical problems, and was rammed and sunk by the light cruiser *Birmingham*. One other U-boat was lost to unknown causes, probably a mine. The results of this first scouting foray by U-boats were a disappointment, inflicting no damage but losing one-fifth of the force. Nevertheless, this five-day patrol proved to German commanders that U-boats could remain at sea for longer periods and could operate over greater distances than had been assumed, which helped to advance more ambitious views as to the possible roles of U-boats.

As it became clear that the Royal Navy was not going to behave as anticipated by charging headlong into German-dominated waters, more distant offensive patrols were conducted. U-boats were sent into the Firth of Forth where their first success was achieved on 5 September 1914, as *U21* under Lieutenant Otto Hersing sank the light cruiser HMS *Pathfinder*. A heavier blow followed on 22 September when *U9*, commanded by Otto Weddigen, sank the three armoured cruisers *Aboukir*, *Cressy* and *Hogue*. On 15 October, the same U-boat attacked and sank the light cruiser HMS *Hawke*. Later in the month *U27* sank a submarine and the converted seaplane carrier *Hermes*. On New Year's Day 1915, *U24* sank the pre-Dreadnought *Formidable*. This was the greatest achievement so far by a submarine, although no Dreadnought had yet been sunk – indeed, none would be sunk by a submarine during the entire war.

These events made it clear to the Admiralty that the submarine threat had been grossly underestimated. The result was not only changes to operations at sea (with high speeds, zigzag courses and destroyer escorts becoming standard procedure) but also a withdrawal

The Baltic saw many clashes at sea between Germany and Russia. The Royal Navy considered various schemes for operations there, including some rather risky amphibious operations. In the end, British involvement was largely confined to submarines, which operated from Russian bases and caused considerable damage and disruption.

by the Grand Fleet from Scapa Flow for much of the period between September and the end of November 1914, while anti-submarine defences there were improved. The world's mightiest expression of naval power had been compelled to retreat by the threat from the submarine; it is difficult to imagine a more striking example of the impact of a new weapon. The naval arm that was of least interest to Tirpitz caused greater concern to the Royal Navy than the High Seas Fleet (on which he had lavished so much financial and political capital) would throughout the war.

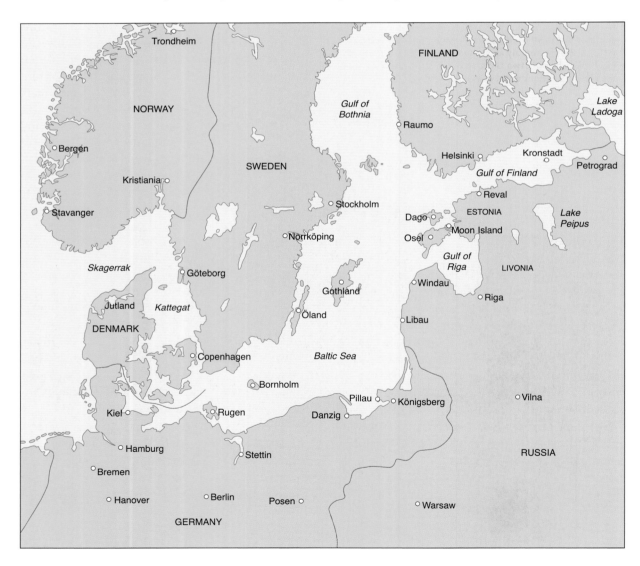

While the Royal Navy found its activities severely constrained by the perceived threat from U-boats, the impact of submarines was far from one-sided. Operations by British submarines caused much the same concern and operational inconvenience to the German Navy as the U-boats caused to the Grand Fleet. While the threat posed by submarines had helped compel the Admiralty to drop the close blockade conducted directly off the enemy bases, the submarine also provided an alternative. While small submarines guarded the British coast against attack,

The crew of HMS *Swift*, a destroyer flotilla leader, commissioned in 1907. She saw extensive service as part of the Dover Patrol, notably an action in April 1917 when, with HMS *Broke*, she sank two German destroyers from a large force aiming to attack anti-submarine forces.

larger and longer-range Royal Navy boats scouted waters close to Germany, including the Heligoland Bight and the Skagerrak, which would have been prohibitively dangerous for surface warships. They achieved some successes, notably *E9*, under Lieutenant Commander Max Horton (who became famous in the Battle of the Atlantic in World War II). On 13 September, this submarine sank the light cruiser *Hela* – later hitting another cruiser with a torpedo that failed to explode – and on 6 October sank a destroyer.

Even a navy that was dominant in the conventional terms of the battlefleet could utilize the valuable ability of submarines to operate where the enemy enjoyed a local superiority. In October 1914, Britain sent three submarines into the Baltic, to disrupt German operations there. One was forced to turn

HMS *Aboukir*. The sinking by a single U-boat of the three old armoured cruisers of the 'live bait squadron' was a great shock to Britain, and clearly demonstrated the dangers for such ships operating in areas where U-boats were present.

back, but two, *E1* and *E9,* succeeded in making the dangerous passage despite mining, heavy German patrols and difficult navigation. The impressive early results achieved by these two boats – damaging a pre-Dreadnought and sinking a destroyer, a collier, a minelayer and a naval transport – resulted in more being deployed in 1915. Four E-class boats braved the straits while four smaller C-class vessels were towed to Archangel and then transported by canal into the Baltic. They operated from Russian bases and achieved a number of successes, not least in helping to disrupt a German amphibious operation against Russia over the summer. *E1* torpedoed and damaged the battlecruiser *Moltke, E8* sank the armoured cruiser *Prinz Albert* and *E19* sank the light cruiser *Undine.* Later, they switched to attacking the German shipments of iron ore from Sweden. Germany had

much the same difficulty in countering submarines as her opponent and, just as the Royal Navy found, the wider disruptive effect of submarine operations was even greater than the direct losses. Training was adversely affected, in an area that had previously been considered safe, and destroyers were switched away from the High Seas Fleet to patrol against submarines.

Submariners on both sides found it difficult to attack enemy warships. While a battlefleet was under way at reasonable speed and following a zigzag course, it was a challenging target for the slow U-boat. It was not possible to maintain submarines on patrol for extended periods, yet if they were dispatched only on definite warning that the opposing fleet had left port, they were usually too slow to get into position in time for an attack. Their low speed and the difficulty of communication between them and surface ships, as well as shore bases, also made it difficult to coordinate their activities with those of the rest of the fleet. Nonetheless, it was clear that an important new element had been added to naval power.

U9 photographed in 1914. On 22 September 1914, *U9* (commanded by Lieutenant Otto Weddigen) came upon three *Cressy*-class armoured cruisers and sank all three in quick succession. This was a considerable achievement, not least since the U-boat was only carrying six torpedoes.

U-BOATS AGAINST COMMERCE

The use of submarines against merchant shipping had not been anticipated before the war other than by a few visionaries such as Fisher. This was largely due to the assumption that they would obey international law, which imposed restrictions on submarine operations – impositions that threatened to make it impossible to use them effectively.

Submarines were bound by 'prize rules' that had been developed for surface raiders. These held that a merchant ship could be stopped, boarded and searched for contraband (that is, war materials). If found to be carrying contraband, the vessel could then be confiscated or sunk – on the condition that the crew were first placed in a position of safety, which putting them in lifeboats would not fulfil unless it occurred very close to the shore. These rules were straightforward for a cruiser or converted auxiliary raider, which would overpower any merchant ship and had either enough personnel to put a prize crew on board a seized ship or had enough space to take onboard the crew of a ship that was to be sunk.

The rules caused great difficulties for submarines, however, since by surfacing to challenge a merchant ship they made themselves vulnerable to attack by a modest armament that would not trouble a cruiser, or even to ramming. Moreover, they could not spare a prize crew (typically having a complement of about 40 officers and ratings) and were too small to take on any captives. There was therefore a tension between observing international law, which meant imposing severe self-limitations, and allowing the U-boats to attack in their most effective manner. It was perhaps inevitable that as Germany began to feel the strain of the war, her strategy would shift towards the latter course.

Though many ships were lost to mines laid by U-boats, the first direct attack on a merchant ship occurred on 20 October 1914, and was conducted strictly in accordance with international law. The small British steamer *Glitra*, en route for Norway, was stopped by *U17*, inspected and scuttled by a boarding party only after the crew were placed in lifeboats, which were then towed to the Norwegian coast (the proximity of which made it acceptable to leave the crew in lifeboats). On 26 October, a different and more ominous attack was carried out, as *U24* torpedoed, without warning, and damaged the French steamer *Amiral Ganteaumme*. The commander believed the people he could see on deck were troops; they were in fact refugees from Belgium, 40 of whom died in the attack.

From November 1914, some commanders in the German Navy began to advocate wider and more systematic attacks on British commerce. As the expected rapid victory on land failed to occur, there was a desire to identify alternative means of pressuring the Allies. Targeting Britain's trade seemed an obvious

The British Blockade

From the start of the war, Britain imposed an economic blockade on Germany to put pressure on its ability and will to continue waging war. It sought to prevent imports of war materials and even food, which also involved seeking to prevent imports into neutral states being re-exported to Germany. The blockade was enforced by cruiser patrols to check merchant ships and, if contraband were found, send them into British ports. These patrols were backed by intensive diplomatic and intelligence efforts. The blockade caused some friction with neutrals, although – much to the indignation of the German Government – less than the U-boat campaign, since at worst it resulted in the seizing and compulsory purchase of cargoes deemed contraband, rather than the death of merchant seamen and civilian passengers. Much war material still reached Germany through neutral countries, but the gradually tightening blockade began to exert severe pressure on her.

option, but as Germany's surface raiders were gradually hunted down and there seemed to be no imminent prospect of the German battlefleet defeating its British counterpart (particularly after its narrow escape at the Battle of the Dogger Bank in January 1915), the U-boats seemed to be the ideal alternative. The restrictions being observed fatally limited the effectiveness of the campaign, it was argued, and should therefore be shaken off. Other senior naval officers and, even more, the civilian members of the German Government (particularly the Chancellor, Theobald von Bethmann Hollweg), opposed any widening of the U-boat campaign that would violate international law. Their principal concern was the risk of alienating neutral powers, perhaps even provoking them to join the war on the side of the Entente. Proponents of submarine warfare replied that observance of the niceties of international law not only jeopardized a potentially war-winning weapon, it also overlooked the fact that such actions could be portrayed as a legitimate response to the British blockade, which itself seemed to be straining accepted international conventions. Why should neutral ships carrying supplies to Britain be left unmolested while those supplying Germany were being intercepted?

As the course of the war failed to take a turn for the better for Germany, and as the British blockade bit harder, pressure in the media and Parliament grew to unleash the U-boats. More naval officers and then finally the Kaiser himself were won over. On 4 February 1915, Germany proclaimed that all waters around Britain would from 18 February be treated as a war zone, with all British ships being sunk without either any warning or any measures to protect the crews. It warned that neutral ships were also subject to attack, since they could not be distinguished from British ships. Some naval officers felt that this statement was too much of a political compromise, since it failed explicitly to state that all shipping, including neutral vessels, was forbidden in the war zone. In practice, the protection for neutrals was considerably watered down by the instructions given to U-boat captains that the safety of their vessel was their first concern, therefore they should not surface to examine a ship and check whether or not it was neutral.

The United States protested strongly and warned the German Government that it would be held accountable for any American ships attacked. As a result, after some bitter debates, the German Government 'clarified' the initial statement, insisting that only enemy vessels, rather than all merchant ships, would be sunk, adding that measures would be taken to ensure the security of neutrals. For Vice Admiral Reinhard Scheer, these modifications for diplomatic consumption 'ruined' the campaign. The navy was ordered to instruct U-boat commanders not to attack neutral-flagged ships unless it was certain that they were enemies using a false flag; yet the instructions passed on to the captains were surprisingly permissive, giving them as much latitude as possible to attack merchant ships. They were ordered to pursue the campaign 'with all possible vigour', but told that they should not attack neutrals – although flags and other markings suggesting neutrality were not to be taken as proof that a ship was truly neutral, and other factors, such as its course, should be taken into account; in addition, commanders would not be held responsible for any mistakes made.

U6, U7, U10 and *U12* photographed in 1913. At the start of the war, the Imperial German Navy had no more than 28 U-boats. None of the four boats pictured here would survive the war: one was sunk by a British submarine, one by a mine, one by a British destroyer and one by another U-boat in a case of 'friendly fire'.

The frequent changes in policy and in instructions to commanders reflected deep divisions within the German Government between its military and civilian members. They were torn between maximizing the impact of the U-boat campaign and minimizing its diplomatic repercussions. Germany was trying to have it both ways, reassuring the United States that American ships would not be deliberately targeted while also explicitly relying on the terror effect of attacks to deter neutrals from trading with Britain. 'Unrestricted submarine warfare' was really a misnomer, since some ships had been torpedoed without warning before 18 February, while even during the height of the campaign, restrictions of some sort were often imposed. The restrictions on U-boat operations were rarely either total or entirely absent, but were rather a matter of degree with considerable variation.

Germany had not envisaged waging war on commerce and had therefore made no plans for it. Similarly, though, Britain had not anticipated the need to defend merchant shipping against submarine attack. When the failure to achieve decisive success on land led Germany to start attacking commerce, both sides had to improvise – with Britain's efforts to do so rapidly becoming the key to her remaining in the war.

THE FIRST 'UNRESTRICTED' U-BOAT CAMPAIGN
The opening of the campaign on 18 February 1915 saw an average of only about five U-boats at sea each day; of the total force in service, some were incapable of long-range operations, others were involved in training crewmen or were under repair. Germany was slow to build more, due to the long-lasting assumption of a short war. Nevertheless, numbers grew, including the smaller UB and UC boats (the latter being minelayers) of the Flanders Flotilla, designed to operate from captured Belgian ports at

Zeebrugge and Ostend. The larger boats operating from the bases of the High Seas Fleet in Germany were well placed for the North Sea, but in terms of reaching the Atlantic, they had a less favourable geographical position than their successors in World War II would enjoy with bases in occupied France and Norway.

On 19 February, the Norwegian tanker *Belridge* was torpedoed and damaged by *U16*, becoming the first neutral vessel to be attacked without warning. The United States protested furiously, since this was a ship belonging to a neutral state, heading from one neutral country (the United States) to another (the Netherlands). The German Government apologized. A few days later, *U8* sank no fewer than five British ships in the English Channel. The campaign was rapidly taking effect and losses mounted.

By the end of 1914, only three merchant ships of 3048 tonnes (3000 tons) in total had been sunk by U-boats (all figures for losses are from Tarrant, V.E. *The U-Boat Offensive 1914–1945*). In January and February 1915, sinkings rose to seven ships totalling over 17,780 tonnes (17,500 tons) and nine ships of 23,165 tonnes (22,800 tons) respectively. In March, as the unrestricted campaign got fully underway, losses rose to 29 ships of 90,935 tonnes (89,500 tons) before falling back in April to 42,165 tonnes (41,500 tons), due to a reduction in the number of U-boats operating. In May, the tonnage sunk soared to over 108,700 tonnes (107,000 tons) – with another 20,300 tonnes (20,000 tons) sunk in the Black Sea – with the June figure even higher at 117,150 tonnes (115,300 tons). These losses, while serious, were lower than the rate of construction of new merchant ships, while the total tonnage available to the Allies was further increased by pressing into service impounded vessels belonging to the Central Powers. This was a one-off bonus, however, while future new construction would be lower due to the reallocation to military production

> 'When the failure to achieve decisive success on land led Germany to start attacking commerce, both sides had to improvise – with Britain's efforts to do so rapidly becoming the key to her remaining in the war'

of shipyards, skilled manpower and raw materials. By May, more than 20 neutral ships had been attacked without warning. That month, however, saw a striking incident that would eventually curtail the first unrestricted campaign.

THE SINKING OF THE *LUSITANIA*

On 7 May 1915, *U20* (commanded by Lieutenant-Commander Walter Schwieger) was heading home after sinking three merchant ships during her cruise.

She sighted the passenger liner *Lusitania*, en route from the United States to Britain. The U-boat happened to be steaming a favourable course for an attack on this fast ship, so the captain submerged and, having recognized the distinctive vessel, ordered an

The result of an attack on a merchant ship. When Germany began to shrug off the restrictions of international law, the rising losses to U-boats began to have an increasing impact. The first campaign ended before large numbers of U-boats were available, but it was a warning of what was to come.

The threat to merchant ships from U-boats was very difficult to counter, given the surprisingly intense opposition from within the Royal Navy to the tried and tested solution of convoy and escort. Britain had little time in which to learn how to conduct an effective anti-submarine campaign.

attack in full knowledge that his target was a passenger liner. The torpedo struck home and blew an enormous hole in the side of the ship. It was followed by a large secondary explosion, caused (according to different theories) by the ship's steam generation plant, coal gas or the detonation of some of the munitions that the ship was carrying as part of her cargo. *Lusitania* sank rapidly, her increasing list as she went down hindering the launch of lifeboats and increasing the casualties. Some 1200 passengers were killed, including 128 Americans. The attack caused outrage among neutrals, particularly the United States, but President Woodrow Wilson was deeply reluctant to become involved in the war and confined the reaction of his government to a strong protest. Nevertheless, American public opinion shifted strongly against Germany – and was considerably less critical thereafter of the impact of the British blockade.

There was much concern among the civilians in the German Government about the impact of such actions, though naval commanders insisted that the policy should continue. Although sinkings, including attacks without warning, continued over the summer, the German Government tightened restrictions somewhat, assuring the United States Government that there would be no more attacks on neutral ships or on passenger vessels of any nationality. The Chief of the Naval Staff, Admiral Bachman, objected that such demanding conditions were unworkable, and insisted for his crews that there be a clear choice between unrestricted warfare and ending the campaign entirely. He was replaced. His concerns that the modified policy would prove impossible to implement in practice were confirmed on 19 August, when the British passenger liner *Arabic*, en route for the United States, was sunk by *U21*, killing 44 people, including three Americans. There was renewed public fury in the United States at this violation of the pledge that no passenger ships would be sunk (a guarantee that was easier to offer than to put into practice). Another sinking of a passenger liner followed on 6 September when *U20* torpedoed the *Hesperian*, killing 32.

Once again, the issue was debated within the German Government. Some in the navy, notably Tirpitz, pressed for attacks without warning to continue while the civilian officials, especially Theobald von Bethmann Hollweg, urged a return to full observation of prize rules. This time, the Kaiser supported the latter viewpoint. On 18 September, U-boats were ordered to cease patrolling the Western Approaches and the Channel, and to act in accord with international law in the North Sea. The first 'unrestricted' U-boat campaign had ended.

The campaign had inflicted painful losses, but not on a scale that threatened Britain's participation in the war. The later part of the campaign had seen merchant ships sunk at a higher rate than new ones were being built, with over 165,615 tonnes (163,000 tons) plus another 15,240 tonnes (15,000 tons) in the Mediterranean and Black Sea sunk in August 1915. There was relief in the Admiralty that the campaign had ended and perhaps also complacency, though the latter sentiment was based on a misunderstanding: the British anti-submarine measures had, despite huge effort, been largely ineffective in meeting the technical and conceptual challenges posed by this new weapon.

Walter Schwieger was the commanding officer of *U20*, which on 7 May 1915 torpedoed and sank the liner *Lusitania*, killing about 1200 civilians. The outcry in the United States over this action compelled the German Government once again to tighten the restrictions on the U-boat campaign. Schwieger was killed in 1917 when his U-boat struck a mine.

The Sinking of the *Lusitania*

The Cunard passenger liner *Lusitania* was more than a ship, she was a symbol. When she was launched in 1906, she was the largest passenger ship in the world, and had been designed explicitly to take back the Blue Riband for the fastest crossing of the Atlantic from German competitors. This she duly achieved, both westbound and eastbound. She was part of a programme by which the British Government provided a subsidy for ships that could be converted to armed merchant cruisers in wartime. As it happened, however, the Admiralty decided that she would not be useful in such a role and she continued as a passenger liner. Other liners had been sunk before the *Lusitania*, but her fame and the large number of people killed (especially Americans) made the reaction more furious.

COUNTERMEASURES

The Allies were fortunate that the U-boat campaign began on a relatively small scale, giving them precious time in which to devise counters. This advantage, however, was outweighed by the difficulty of creating effective means of anti-submarine warfare. The use of U-boats against merchant shipping was an entirely unprecedented and unforeseen type of threat. Experiments had been conducted before the war, but had not been a particularly high priority and had not produced any useful countermeasures.

The most obvious problem was the lack of any means of detecting and attacking submerged submarines. When operating on the surface, U-boats could be spotted – during the day, at least – and were vulnerable to attack by gunfire or even ramming. It was their ability to submerge quickly at the first sign of danger that made them so challenging. The common image of anti-submarine warfare as

depicted in war films shows destroyers using sonar and depth charges to dispatch their prey, but these innovations took some time to emerge: an effective depth charge was not in service until 1916 and Asdic (the original, British name for what the United States called sonar) was invented at the end of the war, though never used operationally. Both of these problems, detection and attack, received a great deal of attention but a solution took time – and meanwhile, losses were mounting.

For detecting submarines, attention initially focused on hydrophones, underwater microphones that could pick up the sound of a U-boat's engines. These were first used in 1916 and represented a step forward but were subject to important limitations: they initially could not give any indication as to the direction of a detected submarine and they required the ship using them to be stationary (very dangerous if submarines were present), to prevent the noise of its own engines

or of water passing its hull from drowning out the sound of any nearby U-boat. Another attempt to reveal the location of submerged submarines was the use of indicator nets, which were equipped with flares or contact mines that would alert patrolling forces if a U-boat became entangled in them.

As for attacking U-boats, the obvious solution was to destroy them in their harbours. The bases in Germany were too well protected to be attacked, so attention focused on those of the Flanders Flotilla in occupied Belgium. During 1915, they were subject to repeated attack by bombing raids and, later in the year, bombardment by purpose-built monitor gunboats. These efforts had little effect, due to the difficulty of

Some countermeasures to the U-boat threat were highly imaginative. This ship is protected by 'dazzle camouflage'. Introduced late in the war, it was designed to make it more difficult for a U-boat commander to judge the course of his intended target and thus harder for him to attack.

achieving the accuracy required and to the heavy protection of the targets.

The U-boats would therefore have to be destroyed at sea. Early use was made of 'explosive sweeps' or

Aircraft against Submarines

The threat from U-boats was met in part by the increasingly widespread use of an even newer technology: aircraft. They included slow, non-rigid airships (or 'blimps'), aeroplanes operating from land bases, seaplanes (which took off from and alighted on the water, using floats attached where a land-based aeroplane would have wheels) and, later, flying boats (which, unlike seaplanes, floated on their main fuselage). Aircraft were able to search large areas of the sea to spot U-boats. They were less effective at attacking any U-boat that was spotted, however, since it was a difficult target for bombs, and air-dropped depth charges did not appear until the next world war. Aircraft could call up warships to attack a U-boat or could simply force it to submerge, reducing its range and effectiveness. The technical characteristics of aircraft improved rapidly during World War I, and hinted at the far greater role they would play in the 1939–45 anti-submarine campaign.

H12 Curtis 'Large America' flying boats attacking a submarine. Aircraft would eventually prove to be a vital element in meeting the threat from U-boats.

'explosive paravanes', which were charges towed underwater that could be detonated if they struck a submerged U-boat. A better solution lay in depth charges, which were dropped behind a patrol ship to explode at a predetermined depth. The idea had been conceived before the war and the first request for them was made shortly before its outbreak, but it took some time to design one and there was then a further delay before it could be made available in the numbers needed.

An alternative approach was to entice the U-boats to launch an attack themselves, luring them to the surface and to approach within range of a trap. Attempts to do this were assisted by the fact that it was appealing for a U-boat commander to surface and to sink a merchant ship with gunfire, or by placing

explosives on board, rather than to use up his limited supply of torpedoes. One version of the U-boat trap used in summer 1915 was to have a trawler towing a submarine; when a U-boat challenged the trawler it would alert the submarine, which could sink the attacker. This practice resulted in the sinking of two U-boats, but others survived to report back and provide warning of this technique.

The second form of the trap built on the long-standing practice of arming merchant ships to give them some capability for self-defence against raiders. A U-boat, highly vulnerable to gunfire, would not approach a ship on the surface that was evidently armed, so the Admiralty devised the Q-ship, a merchant ship with concealed guns, also first used in summer 1915. Believing the Q-ship to be a juicy target, the U-boat would surface and approach, often encouraged by some of the crew faking panic and abandoning ship, at which point the Q-ship would uncover its guns, run up the White Ensign (showing itself to be a warship) and engage the would-be attacker. During the war, Q-ships sank 11 U-boats,

The Short 'improved' Type 184 Seaplane. This was one of the most widely used naval aircraft of the war, with over 900 being built from 1915. It was used for reconnaissance and as a bomber, and also holds the distinction of being the first aircraft to sink a ship with an air-launched torpedo (during the Dardanelles campaign).

which some have seen as a modest return given the large number that went to sea (as many as 180 in 1917). On the other hand, the possibility of vessels being Q-ships forced U-boats to attack from underwater, where their speed was lower than on the surface, using up their torpedoes and thus reducing the number of attacks made on each patrol.

Yet another way to solve the detection and attack problem was to try to prevent the U-boat from reaching the shipping lanes by using mines and barriers. Britain placed considerable faith in minefields, laid off German bases or in narrow waters through which U-boats had to pass to reach their patrol areas. These had less success than hoped: the mines could be swept up by the German Navy, and, in particular, the early mines used by Britain were ineffective, often failing to detonate on making contact with a U-boat or tending to explode when no U-boat was near.

The English Channel was a critical stretch of water for the campaign, partly because of the amount of local traffic between Britain and France, partly

A British convoy leaves port with non-rigid ('blimp') airships. Airships were widely used in support of convoys during World War I. Their great advantage was the ability to remain on station for long periods, although their utility was reduced by their low speed and lack of manoeuvrability.

Convoy – the Early Debate

There was one way to protect valuable ships that had a long history of success: convoy. This involved gathering ships into groups that were guarded by escorting warships, rather than allowing them to sail independently. Some advocated convoy as a means of safeguarding essential merchant ships against attacks by U-boats, yet this response was rejected by the Royal Navy in the early years of the war. Some naval officers felt that modern conditions meant that convoy would no longer work, while others believed that it was merely defensive and trusted offensive patrols to seek out, hunt down and destroy the U-boats. Each time convoy was suggested, a range of arguments was raised against it, while losses rose. At first, they were below the level that would seriously threaten Britain's ability to keep fighting, because of the limited numbers of operational U-boats and the restrictions imposed from time to time on their activities. Yet eventually, the unity of convoy and escort would have to be reconsidered.

The *Arabis*-class sloop HMS *Lupin,* part of the larger *Flower* class, launched in May 1916. The U-boat threat presented an urgent need for small, relatively cheap escort vessels that could be built in the large numbers required. Several dozen *Flower*-class vessels were built as minesweepers and as convoy escorts.

because ships on longer journeys were concentrated there, and also because it was the quickest route for U-boats to reach the Western Approaches. Britain therefore devoted considerable resources to creating a barrier across the Channel, using nets, mines and booms, backed by patrolling warships and airships. This was difficult to achieve due to the strong tides and the weather, and U-boats could simply dive beneath the minefields. The result was not the expected impassable barrier but merely a nuisance, albeit one that caused sufficient inconvenience for the German Navy to order U-boats to avoid this route, and to take the longer alternative around the north of Scotland, between April 1915 and the end of 1916.

A further problem for the Admiralty was the limited number of ships suitable for anti-submarine operations. There were many destroyers, but they were largely occupied with duties supporting the Grand Fleet. In any case, they had been designed for use against torpedo boats and other surface ships and lacked a capability against submarines. Nor did they

exist in the number required. Britain therefore embarked on a rapid construction programme of smaller anti-submarine vessels, such as the 1220-tonne (1200-ton) *Flower*-class sloop. As an interim measure, some 500 trawlers were taken up and armed with guns to form the Auxiliary Patrol. Submarines proved useful in taking on other submarines, sinking some 18 U-boats by the end of the war, but still found it difficult to locate their prey.

Increasing use was made of aircraft, which had two great advantages: their height gave them a view superior to that of any ship, while their speed allowed them to cover a wide area. Britain made considerable use of various types of aircraft, which had different strengths and weaknesses against U-boats. Airships enjoyed a long endurance and an ability to carry heavy loads, including wireless equipment, but were slow and difficult to manoeuvre, making them all but incapable of attacking U-boats. Seaplanes were faster and more manoeuvrable, but gradually gave way to flying boats, which were faster, larger, capable of operating in rougher seas and had more crew members – and hence more eyes watching for U-boats; however, they were vulnerable to attack by enemy aircraft. One major limitation was reach, as much of the U-boat campaign took place in the Western Approaches, which were beyond the range of

British aircraft. This range was further pushed out by creating new air bases in Cornwall and south Wales, as well as establishing bases for seaplanes and flying boats in the Isles of Scilly, but it remained limited.

Each of these issues – locating U-boats, attacking them, preventing their passage to patrol areas and the inadequate number of anti-submarine vessels – was challenging, and together they caused great difficulties. These problems were greatly magnified by a fundamental flaw in the way that the limited number of anti-submarine forces were used. Rather than adopt the familiar technique of 'convoy and escort', by which the Royal Navy had protected merchant ships for centuries, the Admiralty and the great majority of naval officers

rejected its use against U-boats, deriding it as 'defensive', and clung to supposedly 'offensive' patrolling.

Some of the arguments against convoy were respectable, notably the concern that it would mean doing the U-boats' job for them by gathering their targets together, allowing them to attack many ships at once. Besides, the advent of steam power gave merchant ships far greater choice of routes, so it was suggested that they were safer travelling

One of the problems facing the British anti-submarine forces in the early years of the campaign was the lack of any means of attacking a submerged submarine. Depth charges provided the answer to this problem, especially once they became available in larger numbers.

independently. It was also argued that by delaying ships until a convoy could be formed, slowing merchant ships to the speed of the slowest and limiting the number of voyages that could be made, a system of convoy entailed reducing the efficiency of the Allies' scarce shipping tonnage. Merchant crews would not be capable of keeping station, it was felt, especially at night or if the first language of captain and crew was not English. Moreover, having many ships arriving at once followed by long gaps without any arrivals was far from the most efficient use of port facilities. It was also objected that the total number of ships arriving at and departing from Britain's ports was simply too great to be put into convoys.

A German mine-laying submarine. As well as attacking merchant ships and warships directly, U-boats caused significant losses by laying mines off ports or in key stretches of water. This forced the Allies – who conducted their own mine-laying campaigns – to devote enormous resources to sweeping the mines.

Furthermore, convoys would be of little use without escorts, and early on in the war the number of destroyers available was hopelessly inadequate – and there was tough competition for them from the Grand Fleet, which also needed escorts.

It is not quite true that the Admiralty was totally against convoy, as it embraced the system for military transports such as troop ships. Convoy was firmly rejected for merchant vessels, however. The bias for offensive patrolling neglected the principal advantage of the U-boat, which was its stealth in the vast areas in which it could be operating. Offensive patrolling was not, in fact, the active, positive solution that it was portrayed to be. Charging around the seas looking for submarines was in fact remarkably ineffective, particularly when such an obvious alternative existed. The reluctance of the Royal Navy to embrace convoy seems, in retrospect, rather baffling and it came close to costing Britain the war.

THE SECOND U-BOAT CAMPAIGN

The second U-boat campaign began in September 1915 with the reimposition of prize rules following the *Lusitania* and *Arabic* incidents, and went on until 1 February 1917. During this period, the U-boats acted under varying degrees of restrictions. At first, this policy resulted in the German Navy deciding to withdraw most of its U-boats from the North Sea, the Channel and the Atlantic, with a correspondingly low level of sinkings in these areas: between October 1915 and January 1916, the monthly average loss there was just over 17,270 tonnes (17,000 tons).

The efforts of the U-boats were redirected to the Mediterranean, where during the same period the monthly total averaged about 82,800 tonnes (81,500 tons) sunk. The Mediterranean, with the Dardanelles operation underway, offered plenty of targets – few of them from neutral states. There was much British shipping passing through, to or from the Suez Canal, as well as the large amount of traffic to and from France and also Italy, which joined the Entente and entered the war against Austria in May 1915. Germany therefore deployed U-boats in the Mediterranean, some from the High Seas Fleet travelling by sea, while smaller boats were sent in pieces by land to Pola on the Adriatic and were assembled there. The U-boats were helped by the fact that the Allies pursued the same flawed anti-submarine strategy in the Mediterranean that they did elsewhere, relying on offensive patrols while merchant ships were sunk in large numbers. Generally, prize rules were observed in the Mediterranean, although it did not escape the notice of Germany that exceptions were not met with the same American protests that such actions in the Atlantic attracted. Losses became so high that the

The German submarine *U11* in rough seas. The prevailing weather in the North Sea and North Atlantic often meant that the U-boats – not the most seaworthy vessels at the best of times – often had to cope with challenging conditions.

Allies stopped using the Suez Canal, accepting the far longer duration of rerouted voyages around the Cape of Good Hope.

In February 1916, there was another change of policy. The previous month Admiral Henning von Holtzendorff, the Chief of the Naval Staff, had submitted a paper pointing out that the 1915 campaign had damaged Britain, causing shortages in some key raw materials and food, and that a new campaign could draw on a larger force of U-boats and would achieve even more. A restricted campaign, he argued, would cause greater damage than before, but there was no guarantee that it would force Britain to make peace. An unrestricted campaign, on the other hand, would offer the 'definite prospect' of forcing Britain to make peace in six months at the most. Further intra-governmental disputes followed. The German Navy pushed once again for the resumption of unrestricted attacks on merchant shipping, which

The Kaiser, Tirpitz and Holtzendorff in discussion. The extent to which Germany was to obey the conventions of international law – if at all – in the prosecution of the U-boat campaign was the cause of bitter and prolonged disputes within and between the naval leadership and the German Government.

was opposed by civilian members of the government due to wariness about provoking the United States. This bitter dispute resulted in a confused and frequently changing policy. On 1 February 1916, Admiral Scheer (now commander-in-chief of the High Seas Fleet) was told by the Chief of the Naval Staff that a new unrestricted campaign would begin from 1 March. On 23 February, however, he was informed that the Kaiser had been persuaded by the civilians in the government to reverse this decision.

The result of the renewed debate was that from the beginning of March 1916, U-boats were permitted to attack all enemy vessels without warning within the declared war zone around the British Isles and the Western Approaches. Armed merchant vessels could be attacked even outside this area, although only if positively identified as armed, which required a risky close approach for confirmation. No passenger liners were to be attacked without warning. The German Navy chafed over the remaining restrictions – indeed, Tirpitz resigned over the issue – and a number of passenger liners were still sunk, either deliberately or in error due to the confusing orders.

In early March, the balance of opinion shifted once more and the decision was taken to resume the unrestricted campaign from 1 April. Yet again, however, events intervened to complicate policy. On 24 March 1916, *UB29* attacked without warning what her commander believed to be a troop transport. It turned out to be the French-owned ferry *Sussex*. The vessel managed to reach harbour, but the torpedo explosion killed 50 of the 300 passengers on board, including several Americans. Germany initially denied that the attack had been conducted by a U-boat, but when the truth was revealed, there was outrage in the American press and the United States Government sent an official protest, threatening to cut off diplomatic relations unless such attacks ceased. This embarrassing incident strengthened the hand of the civilian opponents of unrestricted warfare, and on 24 April, the U-boats were ordered fully to observe prize rules once again, including giving warning and ensuring the safety of crews. A furious Admiral Scheer decided that this instruction meant that the U-boats could have no practical effect and would suffer many losses due to the increased risk, so he recalled them from the Atlantic and North Sea. This decision seems to have been a bluff, an exercise of brinkmanship seeking to challenge the government and force it to reverse policy again in the face of pressure from Parliament and public opinion. Indeed, even the Naval Staff, believing Scheer to be ignorant of the wider diplomatic factors involved, sought to persuade him to resume operations under prize law, describing his position as 'either everything or nothing'. He refused. The Chancellor held his ground and the decision stood.

Between April and September 1916, therefore, U-boat attacks on merchant ships were in effect confined to the Mediterranean, where losses remained high. Once again, this was a stroke of luck for the British, because while their anti-submarine measures were still woefully inadequate, the number of U-boats was steadily rising, with 36 operational boats in the High Seas Fleet and the Flanders Flotilla by March 1916. In his memoirs, Scheer argued that an unrestricted campaign should have begun at the start of 1916 – when there were enough U-boats to be effective and any delay would only strengthen Britain's defences – or at least immediately after the Battle of Jutland. He commented: 'That we failed to do so fatally affected the outcome of the war.'

For the commanders of the German Navy, the temporary cessation of submarine operations against commerce around the British Isles offered one shred of comfort in that it freed the U-boats for use against the Grand Fleet. Admiral Scheer was now able to include them once again in his plans to reduce the Royal Navy's continuing advantage in capital ships. In May 1916, he planned to use a raid on Sunderland to lure the Grand Fleet into minefields and a U-boat trap. From 17 to 23 May, groups of U-boats took up ambush positions off the main British ports. Other

Part of the funeral procession following the coffin of Lord Kitchener. The Secretary of State for War was perhaps the single highest profile victim of the U-boats. He was killed in the June 1916 sinking of the armoured cruiser HMS *Hampshire*, en route for Russia from Scapa Flow, when she hit a mine laid by *U75*.

boats laid minefields – one of which, west of the Orkneys, on 5 June sank the armoured cruiser HMS *Hampshire*, killing Lord Kitchener (Secretary of State for War), who was en route to Russia. The plan fizzled out as the sortie of the High Seas Fleet was delayed until 30 May; only one U-boat managed to identify a target and fire torpedoes, which missed. It was therefore an intact Grand Fleet that would fight the Battle of Jutland. The indecisive outcome of this battle would persuade Germany to resort once more to unrestricted submarine warfare in a last, desperate attempt to identify a weapon that could win the war.

CHAPTER 4

The Dardanelles and Gallipoli

The situation in the Mediterranean involved a number of players. On the Entente side, the French fleet agreed to take the lead in this theatre, allowing Britain to concentrate on the North Sea and the English Channel, while Austria-Hungary provided the main naval forces of the Central Powers, backed by Germany. Italy and Turkey held the balance of power.

France had a formidable force in the Mediterranean, including two Dreadnoughts and 15 pre-Dreadnoughts, supported by the British Mediterranean Squadron, which at the outset of the war included the battlecruisers *Inflexible*, *Indomitable* and *Indefatigable*. Austria had three Dreadnoughts and nine pre-Dreadnoughts, as well as a number of submarines, based at Pola on the Adriatic. They were backed by the German Mediterranean Squadron under Rear Admiral Wilhelm Souchon, comprising the powerful battlecruiser *Goeben* and light cruiser *Breslau*.

The Allied beachhead at Anzac Cove. The Gallipoli landings were the largest amphibious operation attempted during World War I. They were an attempt to by-pass the problems of the Western Front, and reflected the importance attached to the Eastern Mediterranean and, in particular, Turkey.

The balance between the two sides depended on Italy, which had three Dreadnoughts and six pre-Dreadnoughts. Italy was a member of the Triple Alliance with Germany and Austria, so might be expected to join the war on their side. Yet the Italian Government was well aware of its vulnerability to British and French sea power, and desired to gain Austrian territory, and thus negotiated with both sides for concessions. Although Italy had a pivotal role in the Mediterranean, her intentions were uncertain at the outbreak of war.

Further complicating the picture was the presence of several neutral states, which both sides wished to bring into the war as allies. These included Greece, Bulgaria, Romania and, crucially, Turkey. Britain's interest in Turkey was demonstrated by the sending of a naval mission there in 1908, followed by an agreement to build warships for her. On the other side,

Germany enjoyed rapidly growing economic influence there, as well as maintaining a military mission that was rebuilding the Turkish Army after the losses of the Balkan Wars. The Turkish Government was unstable and divided, with pro-Germany and pro-Entente factions, but gradually the former took the ascendancy. Opinion turned sharply against the Entente in late July 1914, when the British Government decided to seize for its own use two Dreadnoughts that were under construction for Turkey in British shipyards. This action caused all the more outrage because the ships had been partly funded by a Turkish public subscription. A secret treaty was signed between Turkey and Germany shortly before the outbreak of war in August 1914, which guaranteed the former's entry into the war, yet Turkey still hesitated to take that step. Some event would be required to trigger her participation.

THE ESCAPE OF THE *GOEBEN* AND *BRESLAU*

The two German warships in the Mediterranean represented a formidable force. The French fleet was slow to deploy, so the Allied response was led by the British Mediterranean Squadron, commanded by Vice Admiral Sir Archibald Berkeley Milne. He was aware of the complexity of the situation he faced, not least the uncertainty over when war would be declared on Austria and what her fleet would then do, as well as over whether Italy would enter the war and on which side. The British battlecruisers were superior to the German squadron; they would be inferior to the Austrian main fleet unless combined with the French; if Italy joined the Central Powers, then the British and French together might be unable to control the sea.

Milne's orders from the Admiralty were unclear. They implied that his principal objective was to protect French transports carrying their forces from North Africa. Though he was later ordered to shadow the *Goeben*, he was also told not to engage 'superior forces' (though he was not told precisely what this meant). He was further instructed to watch the Adriatic, in case the Austrian fleet should emerge. The location of the German warships was uncertain, but they were expected to head west to threaten French

Rear Admiral Ernest Troubridge served under Admiral Milne in the Mediterranean, commanding a squadron of armoured cruisers. Troubridge was widely blamed for the escape of the German warships, but a Court Martial decided that he had been right not to engage a superior force.

shipping, so Milne tried to balance his competing priorities by sending *Indomitable* and *Indefatigable* towards Gibraltar, while deploying Rear Admiral Ernest Troubridge to guard the Adriatic with his four armoured cruisers.

On the morning of 4 August, *Goeben* and *Breslau* bombarded the French North African towns of Bône and Philippeville. They were then ordered east to Constantinople and headed for the neutral Italian port of Messina in Sicily to coal. At about 10.30am, the two German ships, heading east, passed *Indomitable* and *Indefatigable*, en route for Gibraltar. Since Britain and Germany were not yet at war with each other – war was not formally declared for about another 12 hours – neither side opened fire. The British battlecruisers turned and shadowed the German warships until the afternoon when the latter increased speed and pulled away. The light cruiser *Dublin* remained in contact until about 9pm, when she lost them in fog near Sicily, and the German warships entered Messina.

Milne had been ordered by London to observe Italy's neutrality 'rigidly', so as not to risk antagonizing her, and not to enter waters within 10km (6 miles) of the Italian coast. Crucially, this prevented British warships from following the *Goeben* into the Straits of Messina, which are narrower than this. Milne believed that his prey would head north and then west once again and, since his first priority was to protect the French transports, he deployed his battlecruisers west of Sicily. He informed the Admiralty of his intentions and they made no objection. Hence, on 6 August, when *Goeben* and *Breslau* left Messina heading south and then east, shadowed by the light cruiser HMS *Gloucester*, the only force that could catch them was Troubridge's cruisers.

Troubridge initially intended to engage, but on further consideration, decided that accepting battle in the open seas and in good visibility would violate the order to avoid fighting superior forces. The greater speed of *Goeben* meant that she would be able to avoid battle if the conditions did not favour her, while if they did, her longer-range guns would enable her to knock out the armoured cruisers before they could close to the effective range of their own armament. Troubridge therefore sought to create a situation where *Goeben* lacked room for manoeuvre (by catching her close to shore) or where her range advantage would be reduced (fighting at night or at dawn). When he realized that he could not bring about such conditions, with huge

The *Goeben* and *Breslau*

Goeben was a battlecruiser, a sister ship of the *Moltke*. Displacing 25,400 tonnes (25,000 tons), with a speed of 26 knots (though lower in August 1914 due to mechanical problems) and with ten 11.2-inch guns, she was the single most powerful, best armoured and fastest capital ship in the Mediterranean. Her companion was the light cruiser *Breslau*, a 4570-tonne (4500-ton) light cruiser with twelve 4.1-inch guns. At the start of the war, they were able to take advantage of the confused political and strategic situation, and of errors by the Royal Navy, to escape to Constantinople, where they strengthened German influence and helped to bring Turkey into the war on the side of the Central Powers. They spent the war skirmishing with Russian forces in the Black Sea. Towards the end of the war, the two ships attempted to break out into the Mediterranean. Both hit mines; *Breslau* was sunk, but *Goeben* made it back to port, and continued to serve in the Turkish Navy until 1970.

SMS *Breslau*, a modern, *Magdeburg*-class light cruiser. The escape of the two German warships was a major setback for the public image of the Royal Navy.

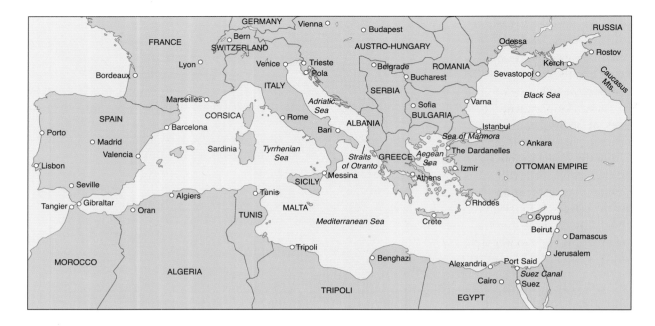

The Mediterranean theatre. Neither the Austrian nor the Turkish fleet made many sorties into the Mediterranean (although the latter was involved in some lively engagements with the Russian Navy in the Black Sea), but it was an important theatre in the U-boat campaign.

reluctance he broke off his pursuit – allowing the German ships to proceed towards the Aegean – and returned to fulfil his other objective of watching the Adriatic. He was the target of bitter criticism from many senior officers, but the outcome of the Battle of Coronel a few weeks later suggests that Troubridge was quite right and that the longer range, heavier gun power and far superior armour of the *Goeben* would almost certainly have prevailed.

By this time, the French fleet had deployed to protect the transports, freeing Milne to head east. However, he first took his battlecruisers into Malta to coal, departing only on 8 August. He had almost reached Cape Matapan when he received a signal sent in error by the Admiralty, ordering, 'Commence hostilities at once against Austria'. As a result, Milne turned away from the Aegean and took up a position guarding the exit from the Adriatic. He informed the Admiralty of his actions, but it was not until the afternoon of the following day that they ordered him

to resume the chase. He did so, though not hurrying since it was still believed that the German warships would soon head west. On the morning of 10 August, the British force entered the Aegean and began searching for its prey among the numerous island harbours. By this time, however, Souchon had finally received permission from the Turkish Government to pass through the Dardanelles Straits – which, since Turkey was neutral, should have been refused according to international treaties. The British force, over 150km (90 miles) to the west, could do little when they learned of this development, beyond establishing a blockade to prevent *Goeben* entering the Mediterranean once again.

Initially, the outcome was seen as something of a success for the Allies. The powerful German squadron had not only been prevented from interfering with valuable shipping, but had also been forced out of the Mediterranean and was now contained, presumably to be interned by neutral Turkey. It was quickly realized,

RIGHT **HMS *Gloucester*. The bravery of her commander, Captain Howard Kelly, in shadowing the German ships after they left Sicily and even exchanging fire in an attempt to slow them down, was described in the *Official History* as 'the one bright spot in the unfortunate episode' for the Royal Navy.**

however, that the *Goeben*'s escape (as it came to be seen) was a serious setback. Its arrival at Constantinople and nominal transfer to the Turkish Navy greatly boosted Germany's prestige and increased the influence of the pro-German faction in the Turkish Government. The latter was able to take a series of actions pushing the country towards war, including throwing out the British naval mission and closing the straits to foreign shipping. Finally, on 29 October, Souchon (with the connivance of pro-German ministers in the Cabinet) launched pre-emptive attacks on Russian Black Sea ports to force the hand of those in the Turkish Government who were still unwilling to go to war against the Allies.

The episode was an embarrassing public failure and a lost opportunity for an early, morale-boosting success. Milne and Troubridge were heavily criticized, and the latter was subjected to a Court Martial, only – to the fury of the Admiralty – for him to be acquitted. Yet the greatest responsibility lay with the Admiralty, which had failed to consider the possibility that the German warships might head for the Dardanelles, despite the ever-closer relationship developing

BELOW **SMS *Goeben*, a *Moltke*-class battlecruiser. Her escape, under the command of Rear Admiral Wilhelm Souchon, greatly embarrassed the Royal Navy. Nominally transferred to Turkish service and renamed *Yavuz Sultan Selim*, she served in the Black Sea for the rest of the war.**

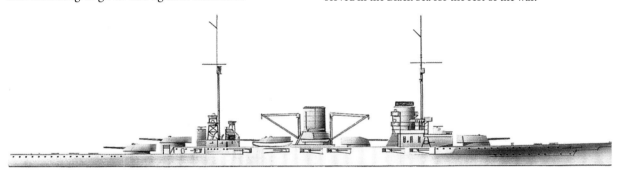

between Germany and Turkey. It then compounded this fault by seeking to exercise very tight control of local commanders, assigning them competing objectives, and sending them ambiguous and simply inaccurate signals. Many of the same factors would cause the disaster of Coronel, with a more tragic cost in lost lives and warships.

AN OPERATION AGAINST THE DARDANELLES?

The Royal Navy's interest in the Dardanelles did not cease with the establishment of a blockade. On 3 November 1914, Britain undertook a brief bombardment of the outer forts guarding the straits, partly to test the effect of naval gunfire against such targets. It inflicted some damage and had a dramatic result when a round detonated the magazine at the fortress of Sedd el Bahr. This action provided a boost to Allied morale, but had two less happy results. First, it led to an over-estimation of the effectiveness of naval gunfire against forts, which marred later operations. Second, it warned Turkey and Germany that reinforcement of the defences of the Dardanelles would be prudent. Accordingly, the static fortifications guarding the straits were supplemented by mobile and concealed gun batteries, far more mines were laid and additional troops were deployed.

Despite the initial embarrassment, the early stages of the naval war in the Mediterranean went reasonably well for the Allies. The Austrian surface fleet was contained in the Adriatic, though its submarines caused growing losses. Attention therefore shifted to exploiting the Allied maritime advantage to influence events on land directly. Much of this effort lay in transporting troops and supplies to Western Europe and to the Middle East. Various ideas also arose about using sea power to undertake operations against the Central Powers. In January 1915, pressure for such a move grew with an appeal from Russia to ease the

difficult situation in which it found itself in the Caucasus by taking action against Turkey.

There was a plausible case for undertaking some sort of operation in the Dardanelles. First, it would allow the Allies to exploit their great advantage over the Central Powers, namely the flexibility and mobility accorded them by sea power, to circumvent the deadlock on the Western Front. Second, an operation there would divert Turkish forces from other areas where they could threaten the Allies, such as Egypt and the vital Suez Canal (which was raided by Turkish troops in February). It would also reduce the military pressure on Russia and on Serbia, another ally. Further, if the straits could be forced and a fleet penetrated into the Sea of Marmara, this would open up a new route for supplying Russia and would also clear the way to Constantinople: the appearance of

Admiral Jacky Fisher. He gave guarded and conditional support to the Dardanelles operation, accepting the use of second-line battleships but insisting that troops would also be needed. He began to oppose the commitment as more forces were sent, which prompted his final resignation as First Sea Lord in March 1915.

Allied battleships there would surely topple the government and force Turkey out of the war. Finally, success might also encourage neutral states in the region – including Italy, Greece, Bulgaria and Romania – to enter the war on the side of the Entente. Action in the Dardanelles promised a bold yet realistic way of achieving a major strategic success that could shorten the war by years.

However, there were counter-arguments that poured cold water on such optimism. First, there were doubts about whether a fleet on its own could force the straits. Even if it reached Constantinople, this would not necessarily drive Turkey out of the war. Moreover, battleships could not remain long in the Sea of Marmara without the support of supply vessels, which would remain highly vulnerable to any remaining defences along the shores of the straits. The battlefleet would also have to run the gauntlet of the defences once again when it returned to the Mediterranean. Its security could only be assured by seizing the heights on either shore, but this would require a considerable commitment of land forces,

which were very scarce, and they would face Turkish defenders who could be easily reinforced.

Arguments favouring action at the Dardanelles tended to leave open the crucial questions of what sort of operation would be undertaken and what resources were available. On these questions, major divisions opened up within the British Government, which cast a cloud over the planning process.

Winston Churchill, First Lord of the Admiralty, was an early convert to the idea of naval action against the Dardanelles, suggesting it as early as November 1914. Admiral 'Jacky' Fisher, the First Sea Lord, raised the possibility of using older battleships, which were not suitable for inclusion in the battlefleet against Germany and could therefore be risked. However, he stressed that the operation would need the support of troops to capture the high ground along the shores of the straits. Yet herein lay the problem. Lord Kitchener, Secretary of State for War, was attracted to the idea of taking action overseas as a means of getting around the Western Front impasse, but he utterly opposed committing troops to any other theatre. He was strongly supported in this by the British Army and the French Government. Kitchener was, therefore, only prepared to back a solely naval operation. Thus, the most senior British naval officer believed that troops were essential for the operation, while the senior soldier refused to countenance their participation.

Churchill was well aware of this difference of opinion and worked around it. He had himself previously written that forcing the straits by warships without troops would be impossible. However, he was very keen for positive action that would restore the navy's reputation, which had been somewhat tarnished by the escape of the *Goeben* and by the Battle of Coronel. In his eagerness, he persuaded himself that a solely naval operation could work, and then turned his formidable powers of persuasion to

Winston Churchill with David Lloyd George, 1915. The operation in the Dardanelles was very much Churchill's baby, as he forced it past half-hearted military opposition and pushed it through an unenthusiastic Cabinet with relentless and ill considered enthusiasm. Its failure ended his tenure as First Lord of the Admiralty.

'Westerners' versus 'Easterners'

During the war, a division opened up among British political and military leaders between 'Westerners' and 'Easterners'. The former insisted that the Western Front was the only possible decisive theatre for the war and resisted what they saw as the pointless diversion of resources elsewhere. Their adversaries argued that, given the impasse in Western Europe, the Allies should look elsewhere for a theatre in which relatively modest forces could tip the balance. The problems that marred the Dardanelles operation were a reflection of this unresolved dispute: the Easterners were strong enough to ensure that the operation went ahead, but the Westerners had enough influence to prevent it being allocated the resources that would give it a good chances of success. This was not the only reason for the failure, but it was a major contributing factor.

dragging others along with him. He envisaged battleships knocking out the forts, clearing the mines and forcing their way through the straits, after which their appearance off Constantinople would cause enough shock and awe to bring down the Turkish Government and force the country out of the war.

Churchill ignored the growing objections of his First Sea Lord and generally failed to take professional advice from senior naval and military officers, who were nearly unanimous in arguing that action by the navy alone would not succeed. He did not consult widely with experts, though giving the impression that he did, and showed a marked tendency to selectively emphasize what he was told (to put it kindly), downplaying any reservations. Churchill's vision and enthusiasm proved seductive to other members of the War Council, not least because of the contrast it offered to the grim situation on the Western Front, and they failed to scrutinize the proposal as much as

they should have. The naval and military officers on the council conspicuously failed to support the proposed action, but nor did they speak out against it, believing that to do so was not their place. Their silence meant that the political leadership acted without a full awareness of the concerns of the senior military and naval leadership. Those who were less enthusiastic about the plan went along with it in the confident belief that Britain could back away if it did not bring rapid results. This was unrealistic, failing to understand that such operations acquire a powerful momentum and become invested with prestige and credibility that makes it difficult to walk away.

Hence, on 13 January 1915, the War Council decided that the Admiralty 'should prepare for a naval expedition in February to bombard and take the Gallipoli Peninsula, with Constantinople as its objective'. This contained two important and distinctly optimistic assumptions, namely that naval action alone could somehow take defended ground and that doing so would somehow leave Constantinople ripe for the taking. Such vague strategic direction was hardly an auspicious start to the undertaking.

THE NAVAL OPERATION

The Dardanelles are a channel linking the Mediterranean and the Sea of Marmara, with the Bosphorus and the Black Sea beyond. They are about 65km (40 miles) long, and about 3km (1.8 miles) wide at the entrance, and then varying in width from less than 1.6km (1 mile) to nearly 8km (5 miles). The straits are dominated by high ground on both the northern (European) and the southern (Asian) shores. The strategic importance of this waterway was clear and it was well protected, with defences organized in three lines. The first, comprising the outer defences, lay at the entrance to the straits. They centred on two forts on the Gallipoli Peninsula at Cape Helles and two more on the opposite (Asian) side of the straits at Kum Kale. The second, more formidable, intermediate defences were a series of gun batteries along both shores of the Dardanelles, supported by searchlights and covering lines of naval mines stretching between the two banks. The final obstacle to a hostile navy

The Dardanelles. The 1915–16 Allied military operation here was one of the most controversial campaigns of the entire war. The case for it, and the way in which it was conducted, is still hotly debated today. For some, it is one of history's greatest missed opportunities.

Lord Kitchener, Secretary of State for War, was keen to see overseas action that might weaken Germany, but refused to send troops when they might have had a decisive role. He eventually relented but his early actions did much to undermine the operation.

came in the form of the inner defences, supporting further minefields that blocked the Narrows, where the width of the channel came down to about 1.2km (0.75 miles). These defences comprised several forts located around the high ground at Kilid Bahr on the Gallipoli Peninsula and at Chanak on the Asian coast. The two main elements of the defences, guns and mines, were designed to be mutually supporting. The gun batteries, well sited on high ground, covered the minefields and would make any attempt to sweep the mines extremely hazardous. Conversely, the mines would compel any attacking warships to remain at such a distance that they would find it difficult to knock out the forts.

The operation was commanded by Vice Admiral Sir Sackville Carden, who had at his disposal a formidable force of 18 capital ships, including the new super-Dreadnought *Queen Elizabeth* and the battlecruiser *Inflexible*, as well as 10 pre-Dreadnoughts and two semi-Dreadnoughts from the Royal Navy, and four French pre-Dreadnoughts. A small force of Royal Marines was available to provide landing parties for brief raids ashore. Carden's plan was not simply to charge into the defences, but rather to reduce them step by step, over about a month. Each stage would see the warships temporarily silencing the guns with long-range fire, followed by minesweepers clearing a path so that the battleships could approach to short range to complete the destruction of the forts.

Before the operation began, senior naval officers continued to push for the involvement of the army to capture the Gallipoli Peninsula. On 16 February, the War Council decided to send out more troops, including the experienced 29th Division, though without any clear idea of what they were to do. Some navy and army officers wanted them to be used jointly with the navy in the main operation, while Churchill saw their role as simply following the navy's success by occupying the peninsula or even Constantinople. Not only was there a muddle over how to use the troops, but also their departure was delayed by several weeks when Kitchener changed his mind over the desirability of removing them from the Western Front. Although he accepted that the army should assist the navy if its

operation became bogged down, he resisted committing troops, thus willing the ends while refusing the means. However, his opposition was slowly worn down: contrary to the assumption that it would be possible to call off the operation if it did not meet early success, the opinion predictably grew that, once begun, it would have to be pushed to a conclusion, so the commitment escalated. This unfortunate model of dithering, unclear roles and delays in providing essential resources was to form the pattern for operations in the Dardanelles.

On 19 February, the Anglo-French force began bombarding the forts of the outer defences. The initial effects were disappointing but eventually the

Turkish fortifications and gun batteries at Chanak Kale fort, part of the inner defences, on the Asian shore. The defences protecting the Dardanelles – combining naval mines, fixed forts and mobile gun batteries – proved remarkably resilient.

bombardment achieved better results, silencing the fire of the outer forts – which the warships easily outranged – and driving off the defenders, allowing Royal Marines to land and destroy the guns. On 26 February, the force moved on to the second stage of the operation, attacking the intermediate defences. This required the ships to enter the straits, where for the first time they became targets for the mobile batteries stationed on both shores. Shelling from these guns forced the warships to keep moving, further reducing the accuracy of their fire. Overall, the accuracy of the naval gunfire proved distinctly poor. The whole operational concept was based on the presumed ability of warships to knock out forts, but the technology of the time meant that they had great difficulty in doing so. This limitation was well known to specialists in naval gunnery and army artillery, but Churchill had failed to consult such men.

The ineffectiveness of naval gunfire meant that the warships would only be able to knock out the forts by approaching to close range. Yet they could not do this because of the presence of mines. These too presented far greater difficulties than had been envisaged, largely because the minesweeping forces provided were quite inadequate. Rather than purpose-designed naval vessels, the plan involved the use of converted fishing trawlers with civilian crews. These boats would have

The French battleship Bouvet *sinking. The pre-Dreadnought participated in the shelling of the intermediate Turkish defences on 18 March. She was hit several times by artillery fire, but was protected by her heavy armour. She then struck a mine, exploded and sank.*

had great difficulty in sweeping mines in the fast currents of the Dardanelles even under the best circumstances. The inability of the battleships to knock out the Turkish gun batteries meant that the

Naval Gunfire at the Dardanelles

Naval gunfire proved ineffective against shore targets at the Dardanelles for a number of reasons. Targets were difficult to locate, as maps were poor and many of the artillery batteries were concealed. Too few aircraft were available to spot for gunfire, and they were early models, lacking wireless sets, and their crews were not trained for the role. The bombarding warships had armour-piercing shells for use against ships that were unsuitable for use against defences ashore, requiring a direct hit for the desired effect. The main problem was that it was simply more difficult to hit a target on land, at long range, with rounds from a naval gun (which were high velocity and low trajectory) than with rounds from a howitzer (which were low velocity and high trajectory) of the sort used so effectively by armies against fortifications on the Western Front. Later developments would vastly improve the ability of warships to destroy targets ashore, but in 1915 this proved extremely difficult.

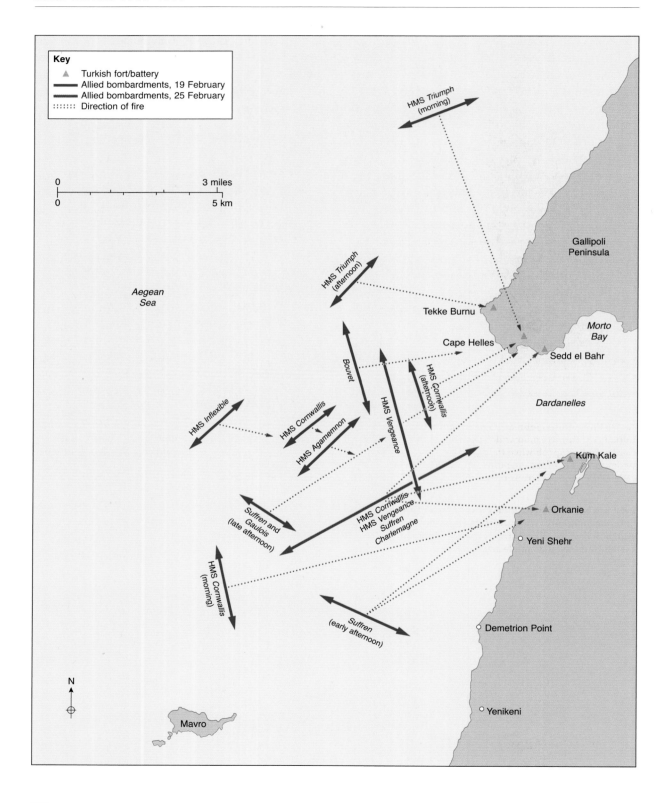

Key
▲ Turkish fort/battery
▬▬▬ Allied bombardments, 19 February
▬▬▬ Allied bombardments, 25 February
∙∙∙∙∙∙ Direction of fire

HMS *Triumph* (morning)

Gallipoli Peninsula

Aegean Sea

HMS *Triumph* (afternoon)

Tekke Burnu

Morto Bay

Cape Helles

Sedd el Bahr

HMS *Cornwallis* (afternoon)

Dardanelles

Bouvet

HMS *Inflexible*

HMS *Cornwallis*

HMS *Agamemnon*

HMS *Vengeance*

Kum Kale

Suffren and Gaulois (late afternoon)

HMS *Cornwallis*
HMS *Vengeance*
Suffren
Charlemagne

Orkanie

Yeni Shehr

HMS *Cornwallis* (morning)

Suffren (early afternoon)

Demetrion Point

N

Yenikeni

Mavro

minesweepers were subject to intense gunfire from short range, creating a situation which their inexperienced crews understandably found impossible. The warships could not knock out the guns until the mines were swept, but nor could the mines be swept until the guns were silenced: the defences were imposing precisely the kind of dilemma on the attackers that their designers had intended.

On 10 March, pressure for faster results from London – due to intelligence that the defenders were running short of ammunition and to fears that German U-boats were about to arrive – led to the tempo of operations being quickened. Several further attempts to sweep the mines were made by night, but once again, the minesweeping trawlers were driven off by gunfire that the warships were unable to suppress. Another variation was planned for 18 March, which would see battleships engage the intermediate and inner defences simultaneously, in daylight, to allow the trawlers to deal with the mines that night. This plan was implemented by a new commander; Carden's health had finally collapsed, so he was replaced by his

ABOVE Vice Admiral John de Robeck (1862–1928) was initially the deputy commander, but replaced Sir Sackville Carden in the top job when the latter's health collapsed under the strain of the operation. He oversaw the disastrous attempt to force the Straits by warships alone.

LEFT The bombardment of the outer forts. The attack on the first line of defences was successful. However, once inside the straits the bombarding warships had to face the additional threats of mines and mobile artillery batteries.

BELOW HMS *Agamemnon* was a *Nelson*-class battleship, the last class of British pre-Dreadnoughts. As such, she had no place in the Grand Fleet and could be spared for operations in the Dardanelles. In November 1918, the Turkish Government signed the armistice on board *Agamemnon*.

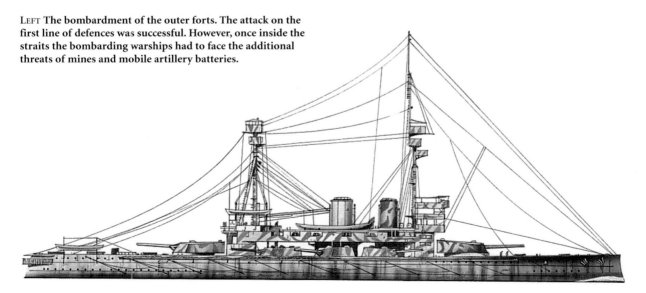

HMS *Irresistible* hitting a mine. The attacking Allies had known of several lines of defensive mines laid by the Turks and their German advisors. However, they were unaware of an additional, newly laid line of mines, which sank the French *Bouvet* and also the British *Irresistible* and *Ocean*.

deputy, Vice Admiral John de Robeck. Commodore Roger Keyes remained in position as chief of staff.

The decisive phase of the naval operation occurred on 18 March. It began with the battleships engaging the principal defensive batteries, and by 2pm the early results were positive. The French battleship *Gaulois* had been badly damaged by a shell, but although most of the mobile Turkish batteries remained largely unscathed, many of the fixed batteries had been silenced and return fire was reducing. At this time, however, the French battleship *Bouvet* was rocked by a huge explosion; she capsized and sank in less than a minute, killing almost the entire crew. The cause was initially unclear, but was wrongly thought to have been a chance shell hit on her magazine. The

battleship *Suffren* was then genuinely hit by a shell, but was saved by an officer quickly flooding her magazine. Nevertheless, by 4pm, the Turkish fire had slackened to the extent that the minesweepers were sent in again, only to come under heavy fire from the mobile batteries. As a line of battleships steamed in to cover the sweepers, they ran into the minefield that had been the true cause of the *Bouvet* sinking – a new field, laid parallel to the shore, unlike the other minefields that stretched across the channel, and nearer to the entrance of the straits. First, the battlecruiser *Inflexible* – already damaged by shellfire – hit a mine, followed by the pre-Dreadnought *Irresistible*. As the other battleships were withdrawing, the pre-Dreadnought *Ocean* was the next to hit a mine and sink, while trying to support the fatally damaged *Irresistible*, which was coming under heavy artillery fire. Despite one French and two British battleships being sunk, and two French battleships and one British battlecruiser being badly damaged (*Inflexible* was able to make it back to port), the mines were still in place and the mobile batteries were still able to cover them.

De Robeck was initially keen to resume the operation and received permission to do so from the War Council. Replacement battleships were sent out from Britain and the minesweeping force was reorganized, with navy crews in the trawlers and some destroyers fitted as sweepers. However, over the next couple of days, de Robeck changed his mind: at a conference on the flagship on 22 March, he informed the other senior commanders that the operation would require the support of the army. He later explained that this decision was because he had seen the limited effect of naval gunfire against forts, he realized that Turkish resistance was stronger than anticipated, and he now acknowledged that troops would be needed to help destroy the defending batteries and to secure the lines of communication for the fleet once it passed through the straits. The newly appointed commander of the land forces, General Sir Ian Hamilton, agreed with de Robeck, but stated that the army would not be ready for a landing until 14 April. Characteristically, Churchill strongly favoured trying again, but his senior admirals would not back him and de Robeck stood firm, while others in London bowed to the unanimous position of the two theatre commanders.

The Turkish and German official histories of the campaign make it clear that the defenders were seriously stretched: morale was low, most of their heavy ammunition was gone and they had few mines left in reserve. The Allied officers who wanted to maintain the offensive argued that the enemy was effectively defeated and that pushing on with the battleships would have achieved success, while any delay only allowed the defenders' morale to recover and reinforcements to arrive and strengthen them.

> 'The warships could not knock out the guns until the mines were swept, but nor could the mines be swept until the guns were silenced: the defences were imposing precisely the kind of dilemma their designers had intended.'

This argument was understandable, but those such as Keyes, who urged de Robeck to press on, seemed to overlook the problem of the mobile batteries; eliminating them would require troops to be landed.

A purely naval operation had, unwisely, been attempted and had failed, so a combined operation involving both the Navy and the Army was needed. However, due to the disjointed planning process and the refusal of Kitchener and others to send out adequate land forces in a timely manner, it was not possible to undertake an immediate landing. Some weeks would be needed to build up additional troops and supplies, and for the transport ships, which had not been loaded for an amphibious operation, to reload at Alexandria. The delay caused by the Allies' inability to conduct a swift landing allowed Turkey to reinforce the peninsula to a strength sufficient to hold it: when the naval operation began, there was just a single Turkish division there, but by mid-April there were six. A smaller force landed early on, with the advantage of surprise, might well have had greater success than the larger force that was eventually to undertake the operation. This was, perhaps, the greatest missed opportunity of the campaign.

PLANNING THE LANDINGS

The Dardanelles were scarcely more promising for an amphibious landing than for a solely naval operation. The vital Gallipoli Peninsula is about 80km (50 miles) long, with difficult terrain rising rapidly from the shore to commanding heights that provide defenders with an enormous advantage. There were few potential landing sites, and those that did exist lacked depth for establishing command, artillery and supply systems for a military campaign. Moreover, the earlier operations had quite forfeited strategic surprise, and Turkey and Germany were rapidly building up their defences.

From the beginning, the Allied expedition was subject to many problems. Hamilton was not given clear strategic guidance about what he was to achieve, and the human and material resources with which he was provided came too little and too late. Just as important, he lacked a proper staff organization to undertake the incredibly complex task of planning and organizing such a demanding operation. There was little coordination between the Navy and Army, whose staffs were not even located together during the planning process. There were frequent disagreements between Hamilton and his subordinate corps and division commanders. The planners lacked accurate intelligence about terrain and the capabilities of the defenders; as is often the case with intelligence failures, the information was available, but simply did not reach those who needed it. There was very poor

'A smaller force landed early on, with the advantage of surprise, might well have had greater success than the larger force that eventually undertook the operation.'

security around the operation, particularly in Egypt, with the result that Turkey and Germany were well informed about developments. Insufficient attention was paid to ensuring the necessary flow of supplies, particularly water, and to dealing with casualties. The Allied forces had far too little artillery, while the lack of ammunition for the small number of guns they had was a constraint throughout the campaign. There was a lack of specialized amphibious shipping and a general paucity of experience in amphibious operations that was hardly surprising, given that the last opposed landing by British forces had been in

1801. Nearly every warning sign that predicts disaster in an amphibious operation can be identified in the run-up to the landings at Gallipoli.

During the naval operation, the head of the German military mission in Turkey, Otto Liman von Sanders, was given command of the rapidly growing defensive forces. He assessed that the most likely locations for the anticipated landings were at Bulair in the north of the Gallipoli Peninsula, and at Kum Kale on the Asian shore. Of the six Turkish divisions available to him, he therefore deployed two to each of these locations. The other area where he believed a landing might be undertaken was at Cape Helles and Gaba Tepe, so he placed one division to defend these locations, with the last division in reserve near Maidos, from where it could advance to Bulair or Helles as required. In each case, he concentrated what he judged had previously been scattered forces, with the main body some distance inland and only small units on the beaches themselves. He used to good

Otto Liman von Sanders was a German general who served as military advisor to Turkey. The successful defence of the peninsula owed much to his careful planning.

effect the time gifted to him by the delays in the Allied operation, improving the roads in the area to ease the movement of his troops and supplies, and strengthening the defences of the likely landing

The naval operations of 18 March against the defences of the straits. Having defeated the outer defences, the Allies moved on to the intermediate defences of the Dardanelles, inside the straits. These proved to be a far more difficult target and the resulting loss of warships ended the purely naval operation.

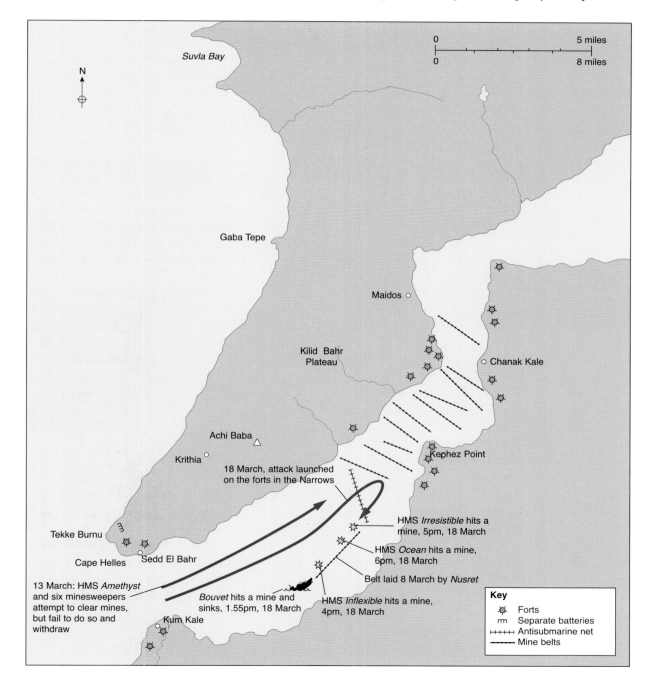

Mustafa Kemal served as a divisional commander under Liman von Sanders. He proved to be a highly capable officer, particularly in taking swift action to cut out the threat from promising Allied offensives. His reputation was greatly enhanced by his contribution in this campaign.

beaches with mines, wires and well dug-in positions for his forces.

The troops at Hamilton's disposal comprised one regular army division, a scratch Royal Naval Division (a mix of Royal Marines and naval personnel), two inexperienced divisions of the Australia and New Zealand Corps – or Anzacs – that were training in Egypt, and one French division. None of these formations was trained or experienced in the demanding role of amphibious warfare.

Hamilton's plan placed the main effort at Cape Helles. This was known to be well defended, but it was the only location with sufficient space on the beaches for the size of force required. His most experienced unit, 29th Division, was to land on several beaches to confuse and disperse the defenders. The main beaches, north to south, were named X, W, and V, with smaller diversionary landings at Y Beach to the north and S Beach to the southeast. A second major landing would see the Anzacs descend about 20km (12 miles) north of Helles, on the western coast of the peninsula. The plan was for the initial forces to seize a bridgehead, through which following forces could move inland, with those from Helles capturing the commanding heights at Achi Baba, while the Anzacs cut off Turkish reinforcements from the north and took the town of Maidos; all of this was to be achieved by the end of the first day. They would then take the Kilid Bahr plateau that dominated the straits, the town of Gallipoli and finally Bulair to secure the peninsula.

These two main landings would be supported by a demonstration (a feint without actually landing) by the Royal Naval Division at Bulair to the north, to hold in place the defenders there, and a diversionary landing by the French division to the south, on the Asian coast. Bulair was assessed as too heavily defended, and too difficult for the navy to provide fire support, for a major landing to be conducted, while forces in Asia would be too vulnerable to counterattack from the interior of Turkey. Hamilton was aware that he had no reserves; this was another effect of the inadequate resources for the expedition.

THE LANDINGS

The landings went ahead on 25 April. At Bulair, the troops approached the beaches under the covering fire of warships and then, as planned, turned away without landing. This action had the desired effect: Otto Liman von Sanders, perceiving what he expected at Bulair, initially believed that the landings to the south were the diversions, and held back his reinforcements for two days, allowing the Allies precious time to build up their bridgeheads. To the south, at Kum Kale, the French force got ashore successfully, held off counterattacks and then withdrew as planned on the night of 26/27 April. They were then set ashore once again to reinforce the position at Helles.

There, the results were mixed, with events going particularly well at the two minor beaches, on either flank. Furthest to the north, Y Beach was added to the plan late, because it seemed to be lightly defended and provided a quick approach to high ground. Surprise was achieved; the forces landed successfully and reached the top of the cliffs, but then stopped in place and at first did not even begin digging in. The officers commanding here lacked clear instructions about what to do next and there was uncertainty over who was in command. Their lack of initiative was compounded by the failure of more senior commanders to send in reinforcements or even supplies of ammunition; urgent requests for such support were not even acknowledged, let alone acted upon. If the British commanders failed to appreciate just how significant a success Y Beach could have become, the Turks made no such mistake. They launched a strong counterattack, supported by artillery, forcing the British force to be withdrawn the next day.

A similar story of unexploited success unfolded at the other end of the line, on S Beach. This landing was only intended as a diversion and because of the inadequate number of landing craft available, only two companies could be inserted here. They achieved surprise and seized the beach quickly with light casualties. However, once again their commanding officers seemed to have little conception of what they should do next and remained in place, rather than pushing on to support the forces landing at the other beaches nearby.

Of the main landings, those at X Beach went reasonably well. This beach was not as strongly defended as the others, and the Turkish forces deployed there were driven off by the covering fire of the battleship *Implacable*. Unlike the other capital ships

The aftermath of one of the landing beaches. As this picture suggests, the beaches along the tip of the Gallipoli Peninsula were far from ideal for opposed amphibious landings, and greatly benefited the defenders. They were captured, with great determination and heavy losses, but this costly success was not exploited.

The landings from the *River Clyde*, at V Beach. A converted collier, the *River Clyde* was designed to act as a 'Trojan Horse' to carry troops to V beach, to supplement the inadequate number of landing craft available. This painting suggests the heavy fire that was directed against the landing troops.

supporting the landings, her captain chose to move her in closer than his orders had envisaged and was therefore able to provide accurate and effective fire support. This assisted the landing forces in establishing themselves ashore and driving off the counterattacks that followed.

Elsewhere at Helles, however, events did not unfold so well. The main landing beaches, W and V, were defended by fairly small forces but their positions had been extremely well prepared, with mines and wire in the water and up the beaches, and then well dug-in defensive positions on commanding high ground, supported by carefully sited machine guns. Hamilton's plan assumed that naval gunfire could destroy the defences but its effect, once again, proved disappointing, not least because the warships were short of the high-explosive shells that were needed for the task.

At W Beach, as elsewhere, the troops were landed from small craft that were towed by steam vessels, but then had to cover the final stretch by rowing. These craft came under heavy fire as they approached the beaches and then the troops became caught in the wire, suffering terrible casualties. A second wave eventually landed north of the main beach, under the shelter of cliffs, and outflanked the defences.

The situation at W Beach was bad; at V Beach it was

worse. Realizing that there were insufficient landing craft available, a solution was improvised by converting a collier, the *River Clyde*, to act as a landing ship that would be run aground close to the shore, carrying with some degree of protection about 2000 troops, who would emerge from specially designed sally ports, with machine guns fitted on the ship to provide covering fire. In an inevitable allusion to a previous conflict fought nearby, this vessel was referred to as a 'Trojan Horse'. In practice, the concept was unsuccessful. It had been realized that the *River Clyde* would not be able to advance right to the water's edge, so arrangements were made to moor other ships alongside to act as a bridge. However, she was not able to approach the beach as closely as the plan had assumed, and the bridging vessels were unable to get into place. This left the troops disembarking from the *River Clyde* having to swim or wade through deep water, under murderous fire from the defenders. Losses at V Beach were so high that the landings had to be stopped until nightfall, and commanders were in serious doubt over whether the beach could be taken. The British forces were able to gain a bridgehead the next morning, capturing the fort of Sedd el Bahr, with the help of naval gunfire and troops from S and W beaches belatedly attacking the defenders from behind – suggesting what might have been achieved if this sort of action had been more generally incorporated in the plan.

Further north, the Anzacs should have landed at Z Beach, or 'Brighton Beach' as it become known, where they would then face a gentle slope to advance inland to the heights that were their initial objective. They were to land at night, to benefit from surprise. However, poor maps, currents that were considerably stronger than expected and the confusion of operating at night resulted in the troops being landed in the wrong location, up to a mile away from the intended position. Units became broken up, further increasing the confusion caused by mounting losses. The Australian and New Zealand troops struggled to advance inland over broken terrain that made it even more difficult to follow maps that were inadequate to begin with. They suffered high losses from Turkish artillery and snipers, for whom the ground was ideal, while the fire support provided by the fleet was very uneven in its impact. Despite the confusion, the Anzacs managed to capture some high ground at Sari Bair but the commander of the Turkish reserve division, Mustafa Kemal, launched a swift counterattack that forced them back. Some unit commanders urged that the Anzacs should be evacuated, but when the corps commander, Lieutenant-General Sir William Birdwood, relayed this to Hamilton, his superior ordered him to stay put and the Anzacs to 'dig, dig, dig'. On 28/29 April, four battalions from the Royal Naval Division, which had conducted the diversionary operation at Bulair, were landed to support the Anzacs in holding the bridgehead, and further British and Indian troops followed later.

'The landings of 25 April suffered from poor planning and failures of command and leadership at several levels, exacerbated by problems in establishing reliable communications.'

The landings of 25 April suffered from poor planning and failures of command and leadership at several levels, which were exacerbated by problems in establishing reliable communications. The result was that considerable sacrifice and individual courage did not get the rewards they deserved. Hamilton and his subordinate commanders were so preoccupied with the admittedly formidable difficulties of getting ashore in an opposed amphibious landing that they focused on this initial stage to the exclusion of what would follow. The result was that where local success was achieved – at Y and S beaches – it was neither reinforced nor exploited, as commanders concentrated instead on the problems at V and W beaches. Matters were not helped by the relationship

The landings at Cape Helles. By the time the failure of the solely naval operation convinced London that the Army would be needed as well, the reinforcement of the defences had made a successful amphibious operation highly unlikely.

between Hamilton and his corps and divisional commanders: he proved too reluctant to intervene and to direct his subordinates, failing to order them to reinforce Y and S beaches, despite being urged to do so by naval officers such as de Robeck and Keyes. Where bridgeheads were established, unit commanders lacked either clear instructions on how to proceed or the initiative to work it out for themselves. Hence, the forces ashore sat tight rather than rapidly pushing inland to exploit the initial confusion of the defenders. As a result, the Turkish forces had time to recover, to bring in reinforcements and to mount effective counterattacks that pushed the Allies back from some of their initial gains. The forces landed at Helles did not succeed in taking the high ground of Achi Baba on the first day – nor would they do so throughout the campaign. Similarly, despite heroic efforts, the Anzacs were unable to take their assigned objectives.

The Allies had managed to land some 30,000 men and to establish bridgeheads that, supported by naval gunfire, they were able to hold against determined counterattacks. Yet this modest success came at a high cost: in the first few days of the operation, 29th

Division had lost nearly 6600 men killed or wounded and the Anzacs nearly 3500. For many historians, the next few days were a missed opportunity: a properly designed plan would have had the attackers push on rapidly to take advantage of the initial confusion and dislocation of the defenders. Despite the problems encountered by the Allies, the Turkish forces were reeling and a little slow to react, but would soon recover if given time; as the Allies built up their forces and supplies, the defenders did the same only at a faster pace. The delays and lack of initiative allowed them to reorganize, bring up reinforcements and further improve their defensive positions.

THE LATER STAGES OF THE CAMPAIGN
With the initial operations having stalled, the Allies now faced the dilemma of how to proceed. Pulling out would have a disastrous effect diplomatically, so they continued to send reinforcements, but at a slow rate and without any clear conception of their purpose. A series of offensives was launched but they tended to be ill planned and hopelessly ambitious given the

The Australian and New Zealand landing at Gaba Tepe. Strong currents resulted in the ANZAC being landed a mile away from where the plan had envisaged. They made some early territorial gains, but were pushed back to their bridgehead by determined Turkish counterattacks.

strength of the Turkish defences and, in particular, the constant shortage of artillery. The situation came to resemble a smaller replica of the Western Front, with trench warfare in which major pushes made negligible gains at enormous cost, while supply problems and, even more so, disease took their toll in lives and morale. Such a war of attrition was not to the benefit of the Allies, not least because the Turks had the advantage of better positions on higher ground, as well as rather easier supply lines.

In Britain, the operation inflicted political casualties. On 15 March, Fisher resigned due to Churchill's insistence on sending further reinforcements, which was the last straw in their deteriorating relationship. The main architect of the expedition did not last much longer, as the formation of a new coalition government on 25 May saw Churchill leave the Admiralty.

The ongoing operation was beset by problems with supplies, partly because the small bridgeheads had long lines of communication back to Greek islands that were 100km (60 miles) or more away, and further back to France, where the nearest railhead was located. These long supply lines were vulnerable to attack, as were the battleships that were providing critical supporting fire to the troops ashore. On 12 May, the pre-Dreadnought HMS *Goliath* was sunk by an intrepid Turkish torpedo boat. This success was followed later in the month as German U-boats began to arrive, with *U21* sinking *Triumph* on 25 May and *Majestic* on 27 May. These losses prompted the rapid withdrawal of *Queen Elizabeth*, with the other battleships following soon after, to be replaced by monitors and cruisers. Improved Allied anti-submarine precautions prevented the loss of further warships, but the U-boats continued to take their toll of merchant shipping in the Mediterranean.

This was one theatre in which the Allies were not the only ones to rely on seaborne communications, as the primitive nature of the road network forced Turkey to make extensive use of ships to supply her own forces at Gallipoli. These presented a lucrative target for any Allied submarines that succeeded in running the gauntlet of the difficult navigation and

heavy defences of the Dardanelles. They were joined in their offensive against Turkish military shipping by Royal Navy seaplanes, which sank several vessels and achieved a significant milestone: on 12 August 1915, a Short 184 seaplane conducted the first ever launch of an air-dropped torpedo, hitting and damaging a supply ship. Attacks on the Turkish supply lines had a useful effect, but could never be decisive unless combined with a major operation on land.

Rather than accept the embarrassment of withdrawing, the Allied governments decided to attempt a renewed offensive. The plan was for British, Australian and New Zealand forces to break out from the northern part of the Anzac Cove area to capture the dominating high ground, cutting off the Turkish forces to the south in preparation for a subsequent advance. When Hamilton learned that he was to receive additional troops, he added to this main element of the plan a new landing by two British divisions at Suvla Bay to the north, which was known to be lightly defended. These operations would be supported by diversionary attacks at the southern end of the Anzac sector and at Helles. This offensive began

on 6 August. The plan for the breakout from Anzac Cove required an unrealistic pace of advance over very difficult ground. Despite heavy losses, widespread confusion and failures of command, some gains were made. However, these were retaken as a result of further prompt action by Mustafa Kemal, the Turkish area commander. The landings at Suvla Bay benefited from the use of armoured, steam-powered landing craft (named 'Beetles'), but in other respects saw a

ABOVE **Armoured motor lighters, nick-named 'Beetles', during the August 1915 landings at Suvla Bay. This operation, intended to work with renewed offensives from the original landing sites, featured many of the failings seen before, notably in leadership and a lack of initiative.**

BELOW **SMS *Kurfürst Friedrich Wilhelm*, a *Brandenburg*-class pre-Dreadnought, was commissioned into the German Navy in 1894. She was sold to Turkey and re-named *Heireddin Barbarossa*. She was sunk by the British submarine *E11* on 8 August 1915, during the Suvla Bay landings.**

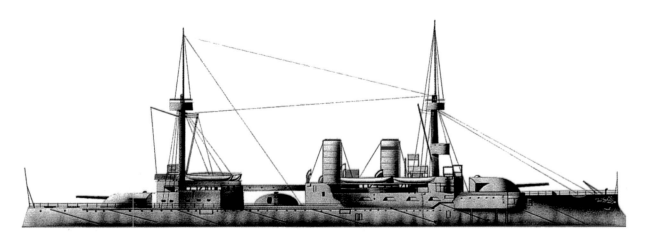

repeat of many of the errors that marred the initial operations. The landings were initially successful, but became disorganized; units became muddled up and officers, trained for the more methodical approach of the Western Front, failed to exploit initial success by

Allied Submarines at the Dardanelles

The first success by an Allied submarine was achieved before the campaign even started; on 13 December 1914, the British submarine *B11* sank the old Turkish battleship *Messudieh* in the straits. More capable boats were sent out, the first of which to penetrate the formidable defences and troublesome waters of the straits and get as far as the Sea of Marmara was the Australian *AE2*, which sank a gunboat before being sunk itself. Other British and French boats followed, notably *E11* and *E14* of the Royal Navy, which caused havoc among Turkish shipping and even attacked the harbour in Constantinople. Four British and four French boats were lost, but they sank another battleship, a coastal defence ship, six smaller warships and over 50 transports, as well as shelling targets and deterring warships from attacking the Allied bridgeheads.

Allied submarines at the Dardanelles made a valuable contribution to the campaign despite the difficult sea conditions and the heavy Turkish defences.

advancing inland and taking the crucial high ground. This lack of initiative allowed the Turks ample time to seize the ridges that were the objective, and to bring in reinforcements. The situation was therefore no better than before, only along a wider front, further exacerbating the existing supply problems.

The failure of this second big effort had worn down support in the government for the operation, while increasingly critical reports in the press created public disillusionment. Once again, the question arose of committing further reinforcements, but they could not be spared from the Western Front. Furthermore, Bulgaria entered the war on the side of the Central Powers in October. This development not only created demands to redeploy Allied forces from the Dardanelles, but also eased the enemy's supply problems by opening routes across land from Germany, which meant that heavy artillery would soon be brought in and turned on the bridgeheads. With winter looming and fear that the existing forces would come under still greater pressure, and no prospect of the arrival of the major reinforcements that would permit a breakout, voices calling for withdrawal became ever louder.

Hamilton opposed this course of action, fearing that a disengagement under fire could cost up to 50 per cent of the force. He was replaced in mid-October by General Sir Charles Munro; the fact that he was known to be a strong 'Westerner' and a long-standing critic of the Gallipoli operation hints at the conclusion that he was expected to draw. Sure enough, he recommended withdrawal. De Robeck agreed, and although he allowed Keyes, always bursting with enthusiasm, to make the case for renewed naval action, he also made clear his own opposition – which was shared by senior admirals at home. Kitchener initially opposed pulling out, but was converted after visiting the area. On 7 December, the Cabinet decided to evacuate Suvla Bay and Anzac Cove, while retaining Helles for the time being.

Of all the different types of amphibious operation, a withdrawal of forces that are in close proximity with the enemy is perhaps the most difficult. It is a formidable challenge to remove a large body of troops while also preventing the enemy from realizing what is afoot and pressing the attack to turn retreat into rout. Given the catalogue of errors in the earlier parts of the campaign, it is all the more striking that the withdrawal from Gallipoli was such a stunning success. At last, an effective plan was meticulously prepared, together with elaborate and imaginative deception plans. By 20 December, the forces at Suvla and Anzac had been evacuated without a single casualty. By then, the decision had been taken to complete the withdrawal by evacuating Helles too, and that was successfully achieved in January, again without losing a man, despite the fact that the same trick was being played a second time. The success of

B11 sinking the *Messudieh*. *B11* was a small, coastal submarine. In December 1914, commanded by Lieutenant Norman Holbrook, she succeeded in penetrating into the Sea of Marmara and sank the Turkish battleship *Messudieh*, earning for her captain the first Victoria Cross – Britain's highest medal for gallantry – ever awarded to a submariner.

Submarine operations and ship losses. Submarines from both sides played an important role in naval operations. German U-boats sank several Allied warships, while a number of Allied submarines succeeded in penetrating the defences of the narrows.

the evacuation was a boost to morale, but scant consolation for the wider failure of the expedition.

There had been several missed opportunities. The initial move against the Dardanelles in February 1915

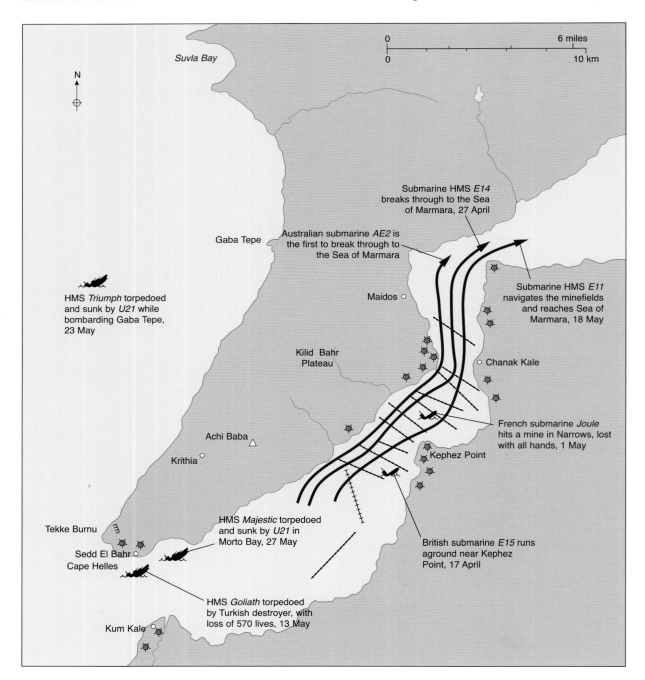

Suvla Bay

N

0 / 0 — 6 miles / 10 km

Gaba Tepe

Submarine HMS *E14* breaks through to the Sea of Marmara, 27 April

Australian submarine *AE2* is the first to break through to the Sea of Marmara

Submarine HMS *E11* navigates the minefields and reaches Sea of Marmara, 18 May

Maidos

HMS *Triumph* torpedoed and sunk by *U21* while bombarding Gaba Tepe, 23 May

Kilid Bahr Plateau

Chanak Kale

French submarine *Joule* hits a mine in Narrows, lost with all hands, 1 May

Achi Baba

Krithia

Kephez Point

British submarine *E15* runs aground near Kephez Point, 17 April

Tekke Burnu

HMS *Majestic* torpedoed and sunk by *U21* in Morto Bay, 27 May

Sedd El Bahr
Cape Helles

HMS *Goliath* torpedoed by Turkish destroyer, with loss of 570 lives, 13 May

Kum Kale

might have enjoyed success if it had been a combined operation involving not only the Navy but also the Army. A far smaller force than the one eventually deployed might have taken the peninsula, lightly defended as it was early on. Failure at this point prevented later operations from achieving surprise, ensuring that they would be conducted against an alerted and reinforced enemy. Nevertheless, at the time of the main landings in April, a better-planned and better-led operation that exploited initial success by pushing inland against a temporarily disorganized

HMS *Majestic* sinking after being torpedoed by *U21*. She was a pre-Dreadnought, dating from 1895, and was used for second-line duties such as escorting troop convoys and coastal bombardment before being sent to the Dardanelles. She provided fire support until *U21* torpedoed her off Cape Helles on 27 May 1915.

opponent might still have achieved the objective of seizing the key high ground. As it was, however, a flawed plan was executed poorly, resulting in a disorganized and ponderous operation that allowed the enemy to recover and reinforce. By the middle of May, given the state of military technology of the time, the Allies were never going to be able to bring to bear sufficient numbers to succeed. By the time the operation ended, it had cost 205,000 British and Empire casualties killed, wounded or sick, plus 47,000 French and some 290,000 Turkish losses.

The Dardanelles operation was an imaginative attempt to exploit the Allies' great strategic advantage of sea power. Success was achievable and might have shortened the war. Its failure ensured that the campaign will remain one of the most controversial expeditions in British naval and military history.

Flawed Concept, or Poor Implementation?

A long-standing debate among historians has focused on whether the fundamental idea behind the Dardanelles expedition was fatally flawed: would military success there truly have brought the strategic benefits that had been so confidently predicted? This line of argument would suggest that the operation was always doomed to failure. More common, however, is the view that there was some genuine potential in the concept, but that it was thrown away by incompetent planning and implementation, and by the failure to provide the necessary resources in a timely fashion. According to this school of thought, there were real opportunities when success was possible, but they were not taken. In the words of the historian Basil Liddell Hart, 'Thus the curtain rang down on a sound and far-sighted conception, marred by a chain of errors in execution almost unrivalled even in British history.'

CHAPTER 5

The Battle of Jutland

Both the Royal Navy and the Imperial German Navy had long anticipated the day when they would finally meet in battle. The British were confident of putting the young challenger in its place, while the Germans looked forward to their fleet establishing its reputation against what had largely been its model. When this long-awaited clash finally occurred, on 31 May 1916, it was the culmination of a rivalry that had grown over 20 years.

The Battle of Jutland – or the Battle of the Skagerrak, as German sources call it – was by far the largest engagement of the war, with 250 warships involved, and was the only occasion on which the main battlefleets fought each other. It was also the last of the great clashes between surface battleships alone, with only the most marginal role played by submarines or aircraft.

In January 1916 Admiral Reinhard Scheer took command of the High Seas Fleet. While Scheer's

HMS *Iron Duke*, Admiral Jellicoe's flagship at Jutland, at sea; she was named after a great soldier, the Duke of Wellington. The battle would finally see the test in action of the great Dreadnought battleships that made up the main battle fleets of Britain and Germany.

Vice Admiral David Beatty, commander of the Battlecruiser Fleet at Jutland. He bore the brunt of the fighting in the early stages of the battle. In general, he acquitted himself well, but made some important errors of judgement that had an important effect on the outcome.

Each side conducted further raids, similar to those discussed in the chapter on the North Sea Raids, in the hope of bringing about an engagement on its own terms. The Royal Navy launched carrier air strikes against Zeppelin bases and the German fleet attacked British patrols and bombarded Lowestoft. All such efforts were frustrated by poor weather or ill luck, or because one side or the other sought to avoid battle. At the end of May, however, a situation arose where each believed that it was ambushing the enemy.

Scheer devised a variation on previous plans. Hipper's force would bombard Sunderland to draw out the British battlecruisers. They would be attacked by U-boats, pre-positioned off their base, and then finished off by the battlefleet before the Grand Fleet could provide support. The operation was postponed to allow repairs to some capital ships, but began on 17 May with the U-boats taking up their positions. However, as so often in the North Sea, deteriorating weather prevented the planned Zeppelin reconnaissance flights on which Scheer was relying for warning should the Grand Fleet approach. Unwilling to call off the operation and with the U-boats reaching the limits of their patrol endurance, Scheer revised his plan. Rather than bombarding Sunderland he would entice Beatty's battlecruisers by attacking British forces patrolling the Skagerrak, where there was less danger of surprise and which was closer to home should it arise. Accordingly, the German battlecruisers left port at about 1am on 31 May. The British fleet had put to sea some four hours earlier, alerted once again by Room 40.

THE OPPOSING FORCES

Beatty's command had been upgraded to the Battlecruiser Fleet in 1915, and comprised three squadrons. One of these had been sent to Scapa Flow to undertake the gunnery practice that was not possible at the battlecruisers' base at Rosyth. To

strategy was the same as his predecessor's – seeking to bring about equality between the opposing fleets by defeating an isolated part of the Grand Fleet – he sought more actively to engineer an engagement in which this could be achieved. Admiral Jellicoe, the British commander-in-chief, was keen for battle, but was well aware that his adversary would do his utmost to avoid a clash with the whole Grand Fleet. He too aimed to create an ambush for the opposing force, far enough from its bases that it could not escape, as the battlecruisers had done at Dogger Bank.

replace it, Beatty had been strengthened with the temporary attachment of the 5th Battle Squadron of the main battlefleet, under Rear Admiral Hugh Evan-Thomas. These were the *Queen Elizabeth* class (minus the lead ship of the class, which was in dry dock), the most powerful warships in the world with the striking power of eight 15in guns, very strong armour and a high speed of 24 knots – although this was still below that of second-generation battlecruisers such as HMS *Lion*. The British scouting force therefore included six battlecruisers and four super-Dreadnoughts, comfortably out-gunning Hipper's five battlecruisers. His role, however, was not to engage in a gunnery duel with the British, but rather to lead them towards the rest of the High Seas Fleet.

The main German force comprised 22 battleships, but six of these were the older, pre-Dreadnoughts of the 2nd Battle Squadron, which were no match for the modern British ships and slowed down the rest of the High Seas Fleet. Scheer initially intended to leave them

behind, but relented because he did not wish to humiliate the crews of a squadron with which he himself had previously served. The addition of the *Queen Elizabeth*-class ships to Beatty's force made it a more lucrative target for Scheer, should he be able to bring it to battle in the absence of the rest of the Grand Fleet.

Beatty, of course, would seek to avoid this situation and to draw Scheer onto the guns of the main Royal Navy battlefleet. With 24 modern Dreadnoughts, Jellicoe's fleet was by some margin the most powerful naval force that had ever put to sea. These battleships were accompanied by the three battlecruisers of the 3rd Battlecruiser Squadron under Rear Admiral Horace Hood. Also included were eight old armoured cruisers, which, like the German pre-Dreadnoughts,

The German High Seas Fleet at sea. The Imperial German Navy was eager to prove itself against the British. At Jutland, it believed that it had finally created the conditions in which it could defeat an isolated part of the Royal Navy, thereby changing the balance of advantage at sea.

were an obsolete type that should have had no place in such a battle. The Grand Fleet not only included ships that should not have been there, but also lacked one that should. It was to have been accompanied by the seaplane carrier *Campania*, which had the speed to keep up with the fleet, as well as a lengthened flight deck to allow her to launch aircraft without having to stop to hoist them onto the sea. However, she was late receiving the order to depart, and when she did put to sea Jellicoe falsely believed that she would be unable to catch his fleet and sent her home. This was regrettable, since her aircraft might have provided Jellicoe with the vital information he was to crave.

The British Grand Fleet at sea. After a series of near misses, the Royal Navy had high hopes that it would this time be able to pounce on the High Seas Fleet, prevent its escape, and give the British public the new Trafalgar that it craved.

The stage was set. The outcome of the battle would be determined by the success of each side in springing its trap. If Scheer could concentrate against Beatty's strengthened force, he could inflict a serious blow to the Royal Navy, bringing the High Seas Fleet closer to numerical parity. Yet if, in turn, he had to face the full power of Jellicoe's Grand Fleet, the German Navy could face catastrophe.

THE PRELIMINARY STAGES

As the British forces headed for their rendezvous on the morning of 31 May 1916, an error was made at the Admiralty in the handling of intelligence that would have major repercussions. Captain Thomas Jackson, Director of Operations, went to Room 40 – of whose work he had a low opinion – and asked where intercepted signals showed a particular German wireless call-sign to be. The staff informed him that it

was in harbour at Wilhelmshaven, which was correct. Jackson actually wished to know where Scheer was; had he explained this, the intelligence experts could have told him that the German admiral only used the particular call-sign about which Jackson had asked when in port, changing to a different one when at sea. The fact that this call-sign was signalling from the harbour did not mean that Scheer was still there. Unfortunately, Jackson asked the wrong question, added his own assumption and wrongly deduced that Scheer and the main body of the High Seas Fleet had not yet departed. This misinformation was passed on to Jellicoe at about 12.30pm, with serious consequences. First, Jellicoe steamed south slowly, delaying his encounter with the German fleet and hence wasting precious daylight – though he had not been hurrying before the signal, so the impact was not as great as is sometimes suggested. Second, and far more significant, when Jellicoe later discovered that the High Seas Fleet was actually at sea, he became inclined to treat subsequent Admiralty intelligence with great scepticism.

Scheer's reconnaissance proved similarly unhelpful. Only one of his carefully deployed U-boats managed to launch an attack on a British warship, and its torpedoes missed. Moreover, the U-boats failed in their equally crucial task of keeping their commander informed: they sent Scheer a series of sketchy reports that left him believing that the Grand Fleet was dispersed, and hence with no inkling of the danger into which his fleet was heading.

The Opposing Forces

There were four main forces involved in the Battle of Jutland. Admiral Beatty commanded the British Battlecruiser Fleet, from his flagship HMS *Lion*. It consisted of six battlecruisers and the seaplane carrier *Engadine*, together with the attached 5th Battle Squadron of four modern super-Dreadnoughts, with light cruisers and destroyers. Admiral Hipper, from his newly built flagship *Lützow*, was in command of the 1st Scouting Group of five battlecruisers and the 2nd Scouting Group of light cruisers, also with attached destroyers. Admiral Scheer's battlefleet comprised 22 battleships – 16 Dreadnoughts (including his flagship *Friedrich der Grosse*) and six pre-Dreadnoughts – which, like the British, were divided into three battle squadrons and were accompanied by light cruisers and destroyer flotillas. The main body of the Grand Fleet, under Admiral Jellicoe on HMS *Iron Duke*, comprised 24 Dreadnoughts, organized in three squadrons. It also included the three-ship 3rd Battlecruiser Squadron, as well as armoured cruisers, light cruisers and destroyers.

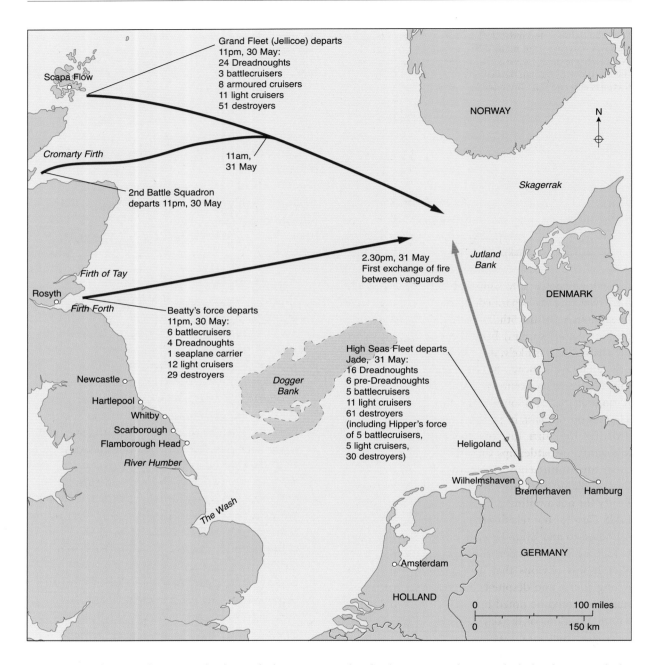

Grand Fleet (Jellicoe) departs
11pm, 30 May:
24 Dreadnoughts
3 battlecruisers
8 armoured cruisers
11 light cruisers
51 destroyers

Scapa Flow

NORWAY

N

Cromarty Firth

11am,
31 May

Skagerrak

2nd Battle Squadron
departs 11pm, 30 May

2.30pm, 31 May
First exchange of fire
between vanguards

Jutland
Bank

Firth of Tay

DENMARK

Rosyth

Firth Forth — Beatty's force departs
11pm, 30 May:
6 battlecruisers
4 Dreadnoughts
1 seaplane carrier
12 light cruisers
29 destroyers

Newcastle

Hartlepool

Whitby

Scarborough

Flamborough Head

River Humber

Dogger
Bank

High Seas Fleet departs
Jade, 31 May:
16 Dreadnoughts
6 pre-Dreadnoughts
5 battlecruisers
11 light cruisers
61 destroyers
(including Hipper's force
of 5 battlecruisers,
5 light cruisers,
30 destroyers)

Heligoland

The Wash

Wilhelmshaven

Bremerhaven   Hamburg

Amsterdam

GERMANY

HOLLAND

0   100 miles

0   150 km

At around 2pm the main bodies of the two battlecruiser fleets were about 80km (50 miles) away from one another, with their light cruiser screens some 25km (15 miles) apart. At this point, a small Danish steamer, the *N.J. Fjord*, played a walk-on part in history. She was spotted at about the same time by the furthest west of Hipper's light forces and the furthest east of Beatty's, both of which changed course to investigate. Warships from both sides therefore sighted each other, reported the presence of the enemy back to their superiors and fired the first shots of the battle just before 2.30pm.

LEFT **The Battle of Jutland – the approach to battle. The complex movements of many different naval forces would eventually see them converge for the long-awaited clash of the British and German battlefleets. The battle would see fortunes ebb and flow, but ended indecisively.**

BELOW **HMS** *Invincible* **was the first battlecruiser to be built anywhere in the world. She had participated in the battles of Heligoland Bight and the Falkland Islands in 1914. At Jutland she was the flagship of Admiral Hood, leading the 3rd Battlecruiser Squadron.**

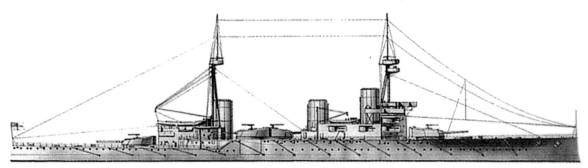

Beatty turned east to support his light cruisers. His force was already separated, as he had allowed the Dreadnoughts of the 5th Battle Squadron to take up a position 8km (5 miles) behind his battlecruisers. In the chase that was likely, their slower speed would see this gap increase. Beatty has been widely criticized for this failure to concentrate his force. His error in stationing was compounded by the failure of Evan-Thomas on *Barham*, in poor visibility, to see the flags ordering the turn towards the enemy; instead of following, his battleships turned onto the next leg of their anti-submarine zigzag, heading away from Beatty. Blame for this incident is shared between Beatty for not awaiting acknowledgment of his order, HMS *Tiger* for not relaying the initial signal as she was supposed to and Evan-Thomas himself for hesitating to follow his commander without explicit orders, even after it was obvious that his squadron was on the wrong course and despite being urged to turn by his staff. (It should be noted in passing that the wireless communications of the day could not transmit voice messages but only Morse code, slowing and complicating the process.) The result of this fiasco was that the most powerful squadron in the world ended up 16km (10 miles) behind Beatty and was therefore delayed in getting into battle.

As soon as contact was confirmed, Beatty ordered *Engadine* to send up a seaplane for reconnaissance. This she did shortly after 3pm, but the carrier was

'Something Wrong with our Bloody Ships'

The most shocking losses for the Royal Navy at Jutland were those of the battlecruisers, which had been the real heart of Jacky Fisher's vision. For some, these losses stemmed from the fact that the ships were not employed as intended: their proper use was demonstrated at the battles of the Falklands and the Dogger Bank, and they should never have been exposed to prolonged fire from heavy guns. Others, however, argued that they had always been envisaged as having a supporting role in a fleet action, so their lack of protection was a serious flaw in their design and in the whole battlecruiser concept. While their armour was considerably weaker than that of their German counterparts, the main problem was more avoidable. Aware that the accuracy of their gunfire was poor, the crews – with the tacit approval of their commanders – ignored safety measures for the handling of ammunition in order to improve their rate of fire. The result was that a hit on a turret carried a great risk of the flash from the explosion detonating a magazine, with catastrophic consequences.

unable to pass on the pilot's reports to the flagship. *Engadine*, which lacked the speed of *Campania*, then proved unable to keep up with the battlecruisers; thus ended the first participation of ship-borne aircraft in a naval battle.

THE 'RUN TO THE SOUTH'

Beatty initially steered southeast in order to cut the enemy off from their bases and prevent them from

escaping as they had at the Battle of the Dogger Bank. He then headed east and was spotted by the German battlecruisers at about 3.20pm. Hipper, for his part, followed the plan by turning south to draw the British battlecruisers towards Scheer. Beatty spotted him just after 3.30pm and gave chase. Thus began the first phase of the battle, known as 'the run to the south'. At this point, the main body of the Grand Fleet was about 100km (60 miles) away, chasing the action. Scheer with the German battlefleet was 80km (50 miles) away, but closing rapidly as the two battlecruiser fleets headed towards him.

Beatty's force delayed opening fire because they overestimated the distance in poor visibility, and

HMS *Queen Mary* exploding prior to sinking. This was the second loss in quick succession of a capital ship in so terrible and sudden a fashion. Hers was the more serious loss, being a more modern battlecruiser than *Indefatigable*.

therefore failed to exploit their range advantage. At 3.48pm Hipper's force opened fire at 14,500m (16,000 yards). Initially, the German gunnery was far more accurate, partly because the light favoured them – with the British showing up clearly against the setting sun, while the German ships were indistinct in the gloom to the east. They also distributed their fire effectively, while the British repeated the error of the Dogger Bank, with two German ships being engaged by multiple British battlecruisers, leaving one to fire undisturbed.

The British suffered the worse. *Tiger* and *Princess Royal* were damaged, as was *Lion*; at 4pm a shell hit on a turret threatened to destroy the ship but the last words of the dying Major Francis Harvey, Royal Marines, ordered the flooding of the magazine, thereby saving her. The German ships were by no means unscathed: *Seydlitz* was hit twice by *Queen Mary*, burning out a turret but the improved post-Dogger Bank precautions against flash saved the ship. *Lützow* and *Derfflinger* were hit too. *Indefatigable* was involved in an intense duel with *Von der Tann*. At about 4.02pm, *Indefatigable* was struck by two salvoes in quick succession, the second of which led to a magazine explosion that destroyed the sinking ship, leaving two survivors from a crew of 1019.

> 'The run to the south lasted a little over an hour and was a German success. Hipper achieved his objective of luring part of the British fleet onto Scheer's main force and had also sunk two British battlecruisers.'

By this time, the *Queen Elizabeth*-class ships had succeeded in closing the gap and swiftly made their presence felt. At about 4pm, they spotted the German light cruisers through the mist, and forced them to pull off with a couple of accurate salvoes. At 4.08pm they were finally able to open fire on the German battlecruisers at a range of at least 17,400m (19,000 yards) and almost immediately hit the enemy ships. Their gunnery was far more effective than that of Beatty's battlecruisers and impressed the Germans, with Scheer later commenting, 'The new enemy fired with extraordinary rapidity and accuracy.' Several of Hipper's ships were hit, forcing them to zigzag and reducing the weight of fire against Beatty's ships; *Von der Tann* lost two turrets and was also hit in the stern, took on water, and was very fortunate not to lose speed, while *Moltke* was hit four times.

A more serious blow fell on the British force. At about 4.20pm the damaged *Lion* briefly veered out of the line, freeing *Derfflinger* and *Seydlitz* to concentrate their fire on *Queen Mary*. At 4.26pm, she was hit by a salvo that was followed seconds later by a magazine explosion that sank the ship in less than two minutes, killing all but 20 of her 1286 crew. After this second loss of a battlecruiser, this time one of the most modern and powerful, Beatty was inaccurately informed that a third of his ships, *Princess Royal*, had blown up. This prompted one of the most famous quotations of twentieth-century naval warfare, as he remarked to Chatfield, his flag captain, 'There seems to be something wrong with our bloody ships today.'

At about the same time as the 5th Battle Squadron opened fire on Hipper's battlecruisers, Beatty ordered his destroyers to make a torpedo attack. As they surged forward, they were met by their German counterparts, engaged on a similar mission, resulting in a fast and confused action between about 4.15pm and 4.45pm. The British destroyers gained the upper hand, preventing attacks on their own battlecruisers, while achieving a torpedo hit on *Seydlitz*, which inflicted only minor damage due to the impressive underwater protection of the German battlecruisers. They also sank two German destroyers, *V27* and *V29*, while two British destroyers, *Nomad* and *Nestor*, were immobilized and were later sunk. At 4.53pm, Beatty recalled his destroyers as the character of the developing battle changed dramatically.

At 4.33pm, Goodenough on HMS *Southampton*, the furthest-advanced British light cruiser, reported the presence of the German battlefleet. This news

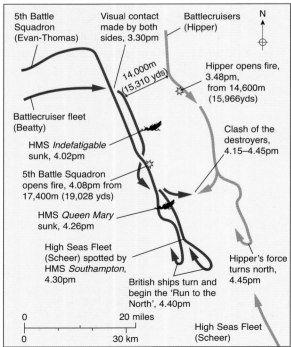

5th Battle Squadron (Evan-Thomas)

Visual contact made by both sides, 3.30pm

Battlecruisers (Hipper)

N

14,000m (15,310 yds)

Hipper opens fire, 3.48pm, from 14,600m (15,966yds)

Battlecruiser fleet (Beatty)

HMS *Indefatigable* sunk, 4.02pm

Clash of the destroyers, 4.15–4.45pm

5th Battle Squadron opens fire, 4.08pm from 17,400m (19,028 yds)

HMS *Queen Mary* sunk, 4.26pm

High Seas Fleet (Scheer) spotted by HMS *Southampton*, 4.30pm

Hipper's force turns north, 4.45pm

British ships turn and begin the 'Run to the North', 4.40pm

0   20 miles

0   30 km

High Seas Fleet (Scheer)

ABOVE SMS *Von der Tann* was the very first of the German battlecruisers and had far heavier armour protection than her British counterparts. This served her well at Jutland, where she was repeatedly hit – all her turrets being knocked out – but survived.

LEFT The initial contact and the run to the south at Jutland. The first stage of the battle saw Beatty chase Hipper's battlecruisers, which were leading him towards the main German fleet. The Germans had the better of it, sinking two British battlecruisers, but narrowly escaped worse losses.

came as something of a shock, since the inaccurate information from the Admiralty had given the impression that it was not at sea. Beatty initially held his course to confirm the report, then at 4.40pm turned to the north, with Scheer to his southeast and Hipper, not yet joined up with his superior, to his northeast. Beatty's destroyers had done their job: together with the fire of the 5th Battle Squadron, they compelled Hipper to fall back on Scheer, buying time for the British battlecruisers to make their turn. At about 4.45pm, the German battlefleet opened fire and a few minutes later, Hipper's force turned north. The roles of the battlecruiser fleets were now reversed, with Beatty doing what Hipper had before – leading the enemy towards his own main force.

The run to the south lasted a little over an hour and was a German success. Hipper achieved his objective of luring part of the British fleet onto Scheer's main force and had also sunk two British battlecruisers. His ships were damaged but still fighting, yet the end of the run to the south came none too early for him, since the effective fire of the *Queen Elizabeth*-class ships was gravely threatening his force. The delay in getting the 5th Battle Squadron into action removed the most powerful squadron in either navy from the early stages of the engagement, for over 15 minutes, when it could have had a huge effect; had they been in action from the outset, Hipper's battlecruisers could well have been wiped out.

THE 'RUN TO THE NORTH'

The second stage of the battle opened with another miscommunication between Beatty's flagship and the 5th Battle Squadron. When Beatty turned his battlecruisers north, he did not initially order the battleships to make the same turn, presumably so as to reduce the distance between the two elements of his force. As they drew level he ordered Evan-Thomas to turn his ships in succession, rather than turning together, which meant that they would take longer to complete the manoeuvre. Furthermore, they would all follow each other around in the same line as they turned, meaning that the closing German battlefleet could concentrate its fire on the point of the turn – through which each battleship would progress – greatly easing their aim. This danger was exacerbated by another error by Beatty's flag officer, Lieutenant Commander Ralph Seymour, who had been responsible for the mistakes during the Scarborough raid and at Dogger Bank, and whom Beatty had refused to replace. Seymour hoisted the flags giving the order to turn, but for some six minutes delayed hauling them down, which would tell Evan-Thomas when to begin the manoeuvre. Once again, Evan-Thomas waited for explicit instructions rather than

Crossing the 'T'

A fleet of warships that could fire broadsides tended to fight in a single line ahead, to maximize its firepower and to make command and control as easy as possible. When manoeuvring in battle, the ideal situation that a commander could achieve was to 'cross the enemy's T' – to be ahead of the advancing enemy, on a perpendicular course; in other words, to be in the position of the line at the top of a capital T. Such a position offered two advantages. First, it allowed the maximum number of one's own guns to fire – the whole broadside of every ship – while the enemy could return fire with only the small number of forward-firing guns on the first few ships of his line. Second, the fire of one's fleet was concentrated on the van of the enemy's force. Nelson's tactics at Trafalgar were unusual because he allowed his 'T' to be crossed, but he had calculated the risks accurately, and the enemy was unable to disable his van before he broke their line. The risks would have been far greater with the longer-range fire of World War I. At Jutland, both commanders wished to cross the enemy's 'T', but only one would succeed – twice.

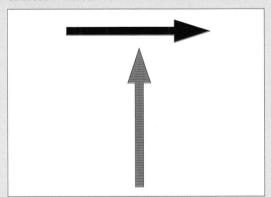

Crossing the enemy's 'T' – the pinnacle of tactical achievement for fleet commanders in the battleship age. The blue fleet has crossed the 'T' of the red fleet.

using his own initiative to start the turn, with each minute carrying his force closer to the approaching German fleet. This problem was caused by Beatty's actions, Seymour's signalling error and Evan-Thomas's hesitation. Its result was to increase greatly the danger to the valuable *Queen Elizabeths*.

Admiral Sir John Rushworth Jellicoe (1859–1935)

 Jellicoe joined the Navy in 1872 and gained extensive experience that twice nearly cost his life – with the sinking of HMS *Victoria* after a collision in 1893, and then with a bullet in the lung during the Boxer Rebellion. He worked closely with Jacky Fisher and helped to design the *Dreadnought* as Director of Naval Ordnance. He was made commander-in-chief of the Grand Fleet in August 1914 despite his great reluctance to replace the previous incumbent, Admiral George Callaghan. Jellicoe was highly intelligent and competent, with a great mastery of technical matters. He was also courteous and modest, though lacking Beatty's social panache, and was genuinely popular with the crews of the Grand Fleet. He was also a great centralizer, unwilling to delegate work to others, and was painfully aware of the heavy responsibility he bore. Historians have a mixed view on his performance at Jutland, praising his deployment, but tending to see his tactics as rather cautious. In December 1916, he became First Sea Lord when he was already worn out by the burdens he had carried, and was dismissed in December 1917. Jellicoe comported himself with great dignity during the Jutland controversy of the inter-war years.

They were accordingly pounded by the heavy guns of the German battlefleet, whose captains could hardly believe their luck at having such an easy target and concentrated their fire against the battleships, while Beatty's faster battlecruisers pulled away. Moreover, in the early stages of the run to the north, although the visibility was generally poor – with increasing amounts of smoke being added to the mist – it continued to favour the Germans. Any damage that appreciably reduced the speed of one ship of the 5th Battle Squadron could only have resulted in its being caught and sunk, like *Blücher* at Dogger Bank. Luckily for them, their 33cm (13in) armour and sturdy construction preserved them from the intense German fire. *Valiant* escaped unscathed, but *Barham* and *Warspite* were slightly damaged, and *Malaya* suffered worst: she took one hit that temporarily reduced her speed, but swift and effective damage control resolved the problem. They also continued to return fire effectively, despite the fact that the German ships were almost invisible to them, further damaging *Derfflinger*, *Seydlitz* and the van of Scheer's fleet.

By about 5.30pm the light conditions had changed to favour the British, as the setting sun was now dazzling the German gunners. Further, the ebb and flow of the battle was on the point of changing once more: at 5.33pm Beatty's lead cruisers made contact with the van of Jellicoe's fleet. Around 5.56pm Beatty himself spotted the lead ships of the Grand Fleet. He then began to push towards the northeast, forcing Hipper to do the same for fear of having his 'T' crossed, thereby concealing from the Germans the fact that the British battlefleet was about to join the battle.

In contrast to the first stage of the battle, the British had considerably the better of the run to the north. This was largely due to the heavy armour and the effective gunfire of the 5th Battle Squadron. Just like Hipper before him, Beatty had succeeded: he made contact with the main body of the German force and then led it towards Jellicoe's Grand Fleet, which would now have its long-awaited chance to smash its rival. He achieved this despite heavy losses that might have shaken a less determined commander. However, Beatty failed in the other, equally important aspect of

ABOVE Damage to the light cruiser HMS *Chester* following the battle. This ship had a close escape: scouting for Hood's battlecruisers, she was badly battered by German light cruisers – suffering nearly 70 casualties – before Hood, in *Invincible*, came to her aid.

BELOW SMS *Lützow*, the same class of battlecruiser as the *Derfflinger*, began the Battle of Jutland as Hipper's flagship. She helped to sink the armoured cruiser HMS *Defence* and the battlecruiser HMS *Invincible*, but the return fire from the latter caused damage that later proved fatal.

his role as commander of the battlecruisers: he neglected to pass on to Jellicoe the crucial information about the enemy's position and course that the commander-in-chief desperately needed.

Jellicoe had received the 2.18pm report that the enemy had been sighted and increased speed. At 4.38pm, he heard the confirmation that the German battlefleet was present, prompting him to signal the Admiralty, 'Fleet action is imminent'. Thereafter, he received a stream of signals that were inaccurate,

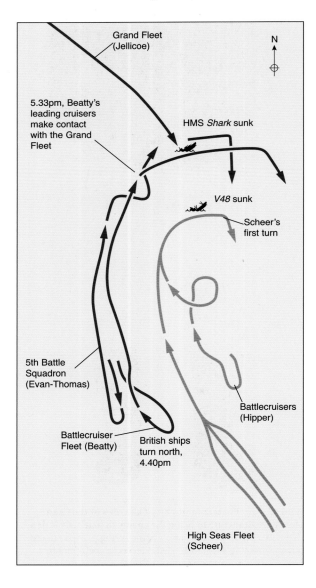

Grand Fleet
(Jellicoe)

N

5.33pm, Beatty's leading cruisers make contact with the Grand Fleet

HMS *Shark* sunk

V48 sunk

Scheer's first turn

5th Battle Squadron (Evan-Thomas)

Battlecruiser Fleet (Beatty)

British ships turn north, 4.40pm

Battlecruisers (Hipper)

High Seas Fleet (Scheer)

incomplete and contradictory. This mattered, since Jellicoe was facing the momentous decision of how to deploy his fleet from its formation for steaming – in six separate columns – to the single line that it would adopt for battle, to bring to bear as many guns as possible. The lack of information prevented him from deciding the direction in which to deploy or when to begin the manoeuvre. It also meant that he encountered the German force earlier than he had anticipated and several kilometres further to the west.

One decision Jellicoe had made earlier was to order Hood's 3rd Battlecruiser Squadron to push on ahead so that it could support Beatty as soon as possible. When it reached him, it had a significant impact in the latest of the many individual engagements that constituted the Battle of Jutland. At 5.27pm HMS *Chester*, which was scouting for the 3rd Battlecruiser Squadron, was surprised by four of Hipper's light cruisers and was damaged. Hood rapidly came to her support and at 5.36pm turned the tables on the German vessels, crippling *Wiesbaden* and damaging *Frankfurt* and *Pillau*. *Chester* was seriously damaged, but made it back home. Hipper's destroyers sought to carry out a torpedo attack, but were fought off by their counterparts in Hood's force, which then went on to make their own attacks. These resulted in the loss of HMS *Shark*, though only after inflicting similarly fatal damage on the destroyer *V48* and hitting the damaged *Wiesbaden* with a torpedo. The unexpected arrival of Hood's battlecruisers, together with the torpedo attacks by British destroyers, persuaded Hipper to fall back on Scheer, thus concealing the arrival of the Grand Fleet as well as buying time for its deployment. By 6.14pm, Hipper had linked up with his superior and was heading north again.

At about this time, Jellicoe made the single most important tactical decision of the battle, indeed of the entire war at sea. He was well aware of the gravity of the decision facing him and that he was making it on

The 'run to the north'. The second of the main stages of the battle saw Beatty drawing the entire High Seas Fleet towards Jellicoe and the British battlefleet. The British ships escaped further loss, with the *Queen Elizabeths* inflicting damage on the chasing German battlecruisers.

the basis of imperfect information, against an enemy which had appeared both earlier and on a different bearing than he had been led to expect. He was equally aware that getting the decision wrong or making it either too soon or too late would place Britain's entire battlefleet in grave danger. This responsibility was his alone, epitomizing the 'loneliness of command'.

Jellicoe's first thought was to deploy to starboard – that is, for the line to form up heading southwest. This would have the advantage of getting into action at closer range and sooner, which was important because daylight was running out. However, it also carried risks. It would allow the German fleet to concentrate its fire on the British van, which would then have comprised its older warships, without the rest of the fleet being able to support it for several minutes. It would also give the Germans an ideal position for launching mass torpedo attacks against part of the British fleet. Deploying to port – having the line form to the southeast – would take longer but offered the advantage of silhouetting the German fleet against the setting sun. It also allowed Jellicoe to cross their 'T' – that is, to achieve the desirable position in a naval battle in which your fleet passes at a right angle ahead of the enemy fleet, allowing all of your guns to fire on his lead ships, which can only fire a small number of guns in reply.

Jellicoe therefore decided to deploy to port. He has subsequently been criticized for this by some historians, notably Churchill, whose assessment was made outside the confusion and danger of battle and with the considerable advantage, that Jellicoe lacked, of perfect knowledge of the position and course of the enemy as well as an awareness of the course of subsequent events. Some critics have suggested alternatives such as forming the line from the centre of the fleet or even deploying into two separate lines, but such manoeuvres would have been enormously complicated when in contact with the enemy, and were not realistic options since they had not been practised beforehand. Most historians – including, strikingly, the authors of both the British and German official histories – have concluded that Jellicoe made the right decision.

A Royal Navy lieutenant in 1916. The crews of the Grand Fleet were desperate to bring the enemy to battle. At Jutland, their training in gunnery and manoeuvring proved effective, but they were hampered by deficiencies in shells and by a lack of initiative among senior officers.

At 6.15pm Jellicoe ordered the Grand Fleet to deploy to port. The manoeuvre – moving from six columns into a single line, 10km (6 miles) long – was conducted well, given the large number of ships in numerous separate squadrons under several different commanders. It was complicated by the ill-fated action of one British commander.

The old armoured cruisers of the 1st Cruiser Squadron, under the command of Rear Admiral Sir Robert Arbuthnot, were ahead of the Grand Fleet. From his flagship *Defence*, Arbuthnot spotted the gunfire from the engagement between *Chester* and the German light cruisers and at 5.50pm hastened to join in, accompanied by HMS *Warrior* – the other two of his cruisers having become separated. He should not have placed himself between the two battlefleets, but with the reconnaissance role of the cruisers fulfilled, he apparently wished to support the embattled British light cruisers. He charged in firing, inflicting further damage on the battered *Wiesbaden*, but then came under heavy fire from Hipper's battlecruisers. *Defence* was torn apart by the bombardment and exploded at 6.20pm, killing Arbuthnot and the entire crew of over 900 men. Her sister ship, *Warrior*, was seriously damaged, and would not have survived but for one of the stranger episodes of the battle.

The 5th Battle Squadron, lagging behind Beatty's battlecruisers, had to rejoin the Grand Fleet. Rather than steer for the head of the line, which would have masked the fire of several British ships, Evan-Thomas elected to join the rear. However, when *Warspite* made the sharp turn that this required, her steering gear – damaged by an earlier hit – became jammed. The result was that she circled, twice, towards the German fleet. In doing so, she attracted almost all of the fire, at short range, of up to 10 German Dreadnoughts. She was damaged, but survived thanks to her heavy armour. She was sent home shortly afterwards, finally making port having had to avoid the torpedoes of one German U-boat and, in return, only narrowly failing to ram that U-boat and one other. The bizarre movements of *Warspite* had the beneficial effect of attracting German fire away from the crippled *Warrior*, which was therefore able to extricate herself. She would sink on the way home, but not before her 900 crew had been taken off by *Engadine*, playing her final role in the battle.

THE CLASH OF THE BATTLEFLEETS

As the main engagement began, the High Seas Fleet enjoyed one last major success. The 3rd Battlecruiser Squadron had successfully forced Hipper to back away and thus covered the British deployment. It now took position in the van, a couple of kilometres ahead of Beatty, with Hood's flagship, *Invincible* – the very first battlecruiser – in the lead. Hood's ships opened fire on Hipper's battlecruisers, to their southwest, which initially could not see them to return fire. The range was only about 8km (5 miles), and the recent gunnery practice of the British battlecruisers seemed to pay off as *Invincible* inflicted eight hits on *Lützow*, causing damage that would eventually prove fatal. *Seydlitz* and *Derfflinger* were also further damaged. Then, at about 6.30pm, the mist suddenly lifted to give the Germans a clear view of their assailants. Their heavy fire again demonstrated the weakness of the British battlecruisers: at 6.34pm, a shell hit a turret on *Invincible*, causing a magazine explosion that literally tore the ship in two. The shallow water in which she sank left her bow and stern jutting above the waves. Just six men survived from her crew of 1031; Admiral Hood was not among them.

> 'As his fleet came under increasingly heavy fire, Scheer became aware that he was facing not merely an isolated detachment of the Grand Fleet but the whole of it. Stretching across the horizon were Dreadnoughts bearing names redolent of centuries of history'

Hipper's 1st Scouting Group had suffered badly from the gunfire of Beatty, Evan-Thomas and now Hood. The extent of the battering they had taken is shown by the fact that when the damage to *Lützow* forced Hipper to disembark and relocate his command, he approached, in turn, *Derfflinger*, *Seydlitz* and *Von der Tann*, only to find that each was too badly damaged to serve his purpose. Finally, he transferred his flag to the relatively undamaged *Moltke*.

By 6.30pm the British warships began to complete their line having already opened fire on any enemy they could see. Visibility was very poor in the mist and smoke, but favoured the British, who could see their opponents against the light western sky, while they were largely hidden in darkness. As his fleet came under increasingly heavy fire, Scheer became aware that he was facing not merely an isolated detachment

SMS *Derfflinger* assisted in the destruction of the battlecruisers *Queen Mary* and *Invincible*. She received more than 20 heavy hits during the battle and was so badly damaged that Hipper was unable to move his flag to her from the doomed *Lützow* – yet she still made it home.

of the Grand Fleet, but the whole of it. Stretching across the horizon were Dreadnoughts bearing names redolent of centuries of history, taken from admirals, generals and famous ships from earlier eras: *Benbow*, *Collingwood* and *St. Vincent*; *Marlborough* and *Iron Duke*; *Bellerophon*, *Temeraire* and *Vanguard*. They had succeeded in crossing the 'T' of the German battlefleet and were firing remarkably effectively, inflicting heavy damage on its leading battleships. The very survival of Scheer's force was in serious jeopardy.

After a few moments in which he seemed stunned and unable to comprehend the unfolding situation,

A lieutenant-captain of the Imperial German Navy in 1916.
The meticulous training of such men withstood the test of
battle. They were cheered by the losses that they had inflicted
on their adversary, but morale began to decline as their
commanders sought to avoid further clashes.

The main fleet action at Jutland. The complicated
movements of the battlefleets saw the British deploy for
action and cross the 'T' of the German fleet. The latter
turned away, then turned back towards the British, before
making its escape a second time. After pausing due to the
threat of torpedoes, Jellicoe gave chase.

Scheer took decisive action to save his fleet. At about
6.35pm he ordered a complex manoeuvre that had
been meticulously practised in case of just such a
situation: the *Gefechtskehrtwendung* or 'battle about-
turn', in which the whole fleet reversed course almost
simultaneously from the rearmost vessel forwards.
This turn, covered by the destroyers with a
smokescreen and torpedo attack, allowed the High
Seas Fleet to break contact and vanish into the mist. It
was heading southwest, away from home, but had
gained a temporary respite from the British fire.

Jellicoe did not at first realize what his adversary had
done. He did not see the turn himself and when, after
a few minutes, it became clear that the German fleet
was not simply hidden in the mist, he could not tell
how far it had turned. Those among his captains who
had observed the Germans make their about-turn
failed to pass on this information. Jellicoe therefore
expected the German fleet to reappear. When it did
not, at about 6.45pm he steered to the south, aiming to
get between Scheer and his route home in the hope of
blocking his retreat and forcing him to resume the
battle. As the British fleet made its turn, HMS
Marlborough was hit by a torpedo, probably fired by
the crippled *Wiesbaden*, killing two crewmen (the only
fatalities suffered by the main body of the fleet during
the entire battle). The damaged Dreadnought was able
to remain with the Grand Fleet for the time being, but
the experience only confirmed Jellicoe's concern about
the threat from underwater weapons.

It was not long before Jellicoe was given his second
chance to have a go at the enemy, due to a remarkable
decision by Scheer. At about 6.55pm he ordered his
fleet to turn back towards the British. He later claimed
that he was eager to resume the battle and to rescue
the *Wiesbaden*, and headed into the British line to
achieve surprise. Such a decision would be sure to
surprise the British because it would have been

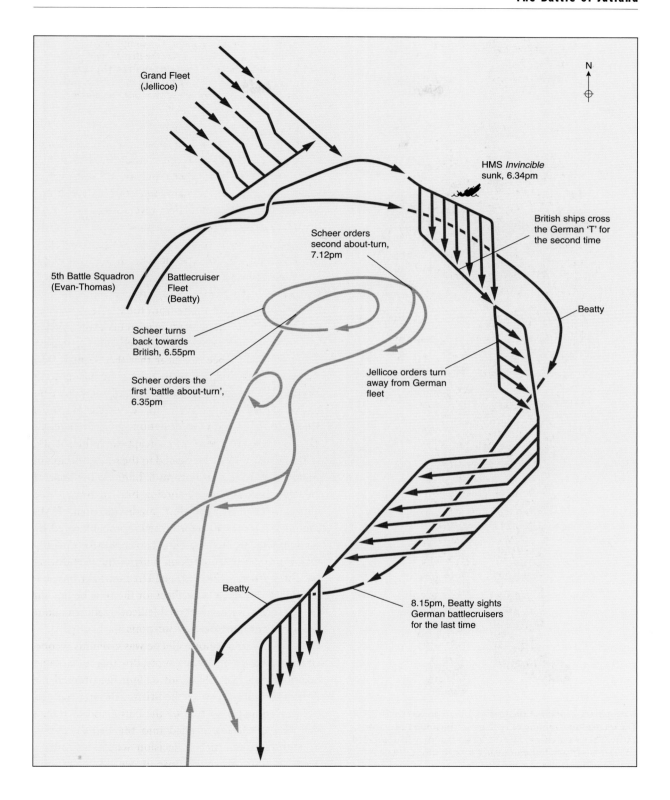

Grand Fleet (Jellicoe)

HMS *Invincible* sunk, 6.34pm

British ships cross the German 'T' for the second time

Scheer orders second about-turn, 7.12pm

5th Battle Squadron (Evan-Thomas)

Battlecruiser Fleet (Beatty)

Scheer turns back towards British, 6.55pm

Scheer orders the first 'battle about-turn', 6.35pm

Jellicoe orders turn away from German fleet

Beatty

Beatty

8.15pm, Beatty sights German battlecruisers for the last time

N

HMS *Invincible* was sunk in shallow water, her bow and stern left jutting in the air. This view, which shocked many men on both sides, provides one of the most striking pictures of the entire war at sea.

suicidally stupid, allowing his 'T' to be crossed a second time, with his battered battlecruisers in the lead. As the historian Julian Corbett put it, this explanation must have been untrue, since 'it cannot be reconciled with his high reputation as a tactician, or even with sanity'. More probably, Scheer realized he could not continue to steer west, away from home and safety, and therefore wished to reverse course; then, having misidentified Hood's battlecruisers as the van of the British battlefleet, he misjudged its location and believed that his new course would take him safely through the wake of the British line.

In any case, his change of course back towards the Grand Fleet was spotted by HMS *Southampton*, which alerted Jellicoe. At around 7.10pm the British fleet crossed the German 'T' for a second time, albeit with its divisions staggered rather than in a single line, so not all of its ships could open fire. Once again the leading German warships were hit repeatedly and found it difficult to return fire against British ships that were all but invisible except for the muzzle flashes of their guns. Hipper's battlecruisers were hit hard yet again, taking at least 25 hits from heavy shells, with the battleships *König, Grosser Kurfürst* and *Derfflinger* also suffering damage.

Scheer realized that he had made a terrible mistake and at 7.12pm ordered a second battle about-turn back towards the west. This manoeuvre, conducted

them easier to avoid, since their relative speed would be far lower if they were chasing the battleships than if they were heading towards each other, while their speed would fall further as they reached the end of their range. In total, 31 torpedoes were fired, of which 20 reached the British line, but not a single one hit. The tactic succeeded – but at the cost of allowing Scheer to complete his turn and to put precious distance between the two fleets, with only about 90 minutes of daylight remaining.

Of all Jellicoe's actions, this one has been most bitterly criticized. Some have argued that he should have turned towards the torpedoes, accepting the risk of having some of his warships damaged or even sunk in order to maintain contact with the German fleet. Critics such as Churchill, writing with his usual magisterial hindsight, have claimed that Jellicoe over-estimated the threat from torpedoes. There was a genuine threat, however, and any critic has to acknowledge that Jellicoe could not know in advance how few torpedoes would be fired; he knew that the full capacity of the German flotilla was over 400 torpedoes, though in the event, not all the German destroyers took part in the attack, and many of those that did were not able to launch their whole load due to the heavy fire from the British fleet.

Jellicoe had no intention of accepting an unnecessary risk. Historians differ over whether his caution was excessive and needlessly threw away the prospect of another Trafalgar, or was wise and showed the same prudence that Beatty had at Dogger Bank when he thought he spotted a periscope. Pressing on would have resulted in damage, perhaps fatal, to some of his ships in return for catching some of the German stragglers. However, the annihilation of the German fleet that some suggest would have ensued is unlikely: most of it would still have escaped due to the poor visibility, the lack of daylight remaining and, particularly, Scheer's evident (and quite proper) determination to avoid another engagement in which his forces would have been at a massive disadvantage.

Jellicoe successfully weathered the torpedo attack, albeit at the cost of allowing Scheer to break contact. He was again unaware of the precise course of the

after a renewed round of heavy British fire, placed enormous demands on his captains and crews, but they succeeded. Scheer evidently recognized just how desperate his position had become: at 7.13pm he ordered his battlecruisers, several of which no longer had any functioning main guns, to charge the British, sacrificing them to cover his retreat. He then altered this order to have them engage the lead British ships and ordered his destroyers to cover him with a smokescreen and a torpedo attack.

It was at this point that Jellicoe made his most controversial decision of the battle, meeting the attacking German destroyers with his own light forces but also turning his capital ships away from the torpedo attack. His rationale was that turning away reduced the threat from the torpedoes by making

HMS *Barham* was a *Queen Elizabeth*-class super-Dreadnought, one of the newest and most powerful warships of the Grand Fleet. At Jutland, she served as the flagship of Vice Admiral Hugh Evan-Thomas in the 5th Battle Squadron, accompanying Beatty's Battlecruiser Fleet.

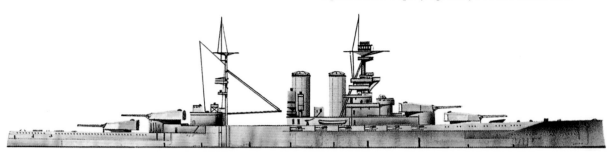

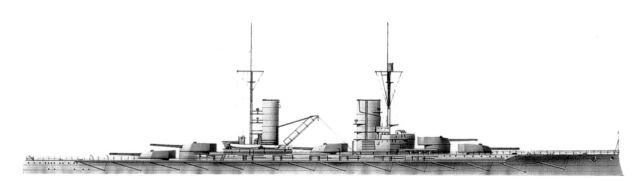

SMS *Grosser Kurfürst*. A *König*-class Dreadnought, she was commission in the week before the outbreak of war in 1914. She was badly damaged at Jutland but survived. Her subsequent career was chequered, being damaged by a British submarine as well as by a collision with another German ship and by running aground. She was scuttled at Scapa Flow in 1919.

German fleet and initially expected to encounter it once more. He sought to pursue it to the west, but when he did not locate it, he turned southwest, again trying to place his fleet between Scheer and the German bases. Meanwhile, Scheer had turned to the south, hoping to avoid the British fleet; further contact seemed inevitable.

At about 8.15pm, shortly before dark, there was another brief engagement as Beatty, ahead of the main British force, sighted Hipper's battlecruisers. The German ships suffered further damage, unable to return fire because they could not see their antagonists. They were saved by the timely intervention of the pre-Dreadnoughts of the 2nd Battle Squadron, which were also damaged by the British battlecruisers but allowed Hipper to extricate himself. Beatty did not pursue, once again showing that he was not as reckless as some have tended to believe. Nevertheless, he did manage to push the German fleet to the west, further from the safety of home. As Marder notes, this was the last time in the war that capital ships engaged each other.

At about 8.45pm, some of the British light cruisers spotted three German battleships and informed Vice Admiral Sir Martyn Jerram, commanding the 2nd Battle Squadron from HMS *King George V*. He refused to open fire, however, suspecting them to be Beatty's battlecruisers. His caution is understandable, but it was another lost opportunity.

NIGHT MOVEMENTS AND SCHEER'S ESCAPE

Jellicoe decided that he would seek to avoid an engagement during the night. He was aware that his forces lacked adequate equipment or training for a night-time action, and was concerned that the greater danger of torpedo attack at night would nullify his numerical advantage. Instead, he would seek to prevent Scheer from getting to the safety of his bases, in order to be in a position to resume the battle the following morning.

He was aware that Scheer had a range of options for his journey home. The first would have been to head northeast, pass through the Kattegat to return home. Jellicoe sensibly dismissed this possibility, since it represented more than twice the distance of the other options and involved too great a risk of losing damaged ships to the pursuing British. The second possible course was south, heading for the channel that had been swept through the British minefields and passing Heligoland. This was unlikely because of the difficultly of locating and navigating the safe passage through the minefield. This left two alternatives: one involved steaming to the southwest, then heading past the mouth of the Ems River and east along the German coast. The last option was to head southeast for the Horns Reef, then passing down the coast of Denmark.

In Jellicoe's opinion, although the latter was the shorter route and hence the more attractive, it was blocked by the British fleet. After the mauling Scheer's force had suffered before, it was unlikely to attempt to break through the Grand Fleet once again. Besides, the last time the Germans had been spotted, they were heading southwest. Jellicoe therefore assessed that the Ems route was the most likely, and took a course that would allow him to cover it. In case Scheer should seek to slip behind him to the Horns Reef, he ordered the minelayer *Abdiel* to lay more mines there. He also stationed his destroyers 8km (5 miles) astern of the battlefleet to intercept any such move.

At 9.17pm Jellicoe ordered the Grand Fleet to take up its formation for night steaming, with Beatty's battlecruisers ahead of the main body, to prevent the Germans from passing in front of it. Jellicoe believed

A lieutenant-captain of a Zeppelin in 1914. The German Navy made extensive use of Zeppelins over the sea to scout for the enemy. Sensitivity to weather conditions reduced this advantage, which could not prevent the Royal Navy achieving surprise on a number of occasions.

that the German fleet was to his northwest. In fact, it was closer than he realized and was on a converging course.

Despite Scheer's later protestations that he was keen to resume the battle, his only concern was to lead his battered fleet to safety. He was well aware that its survival depended on his ability to reach home, which meant that he had to get past the British fleet during the night. From the various possibilities open to him, he opted for the shortest route, via the Horns Reef. This was probably his best decision of the day. However, seeking to head there as early as he did – turning to a south-southeast course at 9.30pm – was dangerous, carrying a high chance of running into the British again.

During the night, Scheer's force was subject to a series of sporadic destroyer attacks, but he refused to be turned aside from his course towards Horns Reef. The two fleets were on converging courses that described a 'V', although as both moved south, the faster British edged ahead, with their lead growing all the time. Around midnight, Scheer crossed in the wake of the Grand Fleet, only about 15 minutes and less than 5 km (3 miles) behind it; such was the narrow margin of breaking through to comparative safety.

Why was the High Seas Fleet able to escape through the rear of the British line? An important factor was that the German ships were far better prepared for fighting at night in terms of equipment (such as effective searchlights and star shells) and training (notably procedures for distinguishing friend from foe). Repeatedly, British ships hesitated to engage a ship they had spotted for fear of attacking one of their

'The two fleets were on converging courses that described a 'V', although as both moved south, the faster British edged ahead, with their lead growing all the time.'

own, resulting in German vessels either escaping or being allowed the great advantage of opening fire first. The British destroyers failed either to prevent the Germans from breaking through or to inflict serious losses on them. Although their attacks were pressed with considerable courage, they were often disorganized, and some of the destroyer flotillas seemed more concerned with maintaining station than attacking the enemy.

There were around a dozen encounters during the night in which fire was exchanged and several others where it might have been but was not. In one, the light cruiser *Southampton* was heavily damaged and left on fire, but not before she torpedoed and sank the German light cruiser *Frauenlob*. In another action, British destroyers sank the light cruiser *Rostock*, then torpedoed the cruiser *Elbing* which, seeking to avoid further torpedoes, was rammed and sunk by the German Dreadnought *Posen*. During these attacks, the British lost the destroyers *Tipperary*, *Fortune* and *Sparrowhawk* (which was damaged by German fire, then in the confusion was rammed by two British ships). HMS *Spitfire* had a lucky escape: her captain realized that he could not avoid a collision with the German Dreadnought *Nassau*, with a tonnage more than 20 times that of his own unarmoured ship, so he chose to ram her. Although badly damaged, *Spitfire* survived the encounter and made it home, carrying a 6m (20ft) section of *Nassau*'s armour plate as a memento. Around the same time, the damaged *Black Prince*, a survivor of the ill fated 1st Cruiser Squadron, was seeking to locate the Grand Fleet when she instead happened on the German Dreadnoughts at point-blank range and was rapidly sunk.

The failure of the destroyers to stop the Germans was compounded by their more startling failure to inform Jellicoe of the enemy's movements. While Jellicoe had neglected to provide the destroyer

SMS *Nassau*, firing at sea. She was the first of Germany's Dreadnoughts and experienced what was perhaps the strangest encounter of the Battle of Jutland. During the night action, she was rammed by the destroyer HMS *Spitfire*, which not only survived but carried away a chunk of her armour plate as a souvenir.

commanders with a clear picture of the situation, they should have displayed sufficient initiative to press the attack when possible and to pass on reported sightings. At about 2am, shortly before dawn, Captain Anselan Stirling of HMS *Faulknor* led the 12th Destroyer Flotilla in a well coordinated torpedo attack that sank the pre-Dreadnought *Pommern*. Unlike the other light forces, Stirling signalled Jellicoe, but his report failed to get through due to German jamming.

It was not only the destroyers that were found wanting. Some Dreadnoughts spotted German

warships, but failed either to open fire or to pass on potentially critical information. At 10.30pm, for example, HMS *Thunderer* spotted *Moltke* – making her way home – but did not open fire due to reluctance to reveal the position of the British fleet. *Seydlitz*, similarly on her own, was sighted several times and eventually broke through the British fleet; no ship opened fire, due to doubts over her identity, and *Seydlitz* limped home, barely afloat, when a couple of salvoes would have finished her. Worst of all, at about 11.40pm, as the German battlefleet passed astern of the British line, *Malaya* identified the *Westfalen*. Her captain, Algernon Boyle, refused the request to open fire, on the spurious grounds that his superior must be aware of the presence of the German ships but had not ordered him to engage.

Vice Admiral Reinhard Scheer (1863–1928)

Scheer joined the Imperial German Navy in 1872, gaining considerable experience and technical mastery, not least in the torpedo branch. Early in the war, he commanded battle squadrons of the High Seas Fleet before succeeding Admiral von Pohl as its commander-in-chief in 1916. He advocated a more active approach to drawing part of the Grand Fleet into an ambush. This resulted in the Battle of Jutland, where he managed to extricate his force from great danger; yet he turned down the Kaiser's offer of ennoblement after the battle. Scheer was made Chief of the Naval Staff in 1918 and conceived the idea of a last great sortie by the battlefleet, only for it to be frustrated by mutiny. His memoirs put a rather favourable gloss on several episodes in the war, Jutland in particular, but show a justifiable pride in the achievements of his fleet. Scheer died in 1928, shortly before he could take up an invitation that he had accepted from Admiral Jellicoe to travel to England and meet.

To be fair, the captains and crews were all exhausted after the trials, stress and danger of battle, as well as the enervating experience of night operations. Less condonable were errors in the Admiralty in not forwarding crucial information. At 11pm Jellicoe was advised by the Admiralty of an intercepted signal giving the German course as south-southeast. This should have pointed to the fact that they were heading for Horns Reef, but Jellicoe dismissed it. This was largely because the error earlier in the day, when he had been wrongly informed that the German battlefleet had not left port, led him to disbelieve intelligence from the Admiralty. (This inclination was increased by an Admiralty signal accurately passing on a message from a German ship that had got its own position manifestly wrong.) Another signal was intercepted, in which Scheer requested Zeppelin reconnaissance over the Horns Reef early the following morning. Inexcusably, the Admiralty failed to pass on this signal or six others that pointed to the actual course of the German fleet. These invaluable pieces of intelligence were not forwarded to the commander-in-chief, but were simply filed away; Marder describes this as 'criminal neglect'. Had Jellicoe seen these signals, he would have been able to realize Scheer's intentions and could have changed course to intercept him the next morning.

HMS *Black Prince* was an armoured cruiser in Arbuthnot's 1st Cruiser Squadron. Separated from the rest of the force, shed missed the action in which her sister *Defence* was sunk and *Warrior* fatally damaged. During the night, she ran into the German battlefleet and was rapidly destroyed.

SMS *Wiesbaden* was involved in the action in which HMS *Chester* was damaged, though she in turn was hit repeatedly by the heavy guns of *Invincible*. She was immobilized and was targeted by other British ships, but returned their fire until she sank.

Jellicoe himself cannot escape all blame. He simply assumed that the noise and light to his stern represented his own destroyers fighting off attempted torpedo attacks by German destroyers; but he could have sought to confirm this. He was also partly responsible for the fact that his crews were inadequately trained for night action and for their captains' tendency to wait for orders rather than displaying initiative.

Around 2.40am on 1 June, just after dawn, Jellicoe turned the fleet north to gather up his light cruisers and destroyers for the battle that he still believed would ensue. His optimism fell sharply at 3am when a Zeppelin appeared overhead. It was driven off by gunfire that was rather more spirited than accurate, but it would surely alert Scheer to the presence of the British fleet, thus enabling him to avoid them. Shortly afterwards, Jellicoe's remaining hopes were dashed when he learned via an Admiralty interception that the High Seas Fleet was well to his northeast, close to the Horns Reef. Scheer had made good his escape. At about 3.30am the German fleet reached the Reef. It passed through the newly laid minefield, which was relatively small due to the fact that HMS *Abdiel* had only been able to lay a few mines in the time available. The Dreadnought *Ostfriesland* was damaged by a mine laid earlier, but still made it home. The fleet also passed safely over the British submarines on its route, which had been instructed to stay on the sea bottom until 2 June.

Jellicoe's forces combed the area for damaged enemy vessels, but found none, as *Lützow* and *Wiesbaden* had sunk during the night. At around 11am the British fleet, frustrated and disappointed, headed for home. On the way, as was traditional in the Royal Navy, many of those killed during the battle were buried at sea. The Grand Fleet arrived home on 2 June, and a few hours later Jellicoe reported to the Admiralty that it was ready for battle once again.

AN ANTICLIMACTIC END

Shortly after the High Seas Fleet arrived home, the German Government released its story first, putting out a triumphalist announcement that claimed a great victory. This statement exaggerated British losses and failed to acknowledge all of the German casualties. In the absence of any British statement, the neutral press and the British newspapers echoed this line. Their interpretation was strengthened by the initial Admiralty communiqué, which took traditional British understatement a little far: the tone was restrained as it listed British losses in full – the

only error being its exaggeration of the number of destroyers sunk – but made no reference to specific German ships sunk, only stating that their losses were substantial. It quite failed to mention that the German fleet had twice fled the British, and that the latter was still at sea, in control of the battlefield and seeking a new engagement, the next morning. Later Admiralty statements gave a fuller account of the action, stressing that the German fleet had fled in poor visibility and that the Grand Fleet had 'driven the enemy into port', as well as making higher claims of Germans losses. This, together with the later

admission by the German Government that it had concealed some of its own losses 'for military reasons' led to neutral press opinion swinging back the other, way as the German Government was accused of what would now be called 'spin'.

So who actually won? The Royal Navy clearly suffered the greater losses – three battlecruisers, three armoured cruisers and eight destroyers, with a total of 6,000 men killed. The High Seas Fleet had lost one battlecruiser, one pre-Dreadnought battleship, four light cruisers and five destroyers, and over 2500 men. The British losses totalled 116,800 tonnes (115,000 tons) and the German, 62,000 tonnes (61,000 tons). In these terms, German claims of victory were understandable. However, taking into account ships damaged, the picture altered. Ten German capital ships were heavily damaged and the extensive repairs they needed meant that they were out of action for longer than the damaged British ships.

The results of battles are not assessed by men killed and machines destroyed but rather by which side achieved its aims. Scheer's objective had been to destroy an isolated part of the Grand Fleet, which he had failed to do. Similarly, though, the Royal Navy had not inflicted a shattering defeat on its enemy, as public

opinion confidently anticipated. In terms of the wider balance, however, the numerical superiority of the Royal Navy actually increased. While the loss of life on the three British armoured cruisers was grievous, the ships themselves were obsolete and their loss did not harm the capability of the Grand Fleet. The loss of four light cruisers was more serious for the High Seas Fleet. Both sides lost one new battlecruiser; the two older British battlecruisers that had been sunk were soon replaced by newly built vessels. When Jellicoe reported his fleet was ready for action on 2 June, this was no mere bravado: he had 24 capital ships available for battle while his opponent could have put to sea just 10. Perhaps more significant, the British advantage was now still greater in the minds of the German commanders. They were well aware of the narrowness of the margin by which they had escaped a shattering defeat, and this was to condition their subsequent activities.

German destroyers of the High Seas Fleet. These ships, like their larger British counterparts, played an important role in the battle, launching torpedo attacks against enemy capital ships as well as countering the enemy's efforts to do so. The German destroyers were critical in helping the High Seas Fleet to escape.

Damage inflicted on SMS *Derfflinger*. This photograph indicates the punishment taken during the battle by many German capital ships, particularly the battlecruisers such as *Derfflinger*. Their strong construction and the defective British shells allowed nearly all of them to reach home regardless.

Although the outcome of the battle was not a decisive victory, its importance was enormous. At the strategic level, the result was a great success for Britain. The purpose of the battle was to contest control of the sea and at its end, the British mastery was if anything stronger than it had been before. The blockade of Germany was in no way lessened and its slow yet strangling effect continued unabated. The German realization that they could not expect success in a future fleet engagement led to a switch to the alternative approach of relying on U-boats for victory, which had the ultimately disastrous consequences explained in the next chapter. The picture is perhaps best captured by an American newspaper, which wrote, 'The German fleet has assaulted its jailor but it is still in jail.'

The outcome of the battle was due to a number of factors. Perhaps the most significant was the poor visibility, exacerbated by the fact that the engagement began so late in the day. While this constraint affected both sides, its impact was to the greater advantage of the side seeking to escape.

Of all of the surviving German capital ships from the encounter, *Seydlitz* had perhaps the luckiest escape. Not only did she come close to foundering on the way home, she had also succeeded in breaking through the British battlefleet to get there.

There were important material weaknesses on the British side, one defensive and one offensive. It is not true that British armour was less effective than that of the Germans; indeed, the evidence suggests that the Royal Navy had the advantage in battleship armour, although the German ships had superior underwater protection. The weakness lay in the battlecruisers. Although the British ships of this type had thinner armour than their German counterparts, they were by no means fragile, with some taking repeated hits by heavy shells yet remaining in action. The critical

failing was in anti-flash protection: while the High Seas Fleet had taken to heart the lesson learned at the Dogger Bank and tightened up procedures, the crews of the British ships tended to shortcut safeguards for handling explosive charges. The result was that a hit in a turret had a high chance of destroying a British battlecruiser, while its German equivalent might lose the turret, but would survive. With proper observation of the established procedures, all of the three British battlecruisers that were lost might have been saved, along with over 3000 lives.

Institutional Failings

Many historians have noted the impact on the outcome of Jutland of institutional failings in the Royal Navy. The argument, made best in Andrew Gordon's masterly book *The Rules of the Game,* is that the long period of peace resulted in the dominance within the Royal Navy of a culture that sapped initiative. The formidable challenges of new technology resulted in excessive centralization and a tendency to play safe and await explicit orders. Such a system was appealing in peacetime, but would inevitably break down under the pressures of war. There were important differences between individual commanders, with Beatty – more like the German Navy – adopting a freer and more decentralized approach, expecting his subordinate captains to show initiative in the pursuit of his broad intentions rather than looking to exercise detailed control over their every action. On the whole, though, the Royal Navy was characterized by centralization and lack of initiative, which contributed to many of the weaknesses at Jutland. Jellicoe contributed to this culture, but was more its victim.

In terms of gunnery, the view that the Royal Navy proved inferior is wrong. The fire of the British battlecruisers tended to be less accurate than the Germans in the early stages of the engagement, but the British battlefleet enjoyed greater success than its opponent. The key British weakness was in defective armour-piercing shells, which at long range often detonated or broke up on hitting armour rather than doing what they were designed to, which was to penetrate the armour before exploding. This flaw, the result of inadequate and unrealistic testing in peacetime, denied the battlefleet the results of its accurate gunfire. Both Scheer and Hipper acknowledged that the poor British shells saved many

The Jutland Controversy

The battle has not only been fiercely debated by disputatious historians, but also resulted in bitter sniping among the British commanders involved and, even more, among their partisans. Beatty came to feel aggrieved about the result of the battle and his admirers insisted that Jellicoe threw away the golden opportunity presented by their hero. In contrast to Jellicoe's dignified restraint, Beatty abused his post-war position as First Sea Lord to establish his opinion as the official version, censoring accounts of the battle that mentioned his errors or praised the role of the battlefleet. The controversy even extended to the *Official History*, with the Admiralty taking the extraordinary step of inserting a note in Julian Corbett's book stating that some of his judgements 'are directly in conflict with their views'. The press took a superficial view, lauding the attractive figure of Beatty, who had always courted them assiduously, rather than the quieter, more austere Jellicoe. Both men had more to be proud of than to regret at Jutland. Strikingly, Beatty insisted, against medical advice, on serving as a pallbearer at Jellicoe's funeral in 1935, hastening his own demise a few months later.

of their ships; with effective shells, it is likely that three more German battlecruisers and two or three battleships would have been sunk.

A number of avoidable errors on the British side also contributed to the indecisive outcome. Greatest among these was the failure of the Admiralty to make effective use of the enormous advantage of signals intelligence. The early error that suggested the German fleet was not at sea inclined Jellicoe to treat later information from the Admiralty with suspicion, while the failure to pass on clear intelligence of Scheer's route home ensured that he would not be

intercepted. The second important mistake was Beatty's failure to ensure that the 5th Battle Squadron was positioned to support his battlecruisers. The earlier participation of this powerful force would probably have saved some or all of the British battlecruisers that were lost, and would have cost Hipper several more of his ships. The third significant failing was in officers repeatedly failing to show the initiative that they should have, either declining to engage the enemy or simply neglecting to pass on to their commander-in-chief information that was clearly critical. For many historians, this weakness was the result of wider organizational weaknesses. On the way home, Beatty amplified his earlier comment, stating, 'There is something wrong with our ships – and something wrong with our system.' He was right on both counts.

Most criticism has been directed against Jellicoe for showing what is claimed to be excessive tactical caution. In fact, he had no great need to take chances, since Britain already had a position of dominance at sea. Moreover, taking a great risk with the fleet would have been unwise, since it would have jeopardized this favourable balance. For his critics, however, taking a limited and calculated risk might have brought about a decisive defeat of the High Seas Fleet. While such an outcome would not have ended the war, it would have produced practical and morale results that might well have shortened it.

Jellicoe was cautious; whether he was too cautious is a fine judgement to make after the event, and there is still nothing approaching a consensus. Churchill exaggerated when he described Jellicoe as the only man on either side who could lose the war in an afternoon, but it must have felt that way to the commander-in-chief. The main problem was that since Scheer was intent on avoiding battle and escaping, there was little that Jellicoe could do to force him to fight at such a disadvantage, particularly with poor visibility and daylight running out.

The popular view at the time, if not that of most Royal Navy officers, was that Jellicoe had let slip a great opportunity. In April 1919, both Jellicoe and Beatty were promoted to Admiral of the Fleet, but then in August Beatty was made an earl while Jellicoe had to be satisfied with the lower rank of viscount. The controversy over the Battle of Jutland escalated further thereafter. Jellicoe had made some errors and Beatty had made more, yet both deserve more credit than blame. The same could be said of the German commanders, and of Hipper most of all, with Scheer showing judgement and determination to extricate his fleet from the trap into which he had led it.

The principal consequence of the Battle of Jutland lay in its impact on the strategy of the two sides. The British approach remained largely unchanged, while the Germans felt compelled to take a dramatic gamble on which the outcome of the whole war depended.

Many of the German battlecruisers and battleships were seriously damaged during the Battle of Jutland, and were only able to put to sea again after months of repairs.

CHAPTER 6

The U-Boats Contained

In 1917, German strategy was not working. Victory seemed no closer on land, while the surface navy had proved incapable of breaking the British blockade, let alone of putting pressure on Britain's war effort. In one last, desperate throw of the dice, Germany turned to unrestricted submarine warfare against merchant shipping.

Before the Battle of Jutland, the German U-boats had switched from operations against commerce to targeting British warships once again, as they had at the beginning of the war. The battle itself did not involve any effective intervention by U-boats, yet in its aftermath, Scheer planned another operation in which they would play a key role.

His plan was similar to the one devised before: the High Seas Fleet would sortie into the North Sea, with eight Zeppelins providing reconnaissance support to ensure that there would be no repeat of May's unpleasant surprise. If the fleet did not encounter a

SMS *Westfalen* was a *Nassau*-class Dreadnought. Whilst participating in the post-Jutland sortie by the High Seas Fleet in August 1916, she was torpedoed and damaged by the British submarine *E23*. Submarines, rather than surface warships, inflicted all of the losses suffered by both sides during this operation.

British warships, but they did not amount to a coherent picture of events. At about 12.30pm, a Zeppelin informed him of a force including capital ships to his south; believing he had succeeded in his aim of isolating part of the Grand Fleet, he abandoned the attack on Sunderland and moved to intercept. In fact, this report turned out to be a misidentification of the Harwich Force light cruisers and destroyers. Disappointing as this must have been, the error was a stroke of good fortune for Scheer, as it meant that he happened to avoid the Grand Fleet and was able to return home safely.

LEFT **Admiral Henning von Holtzendorff, chief of the German naval staff. In 1916 and 1917, he was a keen advocate of unrestricted submarine warfare as Germany's last and best chance to win the war. He was confident that it would defeat Britain in five months, regardless of anything the United States could do. He was forced to resign by ill health in August 1918.**

British force, the battlecruisers would proceed to bombard Sunderland at sunset, returning home overnight, with the aim of drawing out the Grand Fleet into an ambush conducted by 24 U-boats, deployed in five lines. Despite the greater security evident since Jutland, the British were once again aware of the German operation due to the work of Room 40. In response, the Grand Fleet put to sea and, strikingly, the Admiralty deployed 26 submarines to intercept the German force. These drew first blood on the morning of 19 August when *E23* torpedoed the Dreadnought *Westfalen*, which was damaged badly enough to force it to return to port. On the other side, *U52* sank the light cruiser HMS *Nottingham*, and the cruiser *Falmouth* was damaged by *U66* and then finished off by *U63*. Scheer received from U-boats and Zeppelins numerous signals reporting sightings of

The operation is mainly noteworthy because of the participation of no fewer than 50 submarines, which achieved the only successes of the day. Partly as a result, both sides modified their strategy. The Royal Navy now gave to its own submarines the responsibility for patrolling most of the North Sea. Their successes included *E38* damaging the cruiser *München* in October and then in November, *J1* (the first of a new class) torpedoed and damaged the Dreadnoughts *Grosser Kurfürst* and the *Kronprinz*. In April 1918, *E42* damaged the battlecruiser *Moltke*.

For the German part, neither this operation nor another similar one, planned for September but cancelled due to bad weather, did anything to change the unfavourable balance of capital ships. This encouraged the German Navy to advocate that the U-boats be returned to warfare against commerce, waged without restriction. In his July report to the Kaiser on the Battle of Jutland, Scheer argued that while further fleet engagements would damage the Royal Navy, 'even the most successful result from a high-sea battle will not compel England to make peace'; the only way to achieve victory soon was to use U-boats against commerce, and he urged that restrictions be lifted. His views were echoed by other key commanders at a conference in late August 1916. The Chief of the Naval Staff Admiral Henning von Holtzendorff had already advocated a return to unrestricted warfare in February (see Chapter 3) and now pressed it again. Germany and, even more, her allies were in a poor position, he argued, so it was urgent to exploit this powerful weapon. He added that in response to unrestricted attacks, the United States lacked the ability to react

HMS *Nottingham* was a Town-class light cruiser. Commissioned in 1914, she saw action at the Battle of Heligoland Bight, the Scarborough Raid, the Battle of Dogger Bank and the Battle of Jutland. She was torpedoed and sunk by *U52* on 19 August 1916.

effectively while the other neutrals lacked the will and would not go to war unless actually invaded. The civilian members of the government were still unconvinced, believing that there was a considerable risk of provoking war with the United States and with European neutrals, notably Holland and Denmark, at a time when the army was hard pressed by Allied offensives and could not spare any reserves to deal with new enemies. This argument helped to sway the new head of the army, Field Marshal Paul von Hindenburg, who otherwise supported the navy proposal. The conference ended with a decision to postpone any resumption of unrestricted warfare, though in the interim a limited campaign, conducted according to prize rules, would be resumed in British waters from the beginning of October.

THE CAMPAIGN AGAINST COMMERCE RESUMED IN EARNEST

By the time the campaign reopened, the U-boat force had improved in both quantity and quality. By October 1916, the total number of U-boats had grown to 96 including, in the Flanders Flotilla, larger and longer-range boats (the UB-II and UC-II types), which were capable of operating beyond the Channel and into the Atlantic. The new campaign focused on the western approaches to Britain but also involved boats being sent to the Mediterranean, with others deployed against British convoys to Russia, and even saw one U-boat, *U53*, attacking shipping off the coast of the United States. Hence, although the U-boats generally obeyed prize rules (with the exception of the sinking of some passenger ships without warning), losses to merchant shipping quickly climbed to a figure higher than August 1915, the worst previous month (all figures for losses are from Tarrant, V.E. *The U-Boat Offensive 1914–1945*). Total tonnage sunk climbed from 165,720 tonnes (163,100 tons) in August 1916 to 235,215 tonnes (231,500 tons) in

September, and over 346,775 tonnes (341,300 tons) in October. There was a slight fall in November and December to 331,840 tonnes (326,600 tons) and 312,740 tonnes (307,800 tons) respectively. These figures, high though they are, understate the disruption caused to commerce, as many more ships were damaged and required long repairs, while many neutral shipping owners opted to keep their ships in port. Meanwhile, Allied anti-submarine efforts were still largely ineffective, sinking fewer U-boats than were being added by new construction.

The UC boats were coastal minelayers that operated from bases in occupied Belgium as part of the Flanders Flotilla. The UC-II type (shown here), mostly built in 1916, were a considerable advance on the UC-I, with several times the range and the ability to carry 50 per cent more mines.

In October, 24 destroyers were detached from the High Seas Fleet to operate in support of the Flanders U-boats by mounting hit-and-run attacks on the light forces patrolling the Dover barrage. Several of these operations were conducted – for example, one on 26 October sank one British destroyer and six patrol craft. More noteworthy, on 4 November, when two U-boats ran aground and called for help, Scheer sent an impressive force to assist them, including the battlecruisers, the 3rd Battle Squadron of the High Seas Fleet and a flotilla of destroyers. Alerted by Room 40, British submarines were sent in, resulting in the damaging of two German Dreadnoughts by *J1* (mentioned previously). The Kaiser criticized the decision to risk a battle squadron to save two U-boats, saying that it 'showed a lack of a sense of proportion and must not occur again'. Scheer, though, persuaded him that it was right to use the surface fleet to support the U-boats. It is striking how far German naval strategy had changed from the start of the war, when the U-boats were seen as a supporting arm to assist the battlefleet; this had now been reversed.

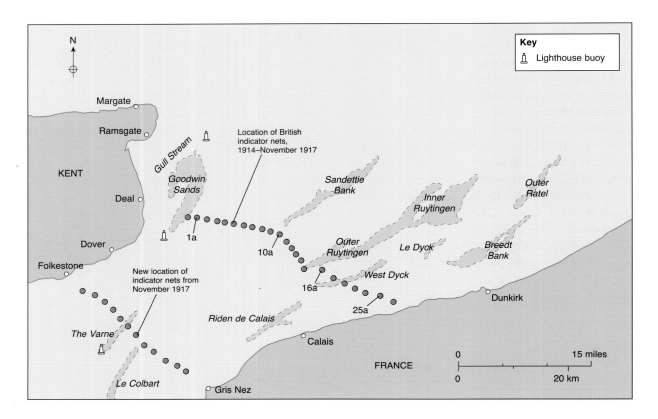

The Dover Straits and the location of the British indicator nets. During 1918 the Dover Barrage, which had previously been rather ineffective, improved hugely and genuinely became a serious impediment to U-boats, to the extent that they were compelled to stop using the most direct route to the Atlantic.

UNRESTRICTED WARFARE RECONSIDERED

The success of this renewed campaign against commerce encouraged the military and naval leadership to press for the lifting of all remaining restrictions. On 22 December, Holtzendorff submitted a further, carefully argued paper, based on painstaking statistical analysis. He concluded that Germany needed to win the war before the end of 1917 and should do so by targeting the British economy, which was sustaining the Allies as a whole. He set a target of sinking 610,000 tonnes (600,000 tons) of British shipping per month, which he believed would also deter two-fifths of neutral shipping from trading with Britain. The effect would be to limit war production, to make it very difficult for Britain to continue overseas military operations and, eventually, to force her to seek peace. Thus, if restrictions were lifted, he calculated, Britain would be defeated in five months.

The German Army, which in September had opposed resuming unrestricted operations, now withdrew its objections. Allied offensives by Britain, Romania and Russia had been contained, freeing reserves to counter any moves by European neutrals to enter the war. More broadly, though, army commanders were as aware as their navy colleagues that the war was not going well, especially for Germany's allies, Austria and Bulgaria. Furthermore, the British blockade was having an increasingly serious impact. Although priority allocation of resources and food ensured that the armed forces were well supplied, the German population was undoubtedly suffering from shortages of food and fuel; many died during the winter of 1916/17, and morale was tumbling.

A strong argument against lifting restrictions on U-boat attacks had been the risk of provoking the United States into entering the war, but assessments of this had changed. Some German leaders were sceptical that the United States, under the idealistic President Woodrow Wilson, would actually declare war, since previous provocations had resulted in much hot air, but little else. Military commanders pointed out that the United States had done nothing to improve the readiness for war of its small armed forces. Besides, the calculation was that the U-boats would knock Britain out of the war before the United States could mobilize and intervene effectively, and its forces could also be attacked when crossing the Atlantic. Given the overall situation of the war, the possibility of the United States joining the Allies was no longer allowed to prevent a decision to unleash the U-boats.

At the General Headquarters conference on 9 January 1917, Chancellor Bethmann Hollweg continued to resist unrestricted submarine warfare, but reluctantly went along with the united front of the navy and the army. The Kaiser was persuaded, and approved the end of all restrictions from 1 February 1917. All shipping, Allied and neutral, would be sunk without warning around the British Isles and well out into the Atlantic, as well as in most of Mediterranean. In a departure from previous practice, designed to increase the psychological impact, the policy was to be announced only the day before it came into effect.

U53 **entered service in April 1916 and survived to the end of the war. After 1916, German construction resources were diverted away from surface ships and towards U-boats. The result was a rapid expansion in the U-boat force.**

This was a truly momentous decision. Previously, German strategy had focused on achieving victory through operations on land. Now, however, the Imperial German Navy was to move to centre stage, though in another reversal of the previous policy, it was the U-boat force rather than the battlefleet that was to play the starring role.

The reaction from the United States was, eventually, just as the more pessimistic voices in the leadership had predicted. The United States broke off diplomatic relations with Germany on 3 February, two days after the resumption of unrestricted warfare, though for a while still hesitated to join the war. Finally, the remaining anti-war sentiment in the United States was swept aside by a combination of further sinkings without warning of American merchant ships in February and March and then by the Zimmermann telegram. This disastrous diplomatic manoeuvre, described in Chapter 2, saw the German Government seek to entice Mexico to declare war on the United States in return for an alliance, subsidies and territorial gains from the southern states. The telegram making the offer was intercepted by Room 40 and passed to the United States Government, which released it to a furious public reaction. On 6 April 1917, the United States finally declared war on Germany. However, by then the predictions of German advocates of unrestricted warfare – that Britain would be defeated before the United States could intervene decisively – seemed likely to be vindicated.

At the beginning of the new, unrestricted campaign the number of operational U-boats had risen to 111,

The British merchantman SS *City of Glasgow* sinks in the Irish Sea after being torpedoed by a German U-boat, 4 September 1918. The crew were rescued by the USS *Beale*, which was one of the US Navy destroyers operating from Queenstown.

and rose further to 120 in April. There was also an increase in the number being built; tellingly, work ceased on two new battleships and four battlecruisers to increase the effort devoted to U-boat construction. Losses had already been high before the lifting of restrictions and they now grew ever worse: 528,750 tonnes (520,400 tons) in February 1917, 573,558 tonnes (564,500 tons) in March and then over 874,105 tonnes (860,300 tons) in April. This was the worst figure of any month in either of the two world wars. In the first three months of this unrestricted campaign, almost two million tonnes of merchant shipping had been sunk and another 3235,315 tonnes (320,000 tons) were removed from use due to damage. Much neutral shipping was held back in port for fear of attack. The effect was gradually strangling Britain, causing shortages in key raw materials, fuel (resulting in the operations of the Grand Fleet having to be curtailed) and even food. During this period, nine U-boats were sunk but 13 new ones were completed. This level of losses was quite simply unsustainable: either some solution to the U-boat threat had to be found or Britain would be forced out of the war, with fatal consequences for the Allies.

COUNTERMEASURES

There were changes at the top of the Admiralty in December 1916, with Admiral Jellicoe becoming First Sea Lord (replaced by Beatty as commander of the Grand Fleet). Reflecting the urgency of the problem, he set up a new Anti-Submarine Division in the Naval Staff, under Rear Admiral Sir Alexander Duff, to bring together and coordinate all of the many different bodies trying to counter the threat.

Some progress had been made with counter-measures. Greater numbers of anti-submarine vessels were now available and the urgent programmes to design means of detecting and attacking submerged U-boats started to bear fruit. By the middle of 1916, anti-submarine vessels began to be fitted with hydrophones (underwater microphones) to detect U-boats and depth charges to attack them. Depth charges achieved their first success in sinking a U-boat in March 1916. However, the early versions available were very limited

President Woodrow Wilson was an idealist, and extremely reluctant to see the United States become involved in a European war. Despite repeated warning to Germany over U-boat attacks against neutral ships and passenger vessels, he delayed declaring war until April 1917.

in their utility, not least due to the requirement that they detonate extremely close to a U-boat to destroy or damage it. The main difficulty, though, lay in the limited supply of depth charges: at the beginning of 1917, an anti-submarine vessel would typically carry just two, which was hopelessly inadequate for the task. By 1918, stocks had increased to a level where a ship could carry as many as 50. By then, the charges could also be set for a wider range of depths, and would be dropped in patterns rather than singly, improving the chance of hitting the target. Ships were also fitted with improved launchers, which could drop charges over the sides as well as over the stern.

As well as new technologies becoming available, further progress was made with existing ones. There were high hopes for submarines as U-boat hunters, not least because they would be more difficult than a warship for the target to spot, and British submarines increased their patrols accordingly. There were some successes, but fewer than hoped because the British submarines found it difficult to locate U-boats, particularly when they changed tactics and began attacking by night. The Admiralty designed a faster submarine, the R class, precisely to hunt U-boats, but it came into service too late to have any impact.

Aircraft also saw considerable advances. Greater numbers of more capable aircraft became available and performed valuable service, especially as aircrew training improved and serviceable if rather unreliable wireless sets were provided. Yet they were hindered by their limited endurance and range, which left the principal U-boat operating areas beyond their reach, and by their lack of an effective weapon, which meant that U-boats could escape by simply diving when they spotted an aircraft. Some sources credit aircraft with sinking just a single U-boat during the entire war and even the more generous accounts mention only four or five, which was a modest return for the resources expended. Nevertheless, these figures do not capture the wider effect of aircraft which, even if they did not sink a sighted U-boat, could force it to dive, running down its batteries and reducing its endurance, or call up warships to make more effective attacks.

Depth charges being launched from the after deck of a US destroyer. Later on in the war, anti-submarine weapons increased not only in numbers but also in quality, which included the ability to launch depth charges rather than simply dropping them over the stern of the ship.

The effort devoted to the U-boat threat extended to administrative measures to increase the availability of merchant shipping. A State Insurance Scheme subsidized insurance, which would otherwise have become prohibitively expensive. Old ships were bought from neutrals and production was expanded, despite the fact that this required the diversion of thousands of ship-building workers from the armed forces and steel from war production, as well as reducing the building of warships. The fact that three planned British battlecruisers and five light cruisers were scrapped to allow more merchant ship construction is a striking sign of the changing priorities of the war at sea. It was an impressive effort, but could not come close to replacing losses.

CONVOY RECONSIDERED

A more fundamental change was needed. Inevitably, the question of convoy and escort was raised once again. Familiar arguments were trotted out against it: merchant ships of differing speeds could not keep together, and would drop out of a convoy; independent sailings were preferable to bringing the U-boats' targets together and thus making their job easier; there were not enough escorts available to protect convoys; and ports would be clogged up by multiple ships arriving all at once. Thus, in November 1916 and again in January 1917, the possibility of

The R class of the Royal Navy (to which *R7*, shown here, belonged) was an imaginative concept: a fast submarine specifically designed to hunt and sink other submarines. They came into service too late in the war to have a significant impact. Many years later, anti-submarine warfare would become a major part of a submarine's duties.

introducing convoy was reconsidered, only to be rejected again. The unfavourable opinion regarding convoy was not confined to a few hidebound old admirals at the top of the service, but was rather the view of the great majority of naval officers.

There were some, however, who believed that it offered useful prospects for success and, crucially, others who were open to persuasion when evidence became available to suggest that a rethink was in order. A key development occurred in January 1917, when a system of convoy was introduced for ships transporting coal from Britain to France, which had been suffering terribly from U-boat attacks. This was self-evidently a critical raw material, while the relatively small scale of the enterprise and the short distances involved made an experiment practicable. These ships were organized into convoys between January and April 1917 and the result was dramatic, with losses tumbling to less than one-fifth of one per cent of colliers making the journey, despite their travelling through the English Channel, where U-boats patrolled intensively. Other tentative experiments with convoys between Britain and Holland and between Britain and Norway offered similarly encouraging conclusions.

As a result of this mounting body of evidence, Admiral Duff of the Anti-Submarine Division changed his mind and recommended that convoy should be brought in for all shipping. He received support from other officers (as well as from politicians, though the change in the Admiralty position pre-dated the intervention of Prime Minister David Lloyd George, who subsequently claimed credit for the new policy). Duff in turn persuaded Jellicoe, who on 27 April set up the Convoy Committee and

ordered another experiment. On 10 May, a group of 16 merchant ships departed from Gibraltar in a convoy, escorted by three armed yachts and two Q-ships, supplemented by an additional eight destroyers when it reached the most likely area of U-boat operations. The convoy arrived in Britain on 20 May, without having lost a single ship. A further test was undertaken a few days later, with a convoy of 12 merchant ships from Hampton Roads on the east coast of the United States. One ship fell behind and was sunk, but the rest arrived safely in Britain. The striking success of these experiments led to further use of convoys in June and July: a total of 354 ships, of which only two were lost, were convoyed across the Atlantic in these months.

The introduction of convoy was by no means a magic bullet, and losses remained high. There was a large fall from April's peak to 626,190 tonnes (616,300 tons) lost in May, but this was due to a reduction in

Germany continued to the end of the war to use armed merchant vessels as auxiliary raiders (such as this one) against Allied commerce. *Möwe* was the most successful of these, capturing 38 Allied merchant vessels, though on the whole their achievements were modest in comparison to those of the U-boats.

the number of U-boats at sea after a peak of effort rather than to the effect of convoy, which was still at an early stage. In June, losses rose again to 707,880 tonnes (696,700 tons). Thereafter, however, although the figures fluctuated, the trend was clearly downwards: 564,415 tonnes (555,500 tons) in July, 479,880 tonnes (472,300 tons) in August, 359,274 tonnes (353,600 tons) in September and 307,455 tonnes (302,600 tons) in November. In December, losses increased to over 417,595 tonnes (411,000 tons), but thereafter fell back again. In May 1918, they were reduced to below 304,815 tonnes (300,000 tons) and only rose above that figure once more, in August. The downward trend concealed a statistic that was in some ways still more significant: the daily tonnage sunk per U-boat at sea was also falling, meaning that they were becoming less effective. This was crucial, because through the summer of 1917, the number of operational U-boats continued to rise, including several larger 'U-cruisers', which could operate still further out into the Atlantic. A key milestone was reached in October 1917, when the number of U-boats sunk first exceeded new construction. Shipping losses were still grievous, but at least the trends were finally moving in the right direction for the Allies.

Why did convoy have such a dramatic, albeit not instant, effect? Several of the arguments that had been used against convoy turned out to be simply wrong, such as the alleged inability of merchant ships to keep station. Others were disproved by re-examining the evidence. For example, it had been thought that large groups of merchant vessels would be more vulnerable than individual sailings to mines, but in practice the reverse was true, since their escorts benefited from the latest information about the location of minefields and could therefore redirect the convoy around the danger. It had also been objected that there was no way

'The submarine was a weapon adopted by every nation. This gave Germany the right to use it in any manner to which it was best adapted. Any use of it which did not take this into account would not make sense.'

Admiral Scheer, 1920

that any system of convoy could possibly cope with all of the 5000-plus ships entering or leaving British ports each week. In fact, however, it was realized that this figure encompassed all ships, including very small vessels and ones making purely local journeys; the most important, large ocean-going ships actually amounted to a far more manageable figure of about 140 each week. This also meant that fewer escorting warships would be needed than had been feared.

Some arguments used against convoy were foolish, notably that it was a 'defensive' activity, unworthy of the proud offensive tradition of the Royal Navy. In fact, by forcing the enemy to come to the warships accompanying the convoy, it solved the critical problem of locating U-boats in the vastness of the oceans, and in that sense it permitted truly offensive action. Moreover, this objection quite misunderstood the principal purpose of anti-submarine operations, which was not to sink U-boats – though this was a highly desirable secondary objective, not least in eliminating experienced commanders and crews – but rather to protect ships. If a convoy reached its destination without being located and effectively attacked, the defenders had achieved their aim, even if no U-boats were destroyed. Conversely, the 'offensive' alternative of hunting for submarines proved ineffective, as the whole rationale for using U-boats was that they were difficult to locate.

The main reason for the success of convoy was not that it permitted the sinking of U-boats, but rather that it denied them the opportunity to attack merchant ships. This key advantage of convoy was demonstrated by the 10 May experiment mentioned previously: the convoy did not encounter a single U-boat on its voyage from Gibraltar to Britain. This was not sheer chance, but rather a reflection of the low probability of a U-boat locating a convoy. Quite

USS *Arkansas*, a *Wyoming*-class battleship commissioned in 1912. In 1918 she became part of the US Navy force that served with the Grand Fleet of the Royal Navy as the 6th Battle Squadron. She was not involved in any battles, but was one of the Allied warships guarding the German High Seas Fleet as it steamed into internment.

contrary to fears that convoys would provide U-boats with a gift by gathering their prey together, the experience of their commanders was that the seas suddenly seemed empty. The Admiralty realized that there was little more chance of a U-boat sighting 20, 30 or even 40 merchant ships in a convoy than of it sighting one single ship – and far less chance of it doing so than of sighting one among 20, 30 or 40 independently travelling vessels. If the U-boat did strike it lucky and spot a convoy, it might only get one chance to attack all of the ships together, rather than stalking them one at a time, and would swiftly come under counterattack by the escorting warships.

Convoy did not have a rapid impact, as it took some time to organize and introduce. It was gradually extended to new routes and new areas, partly in response to changes in the patrol patterns of U-boats, which relocated to waters where convoy was not used.

Initially, the Admiralty concentrated on ships heading to Britain, since they were carrying cargo, and by August 1917, all inward-bound oceanic shipping was protected by convoys. U-boat attacks shifted to attacking outbound ships, since even destroying them without a valuable cargo would prevent them from carrying goods in the future, reducing Britain's shipping resources. By September, this vulnerability was closed off by convoying all outbound shipping too. In October, the extension of convoy to much shipping in the Mediterranean began to stem the high losses there. The following month, experiments began with using convoy for coastal shipping too, both for local traffic and for longer-distance ships that used coastal waters before convoys were formed or after they had dispersed. Once again, the results of the early experiments were so impressive that it was extended, though the number of vessels involved meant that the system was not fully comprehensive until June 1918.

The immediate impact of convoy was also reduced by the shortage of escorts and by their lack of adequate numbers of depth charges. The former problem could have been eased by the greater number of destroyers available with the United States entering the war and with Japan sending a squadron to the Mediterranean. The Royal Navy even detached some destroyers from the Grand Fleet for anti-submarine warfare, in the full knowledge that this would hinder the operations of the battlefleet. These ships were not generally used in support of convoys, however. Many in the navy still clung to the futile practice of offensive patrolling, which continued to absorb a high proportion of the efforts of anti-submarine vessels even after the introduction of convoy. In particular, the fastest destroyers that would have been best able to hunt down U-boats near convoys were wasted in this fashion. There were attempts to make patrolling more effective, such as focussing patrols ahead of the routes of convoys, but this was of little use, since any U-boat could simply submerge until the warships had moved

on. The continuing faith in offensive patrolling was bizarre, since it was not backed by any evidence. Indeed, the available evidence showed that it was utterly ineffective. In mid-June 1917, for example, a major anti-submarine offensive was undertaken north of Scotland, involving a huge effort by a large number of warships. It resulted in 61 sightings of U-boats and 12 attacks, but no damage was inflicted, let alone any sinkings. Better and faster results would have been achieved by strengthening the escort forces of convoys rather than having valuable anti-submarine vessels tearing purposelessly over empty seas.

Shipping losses to U-boats in World War 1. The chart clearly shows the peak of the sinkings in April 1917, as well as the fact that although losses dipped substantially thereafter, they remained uncomfortably high.

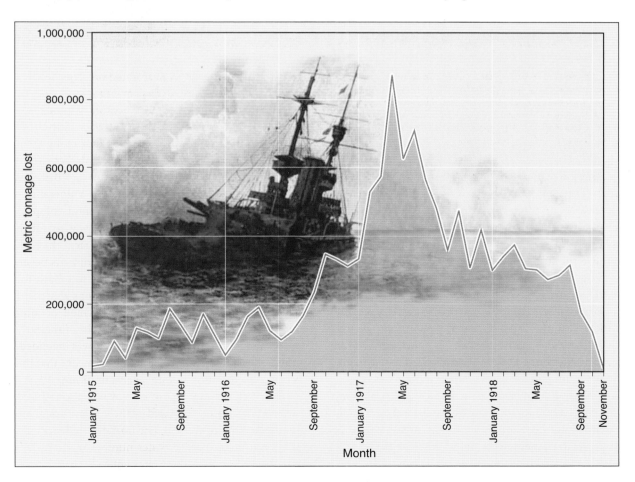

The United States Enters the War

Although it took some time for United States participation in the war to take effect, it was decisive. At sea, it immediately resulted in the release for Allied use of interned merchant shipping belonging to the Central Powers, and brought in the United States Navy, with its destroyers particularly welcome. It added the United States construction capacity for merchant vessels and warships, as well as for munitions. For the war more broadly, it strengthened the Allies diplomatically, and encouraged other former neutrals to follow suit. Most important of all, it added fresh armies to the Allied cause and, due to the improvement of anti-submarine warfare capabilities, the U-boats failed utterly in their crucial role of preventing these forces from crossing the Atlantic. The unrestricted U-boat campaign not only failed to bring Germany victory, it also hastened her defeat.

The long-threatened American declaration of war on Germany changed the shape of the conflict and also played a major role in shaping the subsequent peace.

Besides the introduction of convoy, other factors contributed to the growing success against the U-boats. First, changes within the Admiralty improved the integration of Room 40 within the rest of the Intelligence Division. This allowed signals intelligence to be better exploited, notably information from triangulating the direction of signals and from intercepted messages that revealed the general location of U-boats. Such information could be used to divert convoys away from danger, further reducing the chances of a U-boat locating them.

Second, the considerable effort devoted to laying mines off German bases and along the narrow chokepoints through which the U-boats had to travel began to produce better results. This was largely due to the fact that in spring 1917, Britain finally developed an effective mine for use against submarines, the Mark H, by reverse-engineering a recovered German one. This was followed in 1918 by another mine that could be laid in deeper water. Over 15,000 mines were laid in the Heligoland Bight in 1917 and another 21,000 in 1918. These caused losses and inconvenience,

demanding an enormous German effort for sweeping, yet not enough to seriously reduce U-boat operations. The Dover barrage was also significantly improved, a point to which we shall return.

Third, strenuous efforts were made in non-military affairs to support the anti-submarine effort. Intensive diplomacy brought back into service some of the neutral tonnage that had initially been scared into staying in port. Administrative measures sought to make better use of resources through rationing, as well as increasing domestic food production and restricting imports to the most essential war materials, to free up cargo space. Ships were also reallocated from longer journeys to shorter ones, to squeeze every bit of additional efficiency from the available merchant tonnage. These policies would not have been enough on their own, but they helped to reduce the impact of the German campaign. Indeed, Vice Admiral Arthur Hezlet argued that it was the relatively uncredited activity by the government at home and diplomatically that was the real key to victory, since it bought precious time for the convoy system to spread and take effect.

Finally, the entry of the United States brought its formidable industrial resources to the Allied powers. These produced additional merchant ships and also the large numbers of guns for merchant ships, depth charges and mines that were so badly needed. The United States Navy also contributed growing numbers of anti-submarine vessels – indeed, the awareness that these were about to join the campaign helped to tip the argument within the Admiralty in favour of convoy. The United States Navy shared the obsession of their British ally with offensive patrolling in preference to convoy and escort, but their warships were nonetheless a welcome addition. In May 1917, the first six arrived at Queenstown in Ireland. By the end of August, a total of 35 United States Navy destroyers were based there.

Convoy and escort: the powerful Dreadnoughts of the battlefleet provided indirect support to merchant shipping by preventing enemy heavy warships from breaking out. It was the small escorts, though, that accompanied the convoys on the high seas and protected them from U-boat attack.

The introduction and gradual expansion of the convoy system therefore presented a huge challenge to the U-boat campaign. The outcome of the war would turn on whether the German commanders could devise an effective response. A number were tried. Attacks were concentrated on the significant number of independent sailings. The U-boats also repeatedly changed the focus of their efforts to areas where convoy had not yet been introduced. As noted above, they targeted shipping leaving Britain, and when this gap was plugged they switched away from the Western Approaches to concentrate on the North Sea, the Channel and the Bay of Biscay. As more routes came under the convoy system, they changed tactics to attack in coastal waters. These adaptations help to explain why losses remained so high for so long, yet U-boat successes were on a downward trend as the convoy system expanded.

There were two other ways in which the German Navy might have adapted its tactics to counter convoy, rather than simply persisting in the familiar approach.

A convoy at sea. The convoy-and-escort system was long resisted by many naval officers, but when finally introduced it had impressive effects. When the German Navy failed to find a way to counter it, the U-boats could not deliver the anticipated knock-out blow against Britain.

First, it could have matched the concentration of targets and escorts with its own concentration, by having U-boats attack convoys in groups rather than individually. Such a technique could both overwhelm the escorts of a convoy and also permit the sinking of many or even all of its merchant ships, rather than just one or two as might be achieved by a single U-boat that had the good fortune to happen upon a convoy and evade its escorts. This approach would be followed to great effect by 'wolf packs' in World War II. It was suggested in 1917, but, surprisingly, was not tried until mid-May 1918, when a dozen U-boats concentrated in the Western Approaches. Two were lost (one rammed by a troop ship, one sunk by the British submarine *D4*) in exchange for sinking four merchant ships – a figure which seems even less impressive when set against the fact that nearly 300 merchant ships were convoyed either to or from Britain in this period.

The second way in which German naval strategy could have adapted would have been to seek a better coordination of surface and U-boat operations, rather than having them act largely separately. This is not to say that individual engagements could have been coordinated, which would have been too demanding given the limitations in U-boats' speed and ability to

communicate with surface warships. Rather, a greater effort to send out squadrons of surface units to attack convoys might have overwhelmed their escorts, which tended to be very light forces capable only of taking on U-boats. There were some isolated examples of such operations. On 15 October 1917, two fast light cruisers, *Brummer* and *Bremse*, evaded British forces chasing them and fell on a convoy between Scotland and Norway. They sank the two escorting destroyers and nine of the 12 merchant ships in the convoy. Later, on 11–12 December, four fast destroyers repeated the operation, sinking one escort and driving off the other before sinking all six of the merchant ships present. As a result, heavier forces were deployed to provide distant cover for such convoys. There were also operations by surface raiders in the form of converted merchants,

'As English economic life depended on sea trade, the only means of getting at it was to overcome the [British] fleet, or get past it. The former meant the destruction of the [German] fleet…The U-boats, however, could get past the [British] fleet.'

Admiral Scheer, 1920

including ships that became famous, such as the *Möwe*, *Wolf*, *Seeadler* and *Leopard*. They captured and sank ships, disrupted trade and laid mines even as far away as New Zealand, but their efforts were tiny in comparison to those of the U-boats, with which their operations were not coordinated. The main difficulty with conducting surface operations was that they risked being intercepted by more powerful British forces. While this might provide the opportunity for the German Navy to defeat a locally inferior force, its earlier efforts to achieve such a situation had come close to disaster, and induced a degree of caution.

THE LATER STAGES OF THE U-BOAT WAR

The German response to the introduction and expansion of the convoy system was therefore a combination of seeking out the remaining weak points and also attempting to put as many U-boats to sea as possible. This approach still enjoyed much success, though losses of merchant ships continued to

fall, and by April 1918 it dipped below the level of new Allied construction. Conversely, U-boats were being destroyed faster than they were being built, a trend worsened in its effect on the German Navy by the loss of experienced crews. The U-boat campaign had therefore failed to bring about the anticipated and much-heralded victory – which in turn helped to increase popular disillusionment with the war – while the impact of the United States, which it had brought into the war, was growing. Moreover, the British blockade continued to bite ever harder, having a greater if slower and quieter impact than the U-boat campaign, causing huge damage to popular morale in Germany. The failure of unrestricted submarine warfare to bring about the rapid defeat of Britain placed additional pressure on German land commanders to undertake a major, last-gasp offensive before the full weight of potential United States military power could be brought to bear. The failure of this campaign too brought the end of the war still nearer.

The Allies continued to seek ways to reduce losses further. While many of the more capable anti-submarine vessels were still frittered away on pointless patrols, there were improvements in other aspects of the effort against the U-boats.

Intercepts from Room 40 finally succeeded in overturning the strongly held belief that the Channel barrage was effective. In fact, despite the enormous resources and effort devoted to it, the barrage was simply not working. From 1915 to 1917, it was responsible for sinking just three U-boats, with one more possibly sunk. In November 1917, Rear Admiral Keyes, the former commander of the Harwich Force and chief of staff at the Dardanelles, who was now Director of Plans, produced a highly critical report on the barrage. As a result, in January 1918 he was appointed to the Dover Command as a vice admiral to put his proposals into practice. First, improved minefields were laid across the Channel, between Folkestone and Cap Gris-Nez. Unlike previous attempts to mine these waters, the Royal Navy now had improved mines in far greater numbers. Moreover, the mines were now laid at varying depths and were supported by more patrolling warships, to prevent U-boats from transiting on the surface in order to avoid the mines, and by searchlights and flares to prevent them from doing so by night. The German Navy made some attempts to target the patrolling vessels with hit-and-run attacks by fast

OPPOSITE PAGE **A depth charge exploding. As more escorts were put into service by the Allies, and as depth charges became available in ever greater numbers, losses of U-boats rose dramatically, exceeding the rate of new construction.**

BELOW **A torpedo being launched off Dover by HMS** *Broke*. **On 20 April 1917, a group of German destroyers sought to support the U-boat campaign with an attack on British forces patrolling the Dover barrage. Two destroyer flotilla leaders, HMS** *Broke* **and HMS** *Swift***, intercepted them, sinking two German vessels,** *G42* **and** *G85***.**

Causes of U-Boat Sinkings

In total, some 178 U-boats were sunk during the war. Of these, 37 were lost to unknown causes and 19 to accidents. In terms of enemy action, 47 were sunk by warships (16 by ramming, the rest by guns or depth charges), 18 by submarines, 11 by Q-ships, six by merchant ships (either by ramming or gunfire), two by paravane (an explosive towed device) and one each by explosive sweep, mine net, indicator net and seaplane. Mines accounted for 34 losses, although this might well understate their success, since 17 of the sinkings attributed to 'unknown causes' are presumed to have been due to hitting enemy mines. If correct, this would raise the figure for mines to 51 U-boats sunk. Perhaps most striking is the small figure credited to aircraft, which would be very different to their contribution in World War II.

USS *San Diego*, a *Pennsylvania*-class armoured cruiser, was commissioned in 1907. In July 1918, she was torpedoed and sunk by a U-boat, becoming the biggest warship lost by the United States Navy during its involvement in World War I.

warships, such as on 14 February 1918, when eight patrol ships were sunk. That such raids were undertaken was a testament to the effectiveness of the improved barrier. Several U-boats were sunk and, perhaps more importantly, from mid-February the U-boats of the High Seas Fleet gave up attempting to pass through the Channel, instead taking the longer route around the north of Scotland, which reduced their time on station.

The English Channel was exceptional, however, being a choke point that was both shallow and very narrow – only 32km (20 miles) across. Techniques that were successful here could not necessarily be used to similar effect elsewhere. Jellicoe conceived an attempt to create a mine barrier to interfere with the northern route into the Atlantic. The 'Northern Barrage' was a remarkably ambitious project that envisaged mining over 400km (250 miles) of deep water between the Orkneys and the coast of Norway. Much effort was devoted to this operation, with more than 70,000

mines being laid (four-fifths by the United States), but it had little impact. Another idea was to replicate the Channel barrage in the Mediterranean with a barrier across the Strait of Otranto, directed against U-boats operating from Austrian bases on the Adriatic. This idea failed, partly due to the fact that the deeper water here allowed U-boats to avoid nets and mines by diving beneath them. Indeed, it was worse than useless, since it diverted the efforts of many patrol vessels that might otherwise have been giving more valuable service escorting convoys, which had been introduced in the Mediterranean in October 1917.

Admiral Keyes also concocted a bold plan that sought to take the battle to the bases of the Flanders Flotilla with an amphibious operation against Zeebrugge and Ostend. The aim was to block the exits to the sea from these ports of U-boats and their supporting destroyers based at Bruges, linked to the ports by a canal. The operation was carried out on 23 April 1918 and was largely unsuccessful; it is covered in detail in the next chapter.

By June 1918, the last of the major vulnerabilities of merchant shipping was finally closed off, as nearly all coastal vessels were now in convoy. Indeed, convoying proved even more effective in coastal waters than on the oceans, because aircraft could be used to escort convoys travelling close to home. As elsewhere, the effect of aircraft was less in sinking U-boats than in making their operations more difficult. The U-boats thereafter increasingly tended to attack at night to avoid aircraft, which also helped them to evade escorting surface ships and was a technique that would be generally adopted in the next world war. They moved their area of operation outside Britain's coastal waters, back to the Western Approaches. Between May and October, there was even a minor campaign in American waters, mainly waged by long-range minelayers. They sank the armoured cruiser USS *San Diego*, damaged the battleship *Minnesota* and sank some 111,765 tonnes (111,000 tons) of shipping. Nevertheless, this campaign was more a late gesture of defiance than an effective operation of war.

In August 1918, Admiral Holtzendorff resigned as Chief of the Naval Staff due to ill health, and was replaced by Admiral Scheer, who in turn was replaced

as commander of the High Seas Fleet by Admiral Hipper. By this time, the unrestricted U-boat campaign championed by Scheer had evidently failed. In October 1918, a new German government approached United States President Wilson to seek an armistice, and one of the pre-conditions he demanded before negotiations was an end to attacks on passenger liners. Scheer resisted this, believing that they should be continued as a way of pressuring the Allies, keeping up popular morale in Germany and improving the terms of peace offered. He agreed to the suspension of

HMS *Britannia* sinking. This pre-Dreadnought became the last major warship to fall victim to a U-boat in the war, when she was torpedoed on 9 November 1918 by *UB50*, a coastal U-boat from the German Mediterranean flotilla.

Two Different Campaigns

The campaigns waged by and against the U-boats were quite different in the two world wars, beyond the obvious advances in technology. In World War I, the U-boats had to make long and difficult voyages to reach their patrol areas, whereas in World War II, Germany built bases in Norway and on the west coast of occupied France. In World War II, there was never any question of limiting U-boat operations due to international law. Moreover, better communications allowed them to operate in 'wolf packs', gathering together to attack rather than doing so individually – though this practice also gave more material to the successors of Room 40. The Allies took up convoy from the start of World War II and believed that Asdic (sonar) had solved the detection problem. However, U-boat attacks at night and on the surface caused great difficulties until radar became widely available. Aircraft played a far greater role in the second anti-U-boat campaign, especially longer-range aircraft and those travelling with the convoys in escort carriers. The balance of advantage shifted to anti-submarine warfare, and the U-boat threat was eventually defeated far more comprehensively in the second world war than in the first.

A sinking U-boat. In total, 178 U-boats were sunk during the war, with mines being the leading cause. A similar number, 176, were surrendered to the Allies as a condition of the armistice that ended hostilities.

such attacks, subject to it being matched by concessions in easing the British blockade. Yet with collapse nearing – indeed, the Flanders Flotilla ceased to exist in mid-October as its bases were abandoned in front of the advancing Allies – the German Government was in no position to make any such demand and it ordered a reimposition of prize rules. As he had done before, Scheer reasoned that the campaign against commerce could not now be successful, and recalled the U-boats on 21 October.

Scheer intended to include a force of 22 U-boats in his planned final sortie of the High Seas Fleet at the end of October but the operation was cancelled due to widespread mutinies among the crews of the surface warships. Despite the long and difficult campaign they had waged, and, all the more, given the increased dangers, higher losses and frustrating lack of success of the last few months, it is striking that the U-boat arm did not experience mutinies. Indeed, it was a U-boat that achieved Germany's last naval success of the war, on 9 November, when, off Cape Trafalgar, *UB50* torpedoed the pre-Dreadnought HMS *Britannia*.

Despite the symbolism of this event, the U-boats had failed to win the war for Germany, even though they had demonstrated that Britannia no longer ruled the waves. The surviving U-boats were either interned in neutral ports, scuttled or surrendered to the Allies.

CONCLUSION

The Treaty of Versailles (1919) placed limits on the total size of the German surface fleet, but specifically singled out submarines as a military capability that was prohibited to Germany. The Allies were evidently well aware of which arm had posed the greater threat. The U-boat campaign was the closest thing to a war-winning weapon that Germany devised, and although it was defeated, the result was for some time in the balance, with Britain in a truly perilous position. Had the U-boat force been larger at the beginning of the conflict, or had the shackles of international law been thrown off at an earlier stage, the war's outcome might well have been different.

The impact of the U-boat campaign suggested that a fundamental change had taken place in naval strategy. Contrary to the ideas of historians such as Mahan, a navy that was inferior in the traditional terms of the battlefleet had nonetheless come close to achieving victory through a commercial blockade of

its opponent. The *guerre de course*, war against merchant shipping, had been dismissed by Mahan and had repeatedly proved to be of mere nuisance value, in contrast to the strangling effect of a full naval blockade where the victim's flag is swept from the seas. Yet in World War I, *guerre de course* had been established as a strategic weapon of significance. That it did not succeed was in large part due to the fact that the expansion of Germany's navy had been focused very much along classic lines, building up a battlefleet.

Accounts of the U-boat campaign and the effort to defeat it can sometimes comprise an impenetrable hail of statistics. This was the nature of the struggle, with success and failure not resting on individual engagements, but rather on broad averages. Once a large force of ocean-going U-boats was available and used without limitations, it proved able to sink merchant ships in such numbers that Britain's ability to sustain its allies and remain in the war was

The crew of a U-boat surrendering. The U-boat arm of the Imperial German Navy had genuinely come close to driving Britain out of the war. Just 20 years after the Treaty of Versailles that ended the war, German U-boats would be fighting a renewed Battle of the Atlantic.

genuinely thrown into doubt. Countering the U-boats involved a great deal of creativity, huge effort and enormous resources; new technologies, new organizations, intensive diplomacy, skilled use of signals intelligence and ambitious military operations all played a role. The decisive factor was the eventual adoption of the time-honoured system of convoy and escort. Long delayed, slow to be fully implemented and never wholeheartedly embraced by the Royal Navy, it turned around the key statistics so that losses of merchant tonnage fell and sinkings of U-boats gradually rose. The threat from U-boats had been contained, but not truly defeated, as the next world war was to prove.

CHAPTER 7

The Closing Stages

The final year of the war saw the Allies gradually overcome the U-boat threat while the naval blockade exerted increasing pressure on Germany, while the military balance on land showed signs of shifting. During 1918, one operation stands out – the Zeebrugge raid of 23 April 1918. Although militarily unsuccessful, it cheered public opinion in Britain and among her allies, and has entered national mythology.

Britain had tried various measures to hinder the U-boats, including those of the Flanders Flotilla. This force and a destroyer flotilla were based at Bruges, reaching the sea via a 13km (8 mile) canal to Zeebrugge or a 18km (11 mile) canal to Ostend. Repeated attempts were made to attack this network, but the base at Bruges was well protected against air attack or bombardment from the land, while the technology of the day made it impossible for attacking aircraft or bombarding warships to achieve the necessary accuracy to destroy the canal lock-gates at the two ports.

The German fleet interned in Scapa Flow, the main British fleet base. The proud High Seas Fleet had achieved much during the war, but towards the end was stricken by mutiny.

The alternative to bombardment was to launch an amphibious raid, but Zeebrugge and Ostend were well defended against any such landing. Both ports had many troops in well prepared defensive positions, as well as batteries of coastal artillery totalling over 30 guns at Zeebrugge and 40 at Ostend. The canal exit at Zeebrugge was further protected by the mole – a stone breakwater, over 1.6km (1 mile) long and some 75m (245ft) across its widest point. As well as helping to create the harbour, this edifice had been turned into a minor fortress, with six large artillery pieces, protected by machine guns and troops in defensive trenches.

The blockships at Zeebrugge after the raid. Photographs such as this one, showing the blockships apparently in position, suggested that the operation against the canal had succeeded. However, the practical result was nothing more than a temporary inconvenience.

Despite the difficulties involved, the importance of hindering the U-boats meant that a series of plans for attacking the Belgian ports was considered. These efforts accelerated when Rear Admiral Roger Keyes joined the Admiralty as Director of Plans in December 1917, bringing to the post the same energy and initiative that had seen him devise the raid into the Heligoland Bight at the beginning of the war. He began to modify previous concepts for a raid. Following his appointment as commander of the Dover Patrol on 1 January 1918, he was given responsibility for planning and leading the operation, which he code-named Operation *Z.O.*

The heart of the plan was for a number of old cruisers to be used as blockships, which would be scuttled to obstruct the canal exits into the sea at both Zeebrugge and Ostend; a thick smokescreen would help to cover their approach. However, at Zeebrugge the powerful artillery on the mole was ideally placed to blow the ships out of the water before they could reach their objective. Keyes therefore planned an assault against the mole from a converted cruiser. This element of the plan would primarily be a diversion to allow the blockships to approach the canal, but would also seek to inflict as much damage as possible on the military facilities on the mole. To support the assault an old submarine, filled with explosives, would detonate against the viaduct linking the mole with land, thus preventing the arrival of German reinforcements. Once the blockships had been manoeuvred into position, the forces on the mole would withdraw.

There were some doubts about whether the operation was feasible, but Keyes convinced the Admiralty that it was worth a shot. For the assault

'The raiding force left home on 22 April, the eve of St George's Day. As the motley flotilla departed, Keyes signalled "St George for England".'

troops, he was assigned a battalion of Royal Marines and sought volunteers from among the crews of the Grand Fleet. The main assault ship was to be the old armoured cruiser *Vindictive*. In addition to her existing pair of 6in guns, she was provided with a formidable arsenal to support the attack, including three howitzers, two flamethrowers, batteries of mortars and several machine guns. She was also fitted with an additional upper deck to allow the assault troops to gain access to the parapet over the mole, which they would reach by specially designed 'brows' or ramps. Additional troops were to be carried in two Mersey ferries, *Iris* and *Daffodil*, chosen because their shallow draught would allow them to avoid mines, while their double hulls would make them very difficult to sink. They were given additional armour plate and protection against splinters in the form of sandbags and mattresses. Five old cruisers (three for Zeebrugge and two for Ostend) were chosen to act as blockships and were fitted with extra armour and with scuttling charges, as well as rubble and concrete to make them more difficult to remove. Finally, two old submarines, *C1* and *C3*, were filled with explosives for use against the viaduct. The force comprised over 150 ships and some 1800 men.

The attack had to be conducted at high tide and, ideally, on a moonless night; hence there were only a few days each month when it was possible. Even then it would be challenging to get all of the ships to the right places at the right time because of difficulties of navigation in fast tides and shifting sandbanks, and against enemy fire over the final stages. The operation was launched on 11 April, but at a crucial moment the wind changed and blew away the smokescreen. Keyes took the difficult but necessary decision to call it off. One motor boat was lost, its crew being captured by the Germans. On 14 April, Keyes tried a second time, only to be frustrated once again by high seas and winds. Some senior officers felt the operation should now be cancelled as operational surprise had been lost, but Keyes was keen to press on and even dropped the requirement for a moonless night. The raiding force left home once again on 22 April, the eve of St George's Day. Keyes was not one to overlook a possible reference to the country's patron saint: as the motley flotilla departed, he signalled 'St George for England', to which the captain of *Vindictive* replied, 'May we give the dragon's tail a damned good twist.'

At 10.30pm the ships for the Ostend raid broke away from the main body. About half an hour later, monitors opened fired on the German coastal artillery

batteries, while destroyers took up position outside both harbours to prevent German light forces from interfering with the unfolding operation. Shortly after 11pm the flotilla began to generate the smokescreen that was intended to cover the approach into Zeebrugge harbour. At first it succeeded; the German gunners opened fire when they heard engines approaching but could not see their targets.

At around 11.50pm the wind suddenly shifted, blowing away the smokescreen to reveal *Vindictive* steaming for the mole at a rapidly closing distance of a few hundred metres. The German heavy guns on the

The Zeebrugge raid. This map shows just how formidable and well defended an objective the mole was, and how it shielded the entrance to the Bruges canal. It also indicates the planned and actual location of the assault ships and the blockships.

HMS *Vindictive* during the raid. *Vindictive* was an obsolete *Arrogant*-class protected cruiser, converted to act as the lead assault ship for the attack on the mole at Zeebrugge. She was fitted with additional armour, ramps for the troops and additional weaponry for fire support.

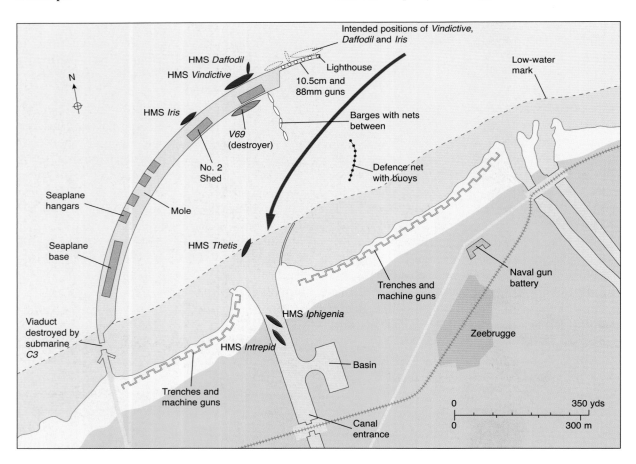

mole opened up at point-blank range and although *Vindictive* returned fire, several of her guns were quickly knocked out and the ship was heavily damaged. Many of the troops onboard were killed, including the naval officer commanding the sailors in the assault party, and both the commanding officer and the second-in-command of the embarked Royal Marines. In an effort to reduce the battering his ship was suffering, her captain shifted course and brought the old cruiser alongside the mole at one minute past midnight on St George's Day. Unfortunately, although this action saved the ship from further damage, it meant that she came alongside a good 275m (900ft) from the intended spot. It had been hoped that from this location, behind the main defensive trenches, the mole guns could swiftly be stormed. The troops would now be exposed in the middle of the mole. Moreover, it proved difficult to hold the ship in place against a fast tide and lively swell. The grapnels that were to have secured her could not be attached to the mole, and she had to be held in position by *Daffodil*, which prevented many of the troops on the ferry from landing. The movement of *Vindictive*, heavy fire from the defenders and damage to the ramps meant that the assault troops got ashore more slowly than was anticipated. Many were killed or wounded before they could disembark. *Iris* got alongside the mole, but encountered similar problems getting her troops onto it because of the height of the parapet above her deck.

One part of the plan did unfold as intended; at about 12.20am the crew of the submarine *C3* succeeded in navigating their way through the harbour and rammed the boat into the viaduct. They then disembarked into motor boats, as planned, and withdrew under increasing German fire. As they did so, the explosive-packed submarine detonated, destroying the viaduct and thereby isolating the mole, cutting communications and stranding any reinforcements.

'At a time when most news seemed bad, the Zeebrugge raid seemed a welcome sign that the Royal Navy was willing and able to conduct an audacious operation against the enemy-held coast.'

Some assault troops did reach the mole and, despite the loss of most of their commanders, launched a number of spirited if sporadic attacks against the defenders. They came under heavy and effective fire from the garrison, protected in well prepared positions, and also from German destroyers moored on the far side of the mole. They could not reach either the artillery batteries or the other intended objectives; however, the main purpose of the assault was to provide a diversion to assist the blockships, which were the real point of the raid. This they achieved. Although the German guns engaged the blockships as they rounded the mole, their fire began later and was lighter than it would have been without the assault from *Vindictive*, *Iris* and *Daffodil*.

Thetis, the leading blockship, was supposed to enter the canal and then steam three-quarters of a kilometre (half a mile) into it, before ramming the lock-gates. As she approached the canal she was badly damaged by heavy gunfire, and then her propeller became entangled in an anti-submarine net. She became impossible to steer, so her captain detonated the scuttling charges. She sank just short of the canal entrance. However, she had drawn the fire of the German gunners and had cleared the nets, thus easing the approach of the other two blockships. The second, *Intrepid*, managed to steam into the canal and scuttle herself in the planned position across the channel. Unfortunately *Thetis* had been instructed only to attack the lock-gates; had *Intrepid's* captain shown a little more initiative, he might have tried to ram them himself – though navigating the channel and avoiding the German fire would not have been easy. The third blockship, *Iphigenia*, also entered the canal, and, despite colliding with *Intrepid* as she manoeuvred into position, scuttled herself across the channel.

At 12.50am, as the blockships sank and their crews were taken off, the recall signal was sounded on the mole, and *Vindictive* re-embarked the survivors from the assault parties. As the ships withdrew, *Iris* was hit hard by the German artillery and the supporting destroyer *North Star* was sunk.

Casualties were heavy, with over 200 men killed (more than 50 by a single shell that struck *Iris* as she withdrew) and 400 wounded, with 13 captured. One destroyer and two motor boats were lost.

The Ostend operation was simpler in conception, since there was no mole and hence no need or opportunity for a diversionary attack. Here, however, the German defenders were better prepared: the captain of the motor boat captured on 11 April was carrying a copy of the plans, so the Germans had been

warned and moved two critical navigation buoys, making the already challenging task of approaching the canal all but impossible. The two intended blockships, *Brilliant* and *Sirius*, were both hit repeatedly by German fire, and then *Brilliant* ran aground. They could go no further so the scuttling charges were detonated, despite the blockships being some distance from the canal. Two later attempts were made, unsuccessfully, to block the canal at Ostend and

German troops aboard HMS *Vindictive* after the Ostend raid. After the St George's Day operation against Zeebrugge and Ostend, the latter was the target of another raid on 10 May, when *Vindictive* was sunk as a blockship. Her bow section is preserved as a monument in Ostend.

The Zeebrugge Mole

The mole at Zeebrugge dominated the harbour and was a major focus of the British raid. It comprised a 530m (1740ft) viaduct adjoining the land, then the curving 1692m (5550ft) mole, with a 238m (781ft) extension at the seaward end with a lighthouse. Any assault was made still more difficult by a high parapet on the seaward side of the mole, the top of which was 9.1m (30ft) above the water at high tide. For the Germans, this was an ideal location from which to defend the lock-gates behind it, and they stationed troops, artillery and machine guns there, protected by trenches and concrete shelters. It was also the location for a seaplane base, munitions stores and U-boat shelters. Little of the mole survives today due to the expansion of the port and the reclamation of the land around it, but part of the structure where the intense engagement of 1918 was fought still exists.

This photograph, from the author's collection, shows what remains of the mole today.

a third was cancelled. No further attempt was made, largely because the increasing effectiveness of the Channel barrage (see Chapter 6) made it unnecessary.

The British initially believed that the Zeebrugge part of the operation had succeeded: aerial photographs seemed to show *Intrepid* and *Iphigenia* lying across the main channel of the canal. In fact, while the blockships caused some initial disruption, the Germans were able to find ways of working around them within a few days and were making full use of the canal by mid-May. This might seem a distinctly modest success in view of the 600 casualties suffered.

The raid, however, was hailed as a triumph – albeit benefiting from considerable embellishment in official accounts. It had an enormously positive effect on morale in the Navy and in the hard-pressed Army, as well as on press and public opinion in Britain and her allies. At a time when most news seemed bad, with the German offensive on the Western Front gaining considerable initial success, the Zeebrugge raid seemed a welcome sign that the Royal Navy was willing and able to conduct an audacious operation against the enemy-held coast. The Admiralty initially baulked at the high number of medals recommended by Keyes – including no fewer than 11 Victoria Crosses, the highest British award for valour – but they gave way in the face of his persistence and public acclaim.

The Zeebrugge operation was a bold and ambitious concept that was conducted with enormous determination and courage. There were significant weaknesses in the planning, however: too much improvisation, insufficient attention to important details and perhaps not enough questioning of optimistic assumptions. It seemed to rest on Keyes's tendency to assume that enthusiasm alone could overcome any difficulty. Nevertheless, even if its military impact was slight, the timely and considerable boost it provided to morale was of great value.

MUTINY IN THE HIGH SEAS FLEET

After the Battle of Jutland, the High Seas Fleet made three further sorties into the North Sea, but these were tentative and suggested an awareness of how narrowly the fleet had escaped heavy defeat. As the emphasis of

German naval strategy switched to the U-boat campaign, morale among the crews of their surface fleet began to fall.

This collapse of morale was partly a reflection of the wider picture for Germany. As the British blockade exerted an ever tighter grip, the German population began to suffer terribly from a lack of food and fuel. Feelings of disillusionment only increased as long-promised success failed to materialize either on land or from the U-boat campaign. Popular dissatisfaction was reflected in growing political unrest across the country and swiftly spread to naval personnel.

The inactivity of the surface fleet led to boredom and meant that sailors were less prepared than before to overlook poor living conditions. Despite the priority given to the armed forces in the allocation of food, the shortages that hit the country in the 1916/17 winter even affected the army and the navy. The effect was magnified by the fact that in many cases, officers received better food than their men, which in turn worsened an increasing distance and lack of sympathy between them. The transfer of many of the more able officers and crew to the U-boat arm, and their replacement with less experienced men, removed what might have been a prop for discipline. Socialist agitation and propaganda found fertile ground as a result of the other sources of dissatisfaction. Initial disciplinary problems led to harsh repression, which only further fuelled the sailors' resentment.

As early as the summer of 1917 disciplinary problems emerged in the High Seas Fleet with protests over living conditions. In July 1917 many of the crew of the battleship *Prinzregent Luitpold* refused orders, with disobedience spreading to the *Friedrich der Grosse* and the cruiser *Pillau*. Further disruption followed in early August in other battleships. The navy blamed this on agitation by political activists; some men were shot, more were imprisoned. Such action only temporarily quietened the grievances.

March 1918 saw a major German Army offensive that enjoyed initial success, but which petered out in July, at huge cost. It was swiftly followed by renewed offensives launched by the increasingly effective British and French armies, and then by United States

Roger Keyes (1872–1945)

Of all the senior Royal Navy officers during World War I, Keyes was the most Nelsonian in spirit. At the outbreak of the war he was commodore of the Submarine Flotilla. He then became chief of staff to the commander of British naval forces off the Dardanelles, where his was always an enthusiastic voice for action. After 15 months with the Grand Fleet and promotion to rear admiral, in September 1917 he became Director of Plans at the Admiralty, where he turned his imagination and energy to the pressing U-boat threat. He was given a direct role in implementing his ideas when he took charge of the Dover Command at the start of 1918. The Zeebrugge raid failed in its aim of stemming the U-boat threat – though it delivered an enormous boost to Allied morale – but his other main project, overhauling the Channel barrage, proved far more successful. Promoted to Admiral of the Fleet in 1930, he left the Navy and became a member of Parliament. In 1940 he was appointed Director of Combined Operations by another old Admiralty hand, Prime Minister Winston Churchill. Keyes was hugely brave and determined, but his great desire for positive action sometimes led him to overlook the practicalities involved.

forces, whose divisions were pouring into Europe, further damaging German military and civilian morale. In addition, the British naval blockade continued to bite, heightening a general war-weariness, while military success seemed ever less likely. The sentiment among the population in

Germany was growing more hostile to the war and the political atmosphere was becoming genuinely revolutionary. The government was riven by internal divisions and was subject to mounting criticism in parliament and press. Then Germany's allies began to tumble: at the end of September 1918, following a successful Allied offensive, Bulgaria agreed an armistice. Shortly afterwards, Turkey opened negotiations with the Allies and, on 30 October, onboard the battleship HMS *Agamemnon*, signed an armistice – one condition of which was to hand over to the Allies the Dardanelles forts that had eluded them in 1915. Austria-Hungary was clearly on the verge of complete collapse.

Matters were little better in the German Navy. In August 1918, Admiral Scheer became Chief of the Naval Staff, with Hipper replacing him as commander-in-chief of the High Seas Fleet. What should have been the culmination of Scheer's wartime

Fireworks from the High Seas Fleet in Wilhelmshaven on the proclamation of the German Republic, November 1918. The mutinous crews of the Imperial Germany Navy helped to contribute to the revolutionary atmosphere that spread though the country in the closing days of the war.

The crew of the SMS *König*. The sailors of the High Seas Fleet had become disillusioned with the country's leadership and with their senior officers, in part because of the passive way in which the surface fleet had been used. Orders for what was seen as a 'death cruise' were the last straw for discipline.

service was soon revealed to be a poisoned chalice. That same month there were what he called 'signs of insubordination' among some crews in the battlefleet. Scheer still believed in using U-boats against British merchant shipping as Germany's last best hope, yet this weapon was soon snatched from his hands. With Germany's war effort clearly on its last legs, the government approached United States President Woodrow Wilson to seek a negotiated end. On 14 October Wilson demanded as a precondition an end to U-boat attacks on merchant ships. The German Government felt it could not refuse and, overruling Scheer's objections, ordered an end to the U-boat campaign against commerce. The situation on the ground was also deteriorating: between these dates, the Germans had evacuated Ostend and then Zeebrugge in front of the advancing Allies.

Scheer decided to use the U-boats with the battlefleet in one last operation against the British.

The plan was for German light forces to attack shipping in the Thames estuary and to bombard the Belgian coast. These activities would, it was hoped, draw out the British battlefleet, which would then be weakened by mines and torpedo attacks before a great, final confrontation off the Dutch coast with the German battlefleet. Hipper was to command a mighty force including five battlecruisers, 18 Dreadnoughts,

12 light cruisers and 70 destroyers. Should the British not emerge, this fleet would head towards Rosyth to confront them.

Scheer believed that this operation might put military pressure on the Allies that would favourably influence the ongoing negotiations for an armistice. He also felt – albeit to a lesser extent than some other officers – that even a valiant defeat, inflicting some losses on the British, would be preferable to meekly surrendering. Such a battle would salvage some pride for the navy and would establish a heroic legacy that might inspire a future fleet. The planned operation, therefore, did have a strategic rationale, albeit a remarkably optimistic one, and was not a mere kamikaze operation or 'death cruise', as it has sometimes been called. It is perhaps understandable, however, that many of the long-suffering crews of the High Seas Fleet did not see it this way. In the febrile

A German U-boat crew in 1917. Despite the harsh conditions and heavy losses that they endured, the discipline of the U-boat arm survived to the end of the war. The commanders of the High Seas Fleet even considered using the U-boats against those of their own capital ships that were controlled by mutineers.

atmosphere of what were clearly the closing stages of the war, the view rapidly spread among the sailors that the planned operation would simply throw away their lives for no worthwhile purpose and was designed solely to disrupt the armistice negotiations. The men who had endured so much over the past four years had simply had enough.

Some isolated acts of disobedience occurred at Cuxhaven and Wilhelmshaven on 27 and 28 October. The disruption escalated on 29 October when the fleet was ordered to raise steam and prepare to leave port for the final operation against the British. Crewmen from *Derfflinger* and *Von der Tann* refused to return from leave, and there was outright mutiny on the Dreadnoughts *König*, *Kronprinz Wilhelm* and *Markgraf*. The unrest spread to more battleships and

escalated on 30 October, to the extent that Hipper was forced to call off the operation. Some men were arrested and the battle squadrons of the High Seas Fleet were dispersed to other ports, though this only spread the problem. On 31 October, U-boats and destroyers threatened to open fire on the battleships *Thüringen* and *Helgoland*; the mutineers went as far as manning the guns of the two Dreadnoughts before backing down. Some of the stricken warships arrived in Kiel on 1 November and the ringleaders were arrested, triggering mass demonstrations by sailors demanding their release. There were suggestions that troops should be used to restore order, but this was impossible since the soldiers were animated by a similar spirit to that of their naval colleagues. By 4 November, a Sailors' and Workers' Council had taken control of Kiel and the red flag was flying over the base. Within a few days, the same occurred at the naval bases of Wilhelmshaven, Cuxhaven and Heligoland, and then at Hamburg and Cologne. A naval mutiny had become a national revolution. On 9 November, the red flag was raised over the Dreadnought *Baden*, the flagship of the once proud High Seas Fleet. When the Kaiser was told that the navy could no longer be relied on, his reply was, 'I no longer have a navy.' The following day, the remaining warships no longer had an emperor, as the Kaiser abdicated and fled to the Netherlands.

Admiral Scheer wrote in his memoirs, with an understandable bitterness, that although the navy was let down by the government, 'we suffered the bitterest disappointment at the hands of the crews of the fleet'.

ARMISTICE, INTERNMENT AND THE END OF THE HIGH SEAS FLEET

During negotiations for an armistice – that is, a temporary suspension of hostilities – the fate of the German Navy became one of the central issues. The Allied navies wanted the High Seas Fleet to surrender as one of the preconditions for a ceasefire. Their governments, however, resisted such a tough stance, fearing that it might result in the Germans opting to continue fighting. The demand relating to the German Navy was therefore moderated: although its entire fleet of U-boats would have to be surrendered to the

SMS *Markgraf* at anchor in Scapa Flow. Given what the battleships and battlecruisers of the High Seas Fleet had been through, their crews were deeply unhappy about being interned under the guns of the Royal Navy. Eventually, they found a way to express their disgruntlement.

Organizing the guard of port protection troops in Hamburg Harbour, 1919. Conditions in Germany remained difficult after the war, during the long armistice negotiations, for civilians and demobilized soldiers alike. The naval blockade was not lifted until the final peace treaty was signed.

Allies, its principal surface units would be interned – that is, they would be disarmed and would fall under Allied supervision, but would still be owned by Germany, pending a final peace treaty. When the conditions were put to Germany, their naval representative objected even to internment on the grounds that the fleet had not been defeated; Admiral Sir Rosslyn Wemyss, the First Sea Lord, commented that in that case, they were welcome to come out and try their luck. For the German Government, with the country wracked by revolution, peace could not come too quickly. The armistice was signed, coming into effect on 11 November 1918.

The war was over. The Grand Fleet was given the order to 'splice the main brace'; that is, in accordance with tradition, to give all crewmen a celebratory tot of rum. There had been no great culminating clash of the battlefleets – to the great disappointment of the British – and the German Navy could claim that tactically, it was undefeated. Strategically, however, the Royal Navy had won: it had neutralized the High Seas Fleet, it had enforced the blockade and it had – just – defeated the U-boat campaign.

The United States wanted the German warships interned in a neutral port, but no neutral state was prepared to host the rebellious fleet. The 74 German warships specified in the armistice agreement would therefore be sent to Scapa Flow, the erstwhile home base of the force that had defeated them.

On the morning of 20 November, the first instalment of 20 U-boats surrendered to the Royal Navy. They were met by destroyers of the Harwich Force and escorted into port – in silence, on the strict orders of Rear Admiral Tyrwhitt. Eventually 176 U-boats made their final journey to Harwich.

The main event occurred on 21 November. *Seydlitz*, the veteran of so many operations and the survivor of so many near escapes, led the High Seas Fleet into internment. Under the command of Vice Admiral Ludwig von Reuter, nine Dreadnoughts, five battlecruisers, seven light cruisers and 49 destroyers steamed to Rosyth. Although their guns had been disabled, the Allies took no chances and seized the chance to display the naval power that had helped to win the war. The German vessels passed through a force of 370 battle-ready warships, mostly from the Grand Fleet – reflecting the balance of effort in the war at sea – but also including a cruiser and two destroyers from France and a battle squadron from the United States. The event was overseen by Admiral Beatty, who felt cheated of his chance for a crushing victory in battle and who had argued for surrender rather than internment. The latter was imposed on

Vice Admiral Ludwig von Reuter had the difficult task of leading the High Seas Fleet into internment, followed by the still more testing role of overseeing it during the peace negotiations. He put his time to good effect, drawing up careful and effective plans to scuttle the fleet.

him by his political leaders, but he blurred the distinction by ordering that the ships of the High Seas Fleet haul down their colours. Reuter protested, but had to accede, and at sunset the ensign of the Imperial German Navy came down across the fleet.

The ships were checked to ensure that they had been disarmed according to the agreement, and then, over the next few days, steamed in groups to Scapa Flow under heavy escort. They were eventually joined there by other ships to make up the agreed 74, including the erstwhile flagship *Baden*, as well as

Sea Power and Victory

For Britain, winning the war at sea was vital if she was to continue fighting. Yet how could sea power contribute to victory in the war as a whole? The attempt to use maritime power to break the deadlock with an amphibious operation in the Dardanelles failed – though sea power helped to sustain campaigns in the Middle East that were, eventually, successful. On the other hand, navies allowed Britain and France to bring to bear in Europe the military and economic power of their overseas empires. It also carried safely to Europe the fresh American forces that helped to turn the tide. Its key contribution to victory, however, was the economic blockade of Germany, which weakened the fighting power and morale of her army and navy, and undermined her home front to the point of revolution. In combination with the long campaigns on land that consumed Germany's military power, the blockade eroded her ability and will to keep fighting. The historian and former army officer Basil Liddell Hart concluded that the Royal Navy did 'more than any other factor towards wining the war for the Allies', because it kept open the seas and, in particular, because it maintained the blockade, 'the decisive agency in the struggle'.

another battlecruiser, one more light cruiser and one destroyer. Scapa Flow became the uncomfortable home for these ships, with skeleton crews for minimum maintenance, during the interminable peace negotiations in Paris. Discipline problems continued, becoming sufficiently serious on the flagship for Reuter to shift his command to the light cruiser *Emden*, the ship named after the earlier light cruiser scuttled in the Cocos Islands in 1914 after her short but successful career as a commerce raider.

The German ships became the source of disagreements among the Allies, with France and Italy each wanting to gain possession of them, the United States wanting to avoid them being transferred to the Royal Navy, and Britain just wanting them destroyed. The German crews had originally assumed that their ships would be returned to Germany at the conclusion of negotiations, but it soon became clear that this was not going to happen. Concern grew that they might have to be surrendered to Britain or that the Royal Navy might pre-empt the diplomatic settlement and seize them by force. Their officers and crews agreed that they would rather have their ships sunk by their own hands than be taken by Britain, so during June 1919, Reuter devised meticulous plans to scuttle the fleet. On 20 June he learned from newspapers that the armistice was to expire the following day (in fact, the deadline was postponed), with Germany having to choose between accepting the proposed treaty or having hostilities reopen. Reuter suspected that this would be the cue for the British to storm his ships, and decided to order the scuttling of the fleet the next day.

The scuttled SMS *Hindenburg* in Scapa Flow, 1919. She was one of the last German battlecruisers, commissioned in 1917, but never saw action. She accompanied the rest of the fleet into internment and was scuttled alongside the other capital ships. *Hindenburg* was salvaged and sold for scrap in 1930.

On the morning of 21 June, the 1st Battle Squadron of the Royal Navy departed for gunnery practice. At 10.30am Reuter sent the pre-arranged signal, 'Paragraph eleven. Confirm.' An hour later all the ships had acknowledged; the Imperial German ensign was raised over the ships once again as they began to sink, their crews having opened them to the sea. The Royal Navy destroyers that were present urgently signalled the battlefleet to return and frantic efforts were made to save the sinking ships; they succeeded with the Dreadnought *Baden*, four light cruisers and 32 destroyers. But the bulk of the High Seas Fleet sank: nine Dreadnoughts, six battlecruisers, four cruisers and 32 destroyers, totalling over 406,400 tonnes (400,000 tons). The warships sunk included names familiar from earlier chapters of this book – the battlecruisers *Seydlitz*, *Moltke*, *Von der Tann*, *Derfflinger* and the Dreadnoughts *Friedrich der Grosse*, *König* and *Grosser Kurfürst*.

The British, though embarrassed, were not too displeased at the outcome, since it removed a thorny political problem over how the German ships should be distributed among the Allies. The French and the Italians were furious. The general reaction among the personnel of the German Navy was not to mourn this sad end for their fleet, but rather to feel proud that it

Surrendered U-boats in Harwich. While the Allied governments were prepared – despite the objections of senior naval officers – to allow the concession of internment rather than surrender to the surface units of the High Seas Fleet, they were adamant that the more threatening U-boats must be surrendered.

had recaptured its honour with one last gesture of defiance, under the noses of their principal enemy. In Scheer's words, 'the stain of surrender has been wiped out from the escutcheon of the German Fleet. The sinking of the ships has proved that the spirit of the fleet is not dead.'

World War I was formally ended by the 1919 Treaty of Versailles. One clause of the treaty required Germany to hand over all eight of her remaining Dreadnoughts, as well as a further eight light cruisers and 42 more destroyers. The future German Navy was not allowed any submarines, nor any warships over 10,160 tonnes (10,000 tons) – and only six this size. Some of the warships that formed the backbone of the Royal Navy in World War I would go on to render sterling service in World War II. In the course of it, they would fight a navy heartened by the spirit of the High Seas Fleet, the leading ships of which were new but carried names such as *Tirpitz*, *Scheer*, *Hipper* and *Von Spee*.

FURTHER READING

Beesly, P., *Room 40: British Naval Intelligence 1914–18* (London, Hamish Hamilton, 1982)

Bennett, G., *Naval Battles of the First World War* (London, B.T. Batsford, 1968)

—— *Coronel and the Falklands* (Edinburgh, Birlinn, 2000)

Brodie, B., *Sea Power in the Machine Age* (Princeton, Princeton University Press, 1943)

Corbett, J.S., *History of the Great War, Naval Operations, vols. 1–3* (London, Longmans Green, 1920–23). *See also* Newbolt.

Dickinson, H., 'The Zeebrugge and Ostend Raids (Op ZO, April 1918)', in T. Lovering (ed.), *Amphibious Assault: Manoeuvre from the Sea* (Woodbridge, Seafarer, 2007)

Falls, C., *The First World War* (London, Longmans Green, 1960)

Goldrick, J., *The King's Ships Were at Sea: the War in the North Sea, August 1914–February 1915* (Annapolis, Naval Institute Press, 1984)

Gordon, A., *The Rules of the Game: Jutland and British Naval Command* (London, John Murray, 1996)

Grove, E.J., *The Royal Navy since 1815: a New Short History* (Basingstoke, Palgrave, 2005)

Halpern, P.G., *A Naval History of World War I* (London, UCL Press, 1994)

Hezlet, A., *The Submarine and Sea Power* (London, Peter Davies, 1967)

—— *Aircraft and Sea Power* (New York, Stein and Day, 1970)

Hickey, M., *Gallipoli* (London, John Murray, 1995)

Hough, R., *The Great War at Sea, 1914–1918* (Oxford, Oxford University Press, 1983)

Joll, J., *The Origins of the First World War* (2nd ed., London, Longman, 1992)

Keble-Chatterton, E., *Q-Ships and their Story* (London, Sidgwick & Jackson, 1923)

Layman, R.D., *The Cuxhaven Raid* (London, Conway, 1985)

Liddell Hart, B.H., *History of the First World War* (London, Cassell, 1970)

London, C., *Jutland 1916: Clash of the Dreadnoughts* (Oxford, Osprey, 2000)

Marder, A.J., *The Anatomy of British Sea Power: a History of British Naval Policy in the Pre-Dreadnought Era, 1880–1905* (London, Frank Cass, 1940)

—— *From the Dreadnought to Scapa Flow: the Royal Navy in the Fisher Era, 5 vols.* (London, Oxford University Press, 1961–70)

Massie, R.K., *Castles of Steel: Britain, Germany and the Winning of the Great War at Sea* (London, Pimlico, 2003)

Mills, S., *Scapa Flow: from Graveyard to Resurrection* (Chesham, Wordsworth, 2005)

Newbolt, H., *History of the Great War, Naval Operations, vols. 4–5* (London, Longmans Green, 1928–31). *See also* Corbett.

Osbourne, E.W., *Britain's Economic Blockade of Germany 1914–1919* (London, Frank Cass, 2004)

Pitt, B., *Coronel and the Falklands* (London, Cassell, 1960)

Rhodes James, R., *Gallipoli* (London, Pimlico, 1999)

Ruge, F., *Scapa Flow 1919: the End of the German Fleet* (London, Ian Allan, 1969)

Scheer, R., *Germany's High Sea Fleet in the World War* (London, Cassell, 1920)

Steel, N. and P. Hart, *Jutland 1916: Death in the Grey Wastes* (London, Cassell, 2003)

Stevenson, D., *1914–1918: the History of the First World War* (London, Penguin, 2004)

Tarrant, V.E., *Jutland: the German Perspective* (London, Arms and Armour, 1997)

—— *The U-Boat Offensive 1914–1945* (London, Cassell, 2000)

Terraine, J., *Business in Great Waters: the U-Boat Wars 1916–1945* (London, Leo Cooper, 1989)

Warner, P., *The Zeebrugge Raid* (London, William Kimber, 1978)

INDEX

Subheadings are arranged in alphabetical order. Page numbers in *italic* denote illustrations. Page numbers in **bold** denote information boxes.

PICTURE CREDITS

AKG Images: 99(left)

Art-Tech/Aerospace: 27(top), 36, 43(bottom), 84, 97, 98, 100, 101, 102, 107, 108, 140, 143, 144, 148, 153(bottom), 157, 164, 171, 183, 187, 188, 215

Art-Tech/MARS: 13, 30, 73, 103, 121, 135(top), 139, 160, 184, 186

Tim Benbow: 210

Bridgeman Art Library: 11(National Gallery, London), 22(Bibliotheque des Arts Decoratifs, Paris, Archives Charmet), 74(top, Royal Geographical Society, London, UK, Courtesy of the de Laszlo Foundation), 207

Cody Images: 12, 14, 18, 23(top), 24(both), 25, 40, 50, 51, 69, 83, 86, 88, 91, 92, 94, 95, 104, 105, 106, 115(bottom), 116, 136, 150, 153(top), 166, 167, 169, 170, 172, 176, 179, 181, 194, 196, 197, 198, 199, 200, 201, 204, 219

Mary Evans Picture Library: 26, 59, 82, 109, 123(top), 132, 152, 202, 211

E. W. W. Fowler: 45, 124, 130, 133, 137

Getty Images: 8, 28, 47(Time & Life Pictures), 62, 68, 72, 117, 129

Getty Images/Popperfoto: 110, 178

Library of Congress: 20, 23(bottom), 33(bottom), 42, 76, 112, 126, 128, 185

Bertil Olofsson/Krigsarkivet: 209

Photos.com: 21, 99(right), 119, 142

Anthony Preston: 17, 87(bottom)

Public Domain: 70

Science & Society Picture Library: 67

SMB Bildarkiv: 19, 53, 55, 60, 63, 64, 80

Suddeutsche Zeitung: 1, 6, 32, 33(top), 37, 48, 49, 52, 56, 61, 65, 93, 113, 120, 175, 212, 213, 214, 216, 217, 218

US Department of Defense: 16, 190, 192, 193

Artworks

Art-Tech/Aerospace: 38, 81, 123(bottom)

Art-Tech/De Agostini: 27(bottom), 43(top), 66, 74(bottom), 75, 79(both), 87(top), 115(top), 135(bottom), 147, 155, 158,162(both), 163

Battle of Jutland 1916 ◇

Battle of Dogger Bank 1915 ◇

East Coast Raids 1914 ◇

Battle of Heligoland Bight 1914 ◇

◇ Cuxhaven Raid 1914

● Scapa Flow

Zeebrugge and Ostend Raids 1918 ◇

◇ Capture of Tsingtao 1914

◇ Battle of Penang 1914

◇ SMS *Emden's cruise* 1914

PACIFIC

OCEAN

INDIAN

OCEAN

Key

◇   *Battles/Events*